OULIPO

A PRIMER OF POTENTIAL LITERATURE

translated and edited by
WARREN MOTTE

Dalkey Archive Press
Champaign · London

Library of Congress Cataloging-in-Publication Data:

Oulipo : a primer of potential literature / edited and translated by
Warren F. Motte, Jr. — 1st Dalkey Archive ed.
p. cm.
Originally published: Lincoln : University of Nebraska
Press, c1986.
Includes bibliographical references and index.
ISBN 1-56478-187-9 (alk. paper)
1. Oulipo (Association) 2. French literature—20th
century—History and criticism. 3. Literature—Societies, etc.—
France. 4. Literature and science—France. 5. Literary form.
I. Motte, Warren F.
PQ22.0809   1998
840'.6'044—dc21   97-51428
CIP

Partially funded by grants from the Services du Conseiller Culturel
and the Illinois Arts Council, a state agency, and by
the University of Illinois, Urbana-Champaign

www.dalkeyarchive.com

For Marie, Nicholas, and Nathaniel

CONTENTS

Preface
to the Revised Edition

· · · · · · · · · · · · · · · · · · · ·

A lot of water has flowed over the dam since the first publication of this *Primer*, a dozen years ago. The Oulipo was impoverished by the death of Jean Queval in December 1990. But it was enriched by the addition of five new members: Bernard Cerquiglini, Michelle Grangaud, Hervé Le Tellier, Oskar Pastior, and Pierre Rosenstiehl. Many rich new works have appeared in French since 1986, as well as English translations of texts by Raymond Queneau, Georges Perec, Italo Calvino, Jacques Roubaud, Marcel Bénabou, and other Oulipians. In this Revised Edition, I have updated and expanded the bio-bibliographical section, entitled "Oulipians and their Works," in order to reflect those recent developments.

On the American front, solid beachheads were established by the Oulipo through events staged by the group in New York and Seattle. My own town, Boulder, was not spared, either: Jacques Jouet took it by storm, single-handedly, in March of 1995—and I'm delighted to report that things have not been quite the same here since. Even as I write these lines, an elite Oulipian commando composed of Marcel Bénabou, Paul Fournel, Jacques Jouet, Hervé Le Tellier, Harry Mathews, and Jacques Roubaud has invaded the Bay Area, in order to liberate San Francisco, Berkeley, and Palo Alto. And if terms such as "lipogram," "holopoem," "javanese stuttering," and "perverb" are not yet household words in the American lexicon, their currency is nonetheless clearly in the ascendant.

As it strides vigorously into its fifth decade, still building literary labyrinths from which it proposes to escape, the Ouvroir de Littérature Potentielle numbers thirty members. For the record (and, I confess, for the characteristically Oulipian pleasure that *enumeration* offers), let me name them here: Noël Arnaud, Marcel Bénabou, Jacques Bens, Claude Berge, André Blavier, Paul Braffort, Italo Calvino, François Caradec, Bernard Cerquiglini, Ross Chambers, Stanley Chapman, Marcel Duchamp, Jacques Duchateau, Luc Etienne, Paul Fournel, Michelle Grangaud, Jacques Jouet, Latis, François Le Lionnais, Hervé Le Tellier, Jean Lescure, Harry Mathews, Michèle Métail, Oskar Pastior, Georges Perec, Raymond Queneau, Jean Queval, Pierre Rosenstiehl, Jacques Roubaud, Albert-Marie Schmidt.

Warren F. Motte, Jr.
November 1997

Noël Arnaud

. . . .

Foreword

Prolegomena to a Fourth Oulipo Manifesto—
or Not

The future of the Oulipo is inscribed in its name. More precisely, its name imposes a *form* on the group, its only manner of being (and of acting). If the Oulipo abandoned this form involuntarily, it would die; voluntary abandon would be suicide: the group would scuttle itself. Having existed for a quarter of a century, it could die honorably, leaving behind it an estimable corpus of works, having proved a remarkable example of stability (twenty-five years is long—and rare—for enterprises of this sort), an example, too (rarer still), of tolerance and unity. Instead of dying, the group might find it convenient simply to disappear, to hide, to close up shop, never again to perform on the cultural stage.

The real present of the Oulipo, that state which is ever so transitory, almost imperceptible between the past and the future, is perhaps distinguished by this question: where is the Oulipo's end? And what would be its "felicitous end" (in the quasi-religious sense of the word)? But the end is also the goal, the vocation; to the distressing question of its end, the Oulipo would respond by returning to first principles, by revivifying its specificity. Its end is in its beginnings. "One cannot wash one's feet twice in the same water," wrote Queneau, paraphrasing the amazed Heraclitus confronted with the phenomenon of a flowing river that prevented him from washing himself twice in the same water. Sophism (before the fact), no doubt, but even if one accepted it as philosophical truth, one could still quench one's thirst from the same water without putting one's feet in the same river: one has merely to walk along the riverbank, on solid ground.

The historians of the Ouvroir de Littérature Potentielle frequently have recalled that the group owes its name to the eminent scholar and sixteenth-century specialist Albert-Marie Schmidt, one of its ten founding members. Let us emphasize the word *ouvroir*, which was preferred to *sémi-*

naire; the latter, drifting away from its first meaning (an establishment wherein young ecclesiastics are educated), began to acquire a secular meaning inherited from the German, designating professional meetings of executives from business, industry, education—in short, from any public or private body desirous of communicating anything at all. Albert-Marie Schmidt's proposal was received enthusiastically and without hesitation. And that is surely one of the singularities of the Oulipo's first years. For an *ouvroir*—a word that has fallen into disuse—once denoted a shop and, as late as the eighteenth century, a light and mobile shop made of wood, in which the master cobblers of Paris displayed their wares and pursued their trade. The word could also denote that part of a textile factory where the looms are placed; or, in an arsenal, the place where a team of workers performs a given task; or a long room where the young women in a community work on projects appropriate to their sex; or a charitable institution for impoverished women and girls who found therein shelter, heat, light, and thankless, ill-paid work, the result of which these institutions sold at a discount, not without having skimmed off a tidy profit, thus depriving the isolated workers of their livelihood and leading them (as it was charged) into vice. Later, and for a short time only, *ouvroir* denoted a group of well-to-do women seeking to assuage their consciences in needlework for the poor and in the confection of sumptuous ecclesiastical ornaments. Curiously enough, it was this last notion, the "sewing circle," that prevailed in the minds of the Oulipians; just like those diligent ladies, Oulipians embroidered with golden thread. Assuredly, Albert-Marie Schmidt (the two of us had occasion to talk about this) was aware of the successive or parallel definitions of the word *ouvroir;* he saw in it above all a secluded place where people work together on a difficult task, where people strive to elaborate new techniques, not knowing whether the latter will produce results or explode sadly like a child's balloon. There was a hint of the Masonic Temple in his vision of our *ouvroir,* but it pleased him to have the Oulipians regard the group principally as a pleasant spot, warm in winter, cool in summer, abundantly provided with food and drink, where people compete in dexterity in the finest sort of needlework. This manual, meticulous, secret, clandestine aspect of Oulipian activities, this aura of the trade guild with its slow and precise elaboration of the "masterpiece" in its newness, its originality steeped in the most ancient lessons of the masters, suited this subtle and perverse spirit. In baptizing the Oulipo, he dictated its future. On 2 February 1963 (he would die three years later), Albert-Marie Schmidt rendered homage to Raymond Queneau in the Protestant weekly *Réforme,* and he continued:

> Having constituted in this fashion a reserve, a treasury of living French, the writer, anxious to reach his reader in his deceitful daily

verity, must strive, if we are to believe Raymond Queneau, to reform the poetics of novels, poems, and essays as they are produced today. To this end, he should try to support them through new structures.

Now a man working alone can imagine and elaborate such structures only with difficulty. This is why Raymond Queneau, intending to help the members of the Republic of Letters out of their difficulties, associated himself with one of the most erudite savants around, Le Lionnais, and founded a secret laboratory of literary structures: the Oulipo (Ouvroir de Littérature Potentielle).

Among those who participate in the work of this closed society of writers modest enough not to insist upon elegant scholarly style are mathematicians, musicians, directors, specialists in electronics, and, as a consultant, a university regent, a specialist on those much-slandered people, the Grands Rhétoriqueurs who, toward the end of the fifteenth century, complicated, with the interdictions of a fertile madness, the armature of their poems.

The "specialist on those much-slandered people," those people whom the Oulipo, from its foundation in 1960, resuscitated, rehabilitated, and installed in the pantheon of its "plagiarists by anticipation," was Albert-Marie Schmidt.

"The Oulipo . . . likes to think," he concluded, "that it is preparing, with fear, laughter, gluttony, intoxication, and trembling, a future for French literature, a future brightened by substantific and medullary discoveries."

Another spring from which we must drink is Raymond Queneau; he tells us to whom the Oulipo addresses itself: "The word 'potential' concerns the very nature of literature, that is, fundamentally it's less a question of literature strictly speaking than of supplying forms for the good use one can make of literature. We call potential literature the search for new forms and structures which may be used by writers in any way they see fit."

Clearly, according to Queneau, the Oulipo works for its own members and for those other writers who deem its discoveries good and useful for their own ends. That these writers were among the best and that, in their indomitable personality, they became active Oulipians, not merely consumers of the Oulipo but inventors of new structures or constraints—Georges Perec, Jacques Roubaud, Italo Calvino, Harry Mathews—that is the richest reward about which Queneau, had he been less modest, might have boasted. It is also the irrefutable proof of the vitality of the Oulipo and the soundness of its approach.

For a long time, the Oulipo shrouded itself in a discretion propitious to its quintessential, somewhat sybaritic manipulations; it was during this time that those writers whom Raymond Queneau wished for surged forth, consolidating and enriching the group.

The day that the Oulipo came out of the shadows, success was lying in wait for it. Happily enough, this success came slowly. Queneau's reputation (and those of a few other less renowned members) as a "practical joker," as a "humorist," the ever so subtly droll character of its first published works, preserved the Oulipo for a while from the stifling and inevitably distorting interest of a public in quest of knowledge.

Academe, in the Oulipo's first decade, blissfully ignored Raymond Queneau and the Grands Rhétoriqueurs, considering them alike to be mere entertainers. It had just begun—in France at least—its infatuation with surrealism and psychoanalysis. In the higher spheres, structuralism applied to analysis and literary creation had begun to consolidate its dogma, and confusion might have arisen between Oulipian research in structures and structuralist theories, prompting François Le Lionnais to suggest a distinction between the two, calling us "structurElists." With all due deference to certain persons, the fact remains that on a few important points (beginning with the way of regarding literary production), structuralist preoccupations—the word "structuralist" taken here in its most general sense (or both generalizing and simplifying at once)—were not wholly unrelated to the preoccupations of the Oulipo. Aside from personal friendships, however, there were no relations between the Oulipo and the structuralists; the latter, moreover, enveloped themselves in a ponderous sobriety that rendered them impervious to Oulipian facetiae. (Personally, I shall except from this one of the founding fathers, Claude Lévi-Strauss, with whom, during these years, I had the privilege of exchanging a delightful correspondence from which it became clear that, to his way of thinking, science was not principally devoted to making people die of boredom.)

Today, the Oulipo finds itself shaken to its foundations by its very success. Even though it violated its first principles in failing to limit the number of members to ten, then to thirteen, its expanded membership remains painfully insufficient to the demands for workshops, lectures, debates, and so forth which flow in from all directions.

If a capitally important problem could be put into abeyance (capitally important since it is a matter of principle: was the Oulipo founded to teach anyone and everyone the art and the means of becoming a poet?), this monopolizing of the Oulipo by pedagogical necessities would cause no difficulties, apart from the considerable time and energies these innumerable workshops take, to the detriment of the invention of new constraints and structures, and to that which the Oulipo itself persists in calling its "creation." Its physiognomy is changing as pedagogy instills itself in its veins. Its personality is dissolving: it is becoming a "writers' workshop" among many other "writers' workshops." Interpreted, once again, in a fallacious manner and with a strong dash of demagogy, Lautréamont's famous maxim, "Poetry must be made by all, not by one," works its magic. Sometimes, allowances are made for the Oulipo's age: it was the first among writers' workshops; it is the granddaddy of writers' workshops. This recognition is dangerous, for it invites a comparison between Oulipian methods and the techniques of a modern pedagogy of "creative writing." The Oulipo was ahead of its time . . . twenty-five years ago . . . and all the more so because nobody at that time was interested in literature under constraint. Now having joined the game of pedagogic competition, it can retain its audience in the lecture halls only by feigning to imitate the theories and terminology taught in the schools. One Oulipian, among the most brilliant, recently recommended that the members of the group take courses in linguistics! One does not become a pedagogue lightly: one must know how to "recycle" oneself.

Will the Oulipo let itself be voluptuously ravished by glory, even if the latter disfigures it? Will it choose between the streetcorner stall of a master cobbler and the claustral life of its first period? Will it adopt a frankly "reactionary" stance? After the fashion of the Roman Catholic Church, sketching out a return to the Mass in Latin, reimposing the cassock on its priests, will the Oulipo pronounce itself in favor of a radical "integrism"? Will it contemplate, perched on its promontory, the mounting tide of computer science (of which vogue the Oulipo is far from innocent; it was, on the contrary, one of the very first to put machines to poetic use, and several of its members have become masterful in the writing of programs and the manipulation of computers)? Will it concede preeminence to the machine? Or will it cut the ties that bind it to the machine, that progressively hold it tighter?

Such are the institutional and private dramas that the Oulipians are acting out as they light the candles on their twenty-fifth birthday cake. Let us wager that the party will be merry. After a few days' regimen, the Oulipians will rise up renewed, restored to their initial vigor, all questions answered, all dramas resolved.

Acknowledgments

· · · · · · · · · · · · · · · · · ·

For grants that facilitated the completion of this project, I thank the American Council of Learned Societies and the Research Council of the University of Nebraska–Lincoln. I am grateful to Keith Bosley for permission to quote his Mallarmé translations, and to Samuel Solomon for his translation of Racine. I appreciate the kindness of all the Oulipians who responded to my inquiries, especially Noël Arnaud, Marcel Bénabou, Ross Chambers, and Harry Mathews, who patiently and generously supplied essential supplementary information. Finally, I should like to offer my warmest (if perhaps by now redundant) thanks to Noël Arnaud, for providing this book with a Foreword.

Introduction

. . . .

Microhistory

In September of 1960, an exceptionally diverse group met at Cerisy-la-Salle on the occasion of a colloquium devoted to the work of Raymond Queneau. The title of these proceedings, "Une nouvelle défense et illustration de la langue française," was in many ways exemplary: if it recalled the Pléiade and its poetic manifesto, it also announced another group, the Ouvroir de Littérature Potentielle. For it was at Cerisy, on the initiative of Queneau and François Le Lionnais, that the Oulipo was conceived. It was born two months later, on 24 November 1960, to be precise, the day of its first official meeting. The ten founding members came from various disciplines: writers, mathematicians, university professors, and pataphysicians.[1] The group began as a subcommittee of the Collège de Pataphysique (although, early on, the *official* affiliation with that group would be dropped), under the title, "Séminaire de Littérature Expérimentale." But at their second meeting, the more modest and (to their way of thinking) more precise title was adopted: "Ouvroir de Littérature Potentielle." Since then, the Oulipo has pursued its research with admirable assiduity. In the last twenty-five years, several more people have joined the group; today, the Oulipo includes twenty-five members.[2]

In its first years, the Oulipo worked in voluntary obscurity. During its first decade, the group's public activities were relatively rare: a presentation of their work to the Collège de Pataphysique in 1961, a special issue of *Temps Mêlés* devoted to the Oulipo in 1964, and, in the same year, a "semi-public meeting" of the group recorded for Belgian radio. In its first decade, however, various members of the Oulipo individually published texts which were in large measure inspired by that group's work, notably Jacques Bens's *41 Sonnets irrationnels* (1965), Jacques Roubaud's є (1967), Jacques Duchateau's *Zinga 8* (1967), Noël Arnaud's *Poèmes Algol* (1968), and Georges Perec's *La Disparition* (1969).

It was in 1973, with the publication of *La Littérature potentielle,* that the Oulipo began to affirm itself openly. The collection offered a representative sampling of Oulipian production, including theoretical texts and exercises. All are relatively short, and as a group they exemplify the two principal directions of Oulipian research: analysis, that is, the identification and recuperation of older, even ancient (but not necessarily intentional) experiments in form; and synthesis, the elaboration of new forms. As François Le Lionnais puts it in the "First Manifesto": "Anoulipism is

devoted to discovery, Synthoulipism to invention. From one to the other
there exist many subtle channels." With the publication of *La Littérature
potentielle*, the Oulipo's timidity slowly began to erode, and the group
began to participate in colloquia and programs of various sorts: a presentation at Reed Hall in 1973, at "Europalia 75 France" in Brussels in 1975,
on France-Culture Radio in 1976, at the Centre Pompidou in 1977, at the
Fondation de Royaumont in 1978, and at the Festival de la Chartreuse de
Villeneuve-lès-Avignon since 1977.

Three important texts have appeared in recent years. In *Oulipo 1960–
1963* (1980), Jacques Bens, the first "provisional secretary" of the group,
published the minutes of the Oulipo's monthly meetings from 1960 to
1963. These documents are both interesting and amusing: if they furnish
material for future literary historians, they also testify eloquently to the
ludic spirit that has consistently animated the group. *Atlas de littérature
potentielle* (1981), a collective effort, responds to *La Littérature potentielle;* like the latter, it includes both theoretical texts and illustrative exercises, offering an update on Oulipian activity since 1973. In *La Bibliothèque Oulipienne* (1981), Slatkine has collected and reprinted the first
sixteen volumes of the Oulipo's "library." This series was created in 1974
on Queneau's initiative; it consists of texts written by members of the
Oulipo and published privately, the edition of each volume being limited
to 150 copies. The texts included in *La Bibliothèque Oulipienne* are intermediary forms; that is, they fall somewhere between the short exercises
of the previous collections and longer works such as Perec's *La Vie mode
d'emploi* and Italo Calvino's *If on a winter's night a traveler*. But like
these other writings, each text in *La Bibliothèque Oulipienne* results from
the application of a given Oulipian principle or theory.

One Hundred Trillion Poems

Of what do Oulipian theories consist? The purpose of the present collection is to respond to that question and to give the English-speaking reader
ingress into the Oulipian labyrinth. The texts have been chosen to provide
a sampler of Oulipian poetic theory, from the polemical language of the
early manifestoes to the more elaborate formulations of a startling literary
aesthetic.

Many of the texts included herein were either produced or inspired by
Raymond Queneau (of whom Roland Barthes said, "His entire *oeuvre*
embraces the literary myth"); more than any other, Queneau nourished
and directed the evolution of the group. Queneau's definition of the Oulipo's work is, moreover, succinct: potential literature is "the search for new

forms and structures that may be used by writers in any way they see fit."
And François Le Lionnais adds, "The Oulipo's goal is to discover new
structures and to furnish for each structure a small number of examples."
It is obvious, then, that Queneau and Le Lionnais conceive of the Oulipo's
vocation in terms of a formal quest. In order to render its parameters more
precisely, one might briefly consider Queneau's *Cent Mille Milliards de
poèmes* (one hundred thousand billion poems), for this work, exemplary
in many ways, echoes throughout the essays in this collection and per-
meates the Oulipian enterprise as a whole: it may be regarded as the semi-
nal Oulipian text.

At first glance, it looks like nothing more than a collection of ten sonnets, but these poems obey formal laws far more vast and rigorous than
those of the traditional sonnet. In fact, they constitute a combinatory ensemble: each line of each poem may replace (or be replaced by) its homo-
logue in the nine other poems. Thus, to each of the ten first lines, the
reader can add any of ten different second lines; there exist therefore 10^2,
or one hundred possible combinations for the first two lines. Given that
the sonnet has fourteen lines, the possibilities offered by the collection as
a whole are of the order of 10^{14}, or one hundred trillion sonnets. The text,
in its *potential* state, thus results from the Cartesian product of fourteen
sets of ten elements each; that is, the combinatory possibilities are exhausted and repetition of combination is excluded. Faced with a work of
this kind, the reader will necessarily encounter a certain number of practical problems. Queneau himself, in the preface, acknowledges the most
thorny among them: the time which a close textual reading demands. According to his calculations, if one read a sonnet per minute, eight hours a
day, two hundred days per year, it would take more than a million centuries to finish the text. François Le Lionnais, in his postface to the work,
notes the same problem, if in a somewhat less brutal manner: "Thanks to
this technical superiority, the work you are holding in your hands represents, itself alone, a quantity of text far greater than everything man has
written since the invention of writing, including popular novels, business
letters, diplomatic correspondence, private mail, rough drafts thrown into
the wastebasket, and graffiti."

This text may engender a whole range of reactions: where certain indi-
viduals see an example of original, conscious, and lucid poetic innovation, others will see only empty acrobatics, pretension, and literary madness. Polemics of this sort frequently surround the experimental text; very
often, the latter draws (or exhausts) the better part of its force therein. The
principal disadvantage of these controversies is that they neglect the capitally important question of textual mechanism. And as interesting as this
whole problematic may be, it will not lead us very far in a consideration

of the *Cent Mille Milliards de poèmes*. Without then entering into a polemic concerning the literary value of this text, we may at least draw one firm conclusion: the *Cent Mille Milliards de poèmes*, in its conception and its execution, stands as the foremost model for the Oulipian enterprise.

First of all, it responds amply to the "analytic" intent, the desire to recuperate and revivify traditional constraining forms. If the sonnet is a far less ancient form than, say, rhopalic verse (a fine example of which is offered by Harry Mathews's "Liminal Poem"), it imposes nonetheless a multiplicity of constraints that are, of course, arbitrary at the outset but become highly codified through use (and it is precisely this "use" that separates the normative text from the experimental). Moreover, given that the sonnet as a poetic form has fallen into disuse, it is not surprising that it elicited the interest of Queneau, who called the death of the *ballade* and the *rondeau* "disasters."

In addition, the *Cent Mille Milliards de poèmes* faithfully reflects the "synthetic" aspect of Oulipian work, the obvious intent behind it being to elaborate a new poetic form, a combinatory form. In fact, this new form, given its basic material, the individual precombinatory sonnet, erects a whole system of meta-constraints: if the traditional metrics remain essentially intact (the combinatory integer being the alexandrine), the rhyme scheme and the syntactic and semantic structures must, on the contrary, bow to the new formal rules imposed by the combinatory ensemble. Each line of the ten master sonnets must be capable of being coherently integrated into a quasi-infinity of derived sonnets.

This leads to a final conclusion about this text: like a hulking iceberg, the *Cent Mille Milliards de poèmes* manifests only a fraction of its bulk. Its reader can accede to a certain number of derived sonnets (the quantity depending on the degree of the reader's initiative, or perhaps on the depth of his or her monomania); turning to mathematics, the reader can determine their exact number. But it is obvious that even in a lifetime of diligent reading, one can read only a small portion of the sonnets theoretically engendered by the combinatory mechanism: *ars longa, vita brevis*. The rest remain in the *potential* state, and this fact, more than anything else, accounts for the status of this text within the Ouvroir de Littérature Potentielle.

Literary Madness and the Canon

Left unanalyzed, this innovation, this seemingly ferocious (post)modernism, would appear to belie the Oulipo's avowed respect for literary tradition. That is, what Oulipians call the "analytic" and the "synthetic" aspects of their work would seem necessarily to be in contradiction. In fact, this is not the case, the apparent problem residing in the word "tradition": the Oulipo manifests enormous respect for the experimentalist tendency within the tradition of literature. Its members have pointed out and paid homage to writers from Lasus of Hermione to the Grands Rhétoriqueurs, from Rabelais to Roussel: these they consider to be their direct antecedents, qualifying the work of those writers, slyly, as "plagiarisms by anticipation," thereby suggesting the desire of the Oulipo to inscribe itself within a certain literary tradition. Georges Perec's "History of the Lipogram," for instance, testifies to the importance he accorded to tradition in the production of *La Disparition,* a 300-page novel written without the letter E. This example, perhaps more clearly than another, shatters the apparent paradox I alluded to, for as Perec's essay suggests, *La Disparition,* received as resolutely avant-gardist, is in fact merely the most recent manifestation of a venerable literary tradition that can be traced back to the sixth century B.C.

In that same essay, Perec protests "a critical misappreciation as tenacious as it is contemptuous":

> Exclusively preoccupied with its great capitals (Work, Style, Inspiration, World-Vision, Fundamental Options, Genius, Creation, etc.), literary history seems deliberately to ignore writing as practice, as work, as play. Systematic artifices, formal mannerisms (that which, in the final analysis, constitutes Rabelais, Sterne, Roussel . . .) are relegated to the registers of asylums for literary madmen, the "Curiosities": "Amusing Library," "Treasure of Singularities," "Philological Entertainments," "Literary Frivolities," compilations of a maniacal erudition where rhetorical "exploits" are described with suspect complaisance, useless exaggeration, and cretinous ignorance. Constraints are treated therein as aberrations, as pathological monstrosities of language and of writing; the works resulting from them are not even worthy to be called "works": locked away, once and for all and without appeal, and often by their authors themselves, these works, in their prowess and their skillfulness, remain paraliterary monsters justiciable only to a symptomology whose enumeration and classification order a dictionary of literary madness.

Perec, like the other members of the Oulipo, is aware that the notion of literary madness is often invoked in order to suppress innovation and thus to maintain the hegemony of the canon. The Oulipo's attitude toward the concept is thus somewhat ambivalent: on the one hand, relying heavily on systematic artifice and formal mannerisms in their own literary praxis, they are open to accusations of literary madness, accusations intended to confine them and their work in the literary ghetto. On the other hand, they profess interest in literary madmen and, more generally (for obvious reasons), in literary marginalia of many sorts. The problem perhaps lies in the definition of literary madness and in the rhetoric in which the notion is couched. Queneau, who studied literary madmen in the 1930s at the Bibliothèque Nationale with a view toward elaborating an encyclopedia of *folie littéraire*, preferred the term "heteroclite." André Blavier, whose *Les Fous littéraires* (1982) follows Queneau's initiative, insists that "the appellation 'literary madman' is used nonpejoratively." For the purposes of his work, moreover, Blavier establishes several criteria for literary madness: the writer in question must be a *fou avéré* (an "established madman," which may seem to beg the question); he must have been entirely ignored by the critics and the general public; his work must have been published in printed form; and, finally, he most probably was a rich bourgeois, since he would have had to pay the publication costs himself.

Jean Lescure, in his "Brief History of the Oulipo," alludes to a discussion that focused upon the notion of literary madness:

> The position of the Oulipo in regard to literature is determined in memorandum #4, minutes of the meeting on 13 February 1961, in the following form: *Jean Queval intervened to ask if we are in favor of literary madmen. To this delicate question, F. Le Lionnais replied very subtly:*
> *—We are not against them, but the literary vocation interests us above all else.*
> *And R. Queneau stated precisely:*
> *—The only literature is voluntary literature.*

We shall have occasion to return to this notion of "voluntary literature"; for the moment, suffice it to say that it is linked to the notion of writing as praxis. It is through this more than anything else that the Oulipo lays its claim to sanity: Georges Perec, asked by an interviewer how he faced the risk of madness while writing, responded that he had been accumulating experiences of literary "madness" for years without having the impression that he was doing anything "madder" than, quite simply, *writing*.[3]

Tradition and Experiment

The Oulipo's relation to the literary establishment is thus problematical. François Le Lionnais addresses this question with ironic relativism:

> The truth is that the Quarrel of the Ancients and the Moderns is permanent. It began with Zinjanthropus (a million seven hundred and

fifty thousand years ago) and will end only with humanity—or perhaps the mutants who succeed us will take up the cause. A Quarrel, by the way, very badly named. Those who are called the Ancients are often the stuffy old descendants of those who in their own day were Moderns; and the latter, if they came back among us, would in many cases take sides with the innovators and renounce their all too faithful imitators.

For the time being, at least, the weight of the canon or, more properly, that of the institutions which codify and guarantee it, is oppressive. And for all the radical refusal and apparent subversion of traditional literary norms, a rather touching yearning also echoes within the Oulipian enterprise. If their indignation at being excluded from the mainstream is genuine, so is their nostalgia for a time when inclusion, rather than exclusion, was the rule. The former sentiment is perhaps more legitimate than the latter, but it is no more insistent in the Oulipo's work, where patently polemical stances are often implied through Adamic language:[4] palindromes, lipograms, tautograms, heretograms, pangrams.

The tension thus engendered results in a curious paradox in Oulipian "analysis": on the one hand, Queneau's work on literary madmen, Blavier's *Les Fous littéraires,* and Perec's "History of the Lipogram," focusing as they do upon writers who must surely stand as the most obscure figures of Western literature, may be read as prolegomena to a systematic erection of an anti-canon. On the other hand, the Oulipo has proclaimed its spiritual affinity to literary figures whose place in the canon is unquestioned by even the most orthodox. In the "Second Manifesto," François Le Lionnais announces this, attenuating the solemnity of an avowal of literary debt through irony: "Occasionally, we discover that a structure we believed to be entirely new had in fact already been discovered or invented in the past, sometimes even in a distant past. We make it a point of honor to recognize such a state of things in qualifying the text in question as 'plagiarism by anticipation.' Thus justice is done, and each is rewarded according to his merit."

Jacques Bens returns to this notion, rendering it somewhat more specific, citing as exemplary plagiarizers-by-anticipation Rabelais, Villon, Marot, and the Grands Rhétoriqueurs. "And we shall not forget that there existed in their time an eminently potential type of literature, the *commedia dell' arte,* which acquired really definite form only at the very moment of its staging."

Perhaps both concerns, the recuperation of obscure literary figures and the work on major figures, are symptomatic of a broader irredentist impulse. This seems clear, for instance, in Jean Lescure's account of an early Oulipian project, a history of experimental literature: that study undoubtedly would have put normative literary hierarchies into question, through savant juxtaposition of the marginal and the mainstream. But it must be noted (a commentary on this whole problematic as eloquent as any other) that the project has thus far failed to bear tangible fruit:

> Our first labors immediately indicated the desire to inscribe the Ou-
> lipo within a history. The Oulipo didn't claim to innovate at any
> price. The first papers dealt with ancient works, works that might
> serve as ancestors if not as models for the work we wanted to begin.
> This led us to consider according a good deal of our efforts to an
> H.L.E., or *Histoire des littératures expérimentales*. Here, we saw the
> notion of experimentation or exercise reappear; at the same time we
> were beginning to realize that which distinguished us from the past:
> potentiality. . . . It's because we had the profound feeling that we
> were not an absolute beginning but rather that we belonged to a tra-
> dition that the Oulipo decided to bring together texts for an anthology
> of experimental literature.

In the "synthetic" dimension of the Oulipo's work, devoted to the elaboration of new poetic structures, an analogous problem presented itself: cultural resistance to innovation. As François Le Lionnais puts it in the "Second Manifesto": "But can an artificial structure be viable? Does it have the slightest chance to take root in the cultural tissue of a society and to produce leaf, flower, and fruit? Enthusiastic modernists are convinced of it; diehard traditionalists are persuaded of the contrary."

On this point, "analysis" would seem to inform and encourage "synthesis," as the Oulipo once again turns to the sonnet, that touchstone of experiment in poetic form. Jacques Roubaud pertinently notes that "the first sonnet, at the moment of becoming a sonnet, is not a sonnet but a Sicilian variant of the Provençal *cobla*. It is only with the thousandth sonnet (or more or less—in any case after many sonnets) that the sonnet appears." Roubaud further states that the sonnet, like other traditional constraining forms, is imperialistic, for it progressively "invades everything." He argues that this process of multiplication is diametrically opposed to the purest concept of *potential* literature, and warns his fellow members against the temptations thereof: "Oulipian constraint, on the contrary, can tend toward multiplicity (toward which, seemingly, it is tending) only in ceasing to be Oulipian."

Multiplicity comes in many colors. Roubaud, I think, speaks for the majority in suggesting that the Oulipo not multiply examples of each new poetic structure it derives; to do so would be, in a sense, to forge the very sort of chains it is trying so diligently to break. But Queneau's *Cent Mille Milliards de poèmes* is surely multiple and at the same time, as we have seen, quintessentially *potential*. Thus, whereas the sonnet leads Roubaud to evoke the specter of rigid cultural codification, other members of the Oulipo see in that form, on the contrary, possibilities of creative liberty. François Le Lionnais alludes to this liberating virtue of form: "Nine or ten centuries ago, when a potential writer proposed the sonnet form, he left, through certain mechanical processes, the possibility of a choice." If the Oulipo has devoted, and continues to devote, much of its effort to an examination of the sonnet form, it is largely because of this "choice." Roubaud notes that "the Oulipian exploration of the sonnet constitutes for Queneau a practical means of . . . 'demonstration' according to constraints." And the demonstration in question takes place in the "analytic" as well as the "synthetic" dimensions, as Queneau's experiments on Mallarmé's sonnets in the present collection will show. The latter author occupies a privileged position in the Oulipian laboratory: with poker face firmly in place, Queneau informs us that "Mallarmé's sonnets are very high-grade material, like the fruit fly in genetics."

The Workroom

Returning to first principles, then, there remains the question of method; here, the image of the laboratory is perhaps not the central one, insofar as the group ultimately chose to call itself neither *Laboratoire* nor *Séminaire* but rather *Ouvroir* de Littérature Potentielle. The French word *ouvroir* has three principal meanings: it denotes the room in a convent where the nuns assemble to work, a charitable institution where indigent women engage in needlework, and a "sewing circle" where well-to-do ladies make clothes for the poor and vestments for the Church (the English word "workroom" thus does not convey the full savor of the term). In choosing it, the Oulipo's intention, like that of much of the work produced by the group in the last twenty-five years, was undoubtedly both frank and ironical. Jean Lescure, in his "Brief History of the Oulipo," playfully suggests why the original appellation was changed: "*Séminaire* bothered us in that it conjures up stud farms and artificial insemination; *ouvroir,* on the contrary, flattered the modest taste that we shared for beautiful work and good deeds: out of respect for both fine arts and morals, we consented to join the *ou* to the *li*."

Moreover, *ouvroir* is etymologically related to the verb *ouvrer,* "to work," in the sense of "working" a given material: wood, copper, stone, and so forth. It is also related to the noun *ouvrier,* "worker"—as Larousse would have it, "a person who, in exchange for a salary, performs manual work for an employer." Last, it is related to *oeuvre;* herein, one can detect the final level of Oulipian taxonomic play. For *oeuvre* has strayed from the etymon in a striking manner: applied to an individual literary text, for instance, it connotes far more than a mere "work"; applied to a body of texts produced by an author, it suggests completion, consecration, canonization if you will. When Perec, for instance, criticizes the literary establishment for its disdain of writing "as practice, as work," he is implicitly opposing *ouvroir* to *oeuvre,* labor to inspiration, collective effort to individual genius, the artisan to the artist.

The notion of the artisanal nature of literary work is central to Oulipian poetics. Jacques Roubaud says, "The claim to craftsmanship reflects an affirmation of amateurism; it is a voluntary archaism." Here, "voluntary" is a key word: Queneau, it will be recalled, invoked it in a discussion of literary madmen as the sine qua non of literature. And the Oulipo's claim to craftsmanship is intimately related to the concept of "voluntary" or "conscious" literature, just as it starkly opposes the myth of literary inspiration. Jean Lescure speaks of Queneau's attack on literary inspiration in *Odile,* and suggests its importance for the Oulipo as a whole:

> If I may refer to the henceforth famous dictum in *Odile,* we can add to this notion the considerable consequences resulting from the fact that: *The truly inspired person is never inspired, but always inspired.* What does this mean? What? This thing so rare, inspiration, this gift of the gods which makes the poet, and which this unhappy man never quite deserves in spite of all his heartaches, this enlightenment coming from who knows where, is it possible that it might cease to be capricious, and that any and everybody might find it faithful and compliant to his desires? The serious revolution, the sudden change this simple sentence introduced into a conception of literature still wholly dominated by romantic effusions and the exaltation of subjectivity, has never been fully analyzed. In fact, this sentence implied the revolutionary conception of the objectivity of literature, and from that time forward opened the latter to all possible modes of manipulation. In short, like mathematics, literature could be *explored.*

And explore it the Oulipians have, from the pyramids of rhopalic verse to the bas-relief of Poe's tomb. As "analysis" nourishes "synthesis," one of the Oulipo's principal goals becomes clearer: as Queneau puts it, the Oulipo intends to elaborate "a whole arsenal in which the poet may pick and choose, whenever he wishes to escape from that which is called inspiration," an elegant formulation of the Oulipo Militant.

Formal Constraint

Erecting the aesthetic of formal constraint, then, the Oulipo simultaneously devalues inspiration. As François Le Lionnais notes, there are many degrees of constraint, ranging from minimal to maximal: "Every literary work begins with an inspiration (at least that's what its author suggests) which must accommodate itself as well as possible to a series of constraints and procedures that fit inside each other like Chinese boxes. Constraints of vocabulary and grammar, constraints of the novel (division into chapters, etc.) or of classical tragedy (rule of the three unities), constraints of general versification, constraints of fixed forms (as in the case of the rondeau or the sonnet), etc."

Clearly, Le Lionnais conceives the range of constraint in terms of a hierarchy. Simplifying grossly, one might postulate three levels: first, a minimal level, constraints of the language in which the text is written; second, an intermediate level, including constraints of genre and certain literary norms; third, a maximal level, that of *consciously* preelaborated and *voluntarily* imposed systems of artifice. No text can skirt the minimal level and remain readable; perhaps no text can wholly avoid the intermediate level. But it is the maximal level that concerns the Oulipo: this is what they refer to in using the word "constraint"; this is what characterizes their own poetic production and, consequently, the model they propose to others.

Implicit in the aesthetic of formal constraint is a rather broad leap of faith in the passage from production to reception. If the Oulipo insists on rigidly constraining formal organization, it is in the belief that this will engender texts of exceptional merit, another avatar of the aesthetic of *difficulté vaincue*. It rapidly becomes clear that this, too, can be conceived as a hierarchy: increasing the difficulty of the problems posed necessarily increases—here is the leap of faith—the merit of its eventual solution. Thus, François Le Lionnais is moved to argue:

> The efficacy of a structure—that is, the extent to which it helps a writer—depends primarily on the degree of difficulty imposed by rules that are more or less constraining.
>
> Most writers and readers feel (or pretend to feel) that extremely constraining structures such as the acrostic, spoonerisms, the lipogram, the palindrome, or the holorhyme (to cite only these five) are mere examples of acrobatics and deserve nothing more than a wry grin, since they could never help to engender truly valid works of art. Never? Indeed. People are a little too quick to sneer at acrobatics. Breaking a record in one of these extremely constraining structures can in itself serve to justify the work; the emotion that derives from its semantic aspect constitutes a value which should certainly not be overlooked, but which remains nonetheless secondary.

If the Oulipo is unanimous in promoting the use of formal constraint, there is, however, some internal debate as to the number of texts resulting from any given constraint. Queneau, as Roubaud sees it, calls for *unicity:* once a constraint is elaborated, a few texts are provided to illustrate it. The group then turns to other concerns, and the texts thus engendered are disseminated to the public. Roubaud himself, we recall, cautions against the proliferation of texts resulting from a given constraint; for him, "the ideal constraint gives rise to one text only." Most severely doctrinaire of all would seem to be Le Lionnais, characterized by Roubaud as an "ultra" because of his insistence that the only text of value is the one that formulates the constraint; all texts resulting therefrom, preaches Le Lionnais, must be banished to the limbo of the "applied Oulipo." Roubaud argues that Le Lionnais's position neglects the deductive aspect of the method, and postulates that "a constraint must 'prove' at least one text."

Regarding the nature of the constraint itself, though, there seems to be widespread agreement. As Roubaud puts it, "A good Oulipian constraint is a simple constraint." Of course, this does not mean that the application of the constraint will be simple; neither does it mean that the text resulting from it will be simple. Consider the case of Georges Perec's *La Disparition*, the novel written without the letter E. What could be simpler than the decision to exclude a letter of the alphabet from a text? Patently, this constraint *is* simple and thus—another leap of faith—elegant. In the passage from conception to application, however, simplicity engenders complexity: as Perec himself notes, "the principle of the lipogram is childishly simple; its application can prove to be excessively difficult."

Roubaud postulates "two principles sometimes respected in Oulipian work": first, that "a text written according to a constraint must speak of this constraint," and second, that "a text written according to a mathematizable constraint must contain the consequences of the mathematical theory it illustrates."[5] He cites *La Disparition* as an example of the first principle, and suggests that it is precisely in this, rather than merely in its length, that the text differs from all previous experiments in the lipogram:

> In what does the Oulipization of this constraint, as old or almost as old as the alphabet, consist? In this, which is a fundamental trait: that, as opposed to the different plagiarists who use the lipogram as a process of translation (Nestor of Laranda and the *Iliad*), process of mnemotechnics, moral or metaphysical formulary . . . the constraint therein is at once principle of the writing of the text, its developmental mechanism, and at the same time the meaning of the text: *La Disparition* is a novel about a disappearance, the disappearance of the *e;* it is thus both the story of what it recounts and the story of the constraint that creates that which is recounted. This highly involuted aspect of constraint (which is undoubtedly not proper to Oulipian constraint, but which is in this case practically pure) is a direct con-

sequence of the Oulipian constraints, which may be formulated in the following manner:

Axiom: Constraint is a principle, not a means.

Perec, for his part, lucidly announces the final virtue of the aesthetic (already hinted at by François Le Lionnais): the liberating *potential* of rigorous formal constraint: "In this sense, the suppression of the letter, of the typographical sign, of the basic prop, is a purer, more objective, more decisive operation, something like constraint degree zero, after which everything becomes possible." This aspect of the aesthetic is startling, since it seems so strongly counterintuitive, and yet Perec and his fellow members appear to be persuaded of it. Perec, whose considerable poetic production might serve as a casebook on systematic artifice, even goes so far as to suggest that writing a poem "freely" would be more problematical for him than writing according to a system of formal constraint: "I don't for the moment intend to write poetry other than in adopting such constraints. . . . The intense difficulty posed by this sort of production . . . palls in comparison to the terror I would feel in writing 'poetry' freely."[6]

Granted that formal constraint becomes the hallmark of the Oulipian text, Paul Braffort is led to characterize the Oulipo's work as "non-Jourdanian literature."[7] The allusion, of course, is to Molière's *Bourgeois Gentilhomme*, II, iv, where Monsieur Jourdain discovers to his astonishment that "everything which is not prose is poetry, and everything which is not poetry is prose." Braffort's comment is both amusing and highly ironic, but it nonetheless advances the rather serious suggestion that traditional taxonomy is no longer sufficient in distinguishing between "quasi-amorphous texts and texts produced according to rigorous constraints." To offer a concrete illustration of this, one might argue, for instance, that *La Disparition* resembles Harry Mathews's "Liminal Poem" more closely than it resembles *Eugénie Grandet;* or that the *Cent Mille Milliards de poèmes* is fundamentally more similar to Italo Calvino's novel *If on a winter's night a traveler,* or even to Scève's *Délie,* than it is to Nerval's *Chimères.* Through all these pyrotechnics, the Oulipo's message is at once becomingly modest and outrageously bold; Jean Lescure has offered a lapidary formulation thereof: "What the Oulipo intended to demonstrate was that these constraints are felicitous, generous, and are in fact literature itself."

Mathematics

Oulipian systems of formal constraint are often based on the alphabet. But in many cases, as the reader has undoubtedly begun to suspect, the nature of Oulipian constraint is mathematical. At the center of the group's poetics is the idea of the essential analogy of mathematics and literature. Much of their work may be seen as an attempt to demonstrate the complementarity of these two modes of discourse, which are thought by many to be mutually exclusive. While the reciprocal relations of music and literature have received a considerable amount of attention—one could catalogue examples from Orpheus to *Doctor Faustus*—the same is not true of mathematics and literature, although some suggest that mathematics is the link between literature and music, and music is what poetry aspires to. Arguably, the connection between architecture and literature (which seems clear, for instance, in the architectonic elegance of fixed form poetry, and is demonstrably insistent on the thematic level in many works whose formal organization would appear to be less rigorous, the most salient example being Hugo's *Notre-Dame de Paris*) is essentially a connection between literature and mathematics.

In spite of this resistance, the notion of the analogy of mathematics and literature has always existed on the margins of the latter, and this aspect of the Oulipian enterprise has a certain number of authoritative antecedents. Pythagoras, for example, taught that number was the essence of all things, and that any relation, from natural relations to those occurring in music and poetics, could be expressed mathematically. Plato, in the *Meno* and the *Republic,* argues that geometry is the foundation of all knowledge: this belief, and the consequences for aesthetics that arise from it, revived in the neo-Platonic disputes of the Middle Ages. In the Renaissance, the aesthetics of mathematics and the mathematics of aesthetics are clear in the work of Leonardo. Later, in France, Descartes, Pascal, and d'Alembert were both writers and mathematicians. In Germany, Schopenhauer (in *World as Will and Idea*) suggested the similarity of poetical and mathematical conceptualization. Lautréamont, in his *Poésies,* argues that "poetry is geometry par excellence," using that notion in a global and singularly vituperative attack on Romanticism. But it is perhaps Lewis Carroll who best achieves what François Le Lionnais refers to as the "amalgam" of mathematics and literature: that is, the conscious application of one to the other, the exploitation of their *potential* for interpenetration. In our own century, Valéry studied mathematics as "a *model* of acts of the mind," and Ezra Pound, in his *Spirit of Romance,* declares that "poetry is a sort of inspired mathematics." Finally, the mutual complementarity of literature and mathematics has been elaborated at some length by Scott Buchanan, in *Poetry and Mathematics,* although it must be noted that his point of view betrays a distinct bias toward mathematics.

François Le Lionnais situates the Oulipo's contribution to this tradition as follows: "Visited by mathematical grace, a small minority of writers and artists (small, but weighty) have written intelligently and enthusiastically about 'the queen of sciences.' Infinitely rarer are those who—like Pascal and d'Alembert—possessed double nationality and distinguished themselves both as writers (or artists) and as mathematicians. Outside, perhaps, of Lewis Carroll and some Oulipians, I know of only Raymond Queneau who has brought about in his work, to such a fine degree, the intimate amalgam of poetical inspiration and mathematical sense of structure."

The notion of "double nationality" is singularly appropriate in the case of the Oulipo, for the group harbors many fine amateur mathematicians as well as three professionals: Jacques Roubaud, Claude Berge, and Paul Braffort, whose fields of specialization are, respectively, pure mathematics, graph theory, and artificial intelligence. It is thus wholly logical to find that whereas the antimathematical prejudice in literature is often articulated around the more pernicious fear of the mechanistic model that subtends it, the Oulipo embraces this mechanistic model. In doing so, its members are conscious of working against the grain of contemporary poetics, yet they remain convinced that mathematics is functional in even the most apparently amathematical text. Queneau himself noted a very elemental level of this function: "The poet, however refractory toward mathematics he may be, is nonetheless obliged to count up to twelve in order to compose an alexandrine."

Roubaud, for his part, notes the influence of Nicolas Bourbaki's *Eléments de Mathématique* on the Oulipo, calling the former "a sort of mathematical surrealism." Roubaud further characterizes the essential stance of the group in this regard: "To comport oneself toward language as if the latter could be mathematized; and language can be mathematized, moreover, in a very specific fashion." This leads him to formulate a series of conjectures and principles: "Arithmetic applied to language gives rise to texts"; "Language producing texts gives rise to arithmetic"; "A constraint is an axiom of a text"; "Writing under Oulipian constraint is the equivalent of the drafting of a mathematical text which may be formalized according to the axiomatic method." The polemical, reactive intent of these statements is obvious—they of course rejoin the broader attack on the notion of literary inspiration—but apart from that, the theory they expose corresponds very closely to Oulipian praxis, as several of the essays in the present collection will demonstrate. They may also suggest the long march from simple arithmetic to the form of higher mathematics that Oulipo privileges in its work: combinatorics. Claude Berge, in "For a Potential Analysis of Combinatory Literature," has offered a definition of combinatorics, suggesting the importance of the discipline within Oulipian poetics:

One has to wait until 1961 for the expression *combinatory litera-ture* to be used, undoubtedly for the first time, by François Le Lionnais, in the postface to Raymond Queneau's *Cent Mille Milliards de poèmes*. Literature is a known quantity, but combinatorics? Makers of dictionaries and encyclopedias manifest an extreme degree of cowardice when it comes to giving a definition of the latter; one can hardly blame their insipid imprecision, since traditional mathematicians who "feel" that problems are of combinatory nature very seldom are inclined to engage in systematic and independent study of the methods of resolving them.

In an attempt to furnish a more precise definition, we shall rely on the concept of *configuration;* one looks for a configuration each time one disposes of a finite number of objects, and one wishes to dispose them according to certain constraints postulated in advance; Latin squares and finite geometries are configurations, but so is the arrangement of packages of different sizes in a drawer that is too small, or the disposition of words or sentences given in advance (on the condition that the given constraints be sufficiently "crafty" for the problem to be real). Just as arithmetic studies whole numbers (along with the traditional operations), as algebra studies operations in general, as analysis studies functions, as geometry studies forms that are rigid and topology those that are not, so combinatorics, for its part, studies configurations. It attempts to demonstrate the existence of configurations of a certain type. And if this existence is no longer in doubt, it undertakes to count them (equalities or inequalities of counting), or to list them ("listing"), or to extract an "optimal" example from them (the problem of optimization).

It is thus not surprising to learn that a systematic study of these problems revealed a large number of new mathematical concepts, easily transposable into the realm of language, and that the pruritus of combinatorics has wrought its worst on the Oulipian breast.

Here, it should be noted that Oulipian aesthetics rejoins the critical avant-garde: in the mid-1960s, critics such as Umberto Eco and B. A. Uspenski began to apply the name "combinatorics" to the permutational phenomena in certain narrative forms (these phenomena and their combinatoric nature having of course been pointed out, much earlier, by Vladimir Propp, but without using the magic word). The term gradually came to acquire the critical vogue that it enjoys today. Many of the essays in the present collection testify to the Oulipo's concern with combinatorics: Queneau's "A Story as You Like It" and "The Relation X Takes Y for Z," Italo Calvino's "Prose and Anticombinatorics," Paul Fournel's "The Theater

Tree: A Combinatory Play," Harry Mathews's "Mathews's Algorithm," and Bens, Berge, and Braffort's "Recurrent Literature" all speculate upon, or exploit, combinatoric theory and its *potential*.

If the Oulipo insists upon combinatorics in its poetics, it is perhaps because combinatorics, whose status as a mathematical discipline is now established, is demonstrably functional in many literary structures, even some of the most traditional ones. That is, combinatorics offers a privileged locus for the interplay of mathematics and literature. All of this, perhaps inevitably, granted the practical problems inherent in the manipulation of complex combinatoric structures, leads to experimentation with computers. Queneau, in "Potential Literature," which dates from early 1964, says that the constant *lamento* of the group at that time was its lack of access to sophisticated machinery. Since then, things have changed for the Oulipo, as they have for many of us; Paul Fournel's "Computer and Writer: The Centre Pompidou Experiment" seems to suggest that the Oulipo in the future progressively will be drawn toward a more systematic exploration of the literary possibilities offered by the computer.

Aleatorics and Anti-Aleatorics

If the image of the computer has undoubtedly caused many literati to shudder, conjuring up as it does the machine and its ghost, it must be noted that it is because of the *potential* the computer furnishes to the mechanistic model that the Oulipians are drawn to it. The computer constitutes thus another arm in the arsenal they deploy against the notion of inspiration and, in a broader sense, against the avowed *bête noire* of the Oulipo: the aleatory. For another way of considering the Oulipian enterprise is as a sustained attack on the aleatory in literature, a crusade for the maximal motivation of the literary sign. All of their work, from short exercises in highly constraining form to far longer texts resulting from the application of Oulipian theory, from the indications of a nostalgic longing for a mythological primitive language to their insistence on *voluntary* or *conscious* literature, may be read in this light. As Jacques Bens expresses the position: "The members of the Oulipo have never hidden their abhorrence of the aleatory, of bogus fortunetellers and penny-ante lotteries: 'The Oulipo is anti-chance,' the Oulipian Claude Berge affirmed one day with a straight face, which leaves no doubt about our aversion to the dice shaker. Make no mistake about it: potentiality is uncertain, but not a matter of chance. We know perfectly well everything that can happen, but we don't know whether it will happen."

Jacques Roubaud echoes Bens, in a discussion of Queneau's notion of *voluntary* literature: "The intentional, voluntary character of constraint to

which he insistently alludes time and again is for him indissolubly linked
to this lively refusal of the frequent equation of chance and freedom." The
seeming paradox we noted in Oulipian aesthetics, the belief that systems
of formal constraint—far from restricting a writer—actually afford a field
of creative liberty, is again apparent here. Queneau affirms, "The classical
playwright who writes his tragedy observing a certain number of familiar
rules is freer than the poet who writes that which comes into his head and
who is the slave of other rules of which he is ignorant." The Quenellian
vision of liberty is classical in this sense, insofar as its enabling condition
is lucidity. His attack on the aleatory springs in part from his reaction
against the surrealists, a group with which he was briefly associated and
from which, like many others, he was summarily excommunicated. The
surrealists erected the aleatory and the psychological construct based on
it, the unconscious, as a means of transcendence; it becomes rapidly clear
that Queneau's aesthetic is diametrically opposed to theirs. His attack on
chance reflects, says Roubaud, "rejection of the mystical belief according
to which freedom may be born from the random elimination of constraints."

And yet, in this play of terms—in which "aleatory," "random," "inspiration," and "ignorance" are opposed to "conscious," "voluntary," "constraint," and "lucidity"—tensions and even contradictions exist, for the
aleatory cunningly seems to insinuate itself even where efforts to exclude
it are most diligent. Roubaud recognizes this and tries to explain it, using
as an example Queneau's fascination with the series of prime numbers
(called by François Le Lionnais "those rebel angels"): he argues that Queneau became interested in them precisely because they "imitate chance
while obeying a law"; consequently, chance is exorcised, since it is recognized for what it is and thus is mastered. His argument suggests a far
thornier question going directly to the heart of Oulipian poetics: what if
the law itself is aleatory—for instance, the mathematical law that permits
us to engender the series of prime numbers or, analogously, the system of
constraint through which an Oulipian text is generated? Speaking specifi-
cally of the Oulipian aesthetic of formal constraint, Roubaud is forced to
admit a contradiction: "Queneau's attitude (and that of the Oulipo) toward
traditional constraints, if it is less bold and naive than Bourbaki's, reflects
nonetheless the inherent ambiguity of the procedure: on the one hand, the
eminently arbitrary character of constraints is revindicated; at the same
time traditional constraints are marked as arbitrary, but, precisely because
they are traditional and solidly anchored in history, they guard a power of
fascination that situates them elsewhere, beyond the arbitrary . . . it is
difficult to get out of this."

Jacques Bens touches upon the same problem in a discussion of Queneau's work:

Before soliciting any other sort of potentiality, I would like to respond to an objection that came to my mind as we went along. "It is well known," one might object, "that Raymond Queneau constructs his novels with obstinate and laborious rigor, and cannot tolerate leaving anything to chance (he himself says it). How can one reconcile such rigor with the vagueness, the incertitude, the approximations that necessarily accompany potentiality?"

I believe, actually, that the contradictions exist solely in appearance. Or rather that there is no contradiction: it is the problem that is ill-formulated. For the writer never claimed that he detested incertitude itself but merely that incertitude born of chance, which is not at all the same thing.

On the other hand, it might very well be the same thing, and in any case the distinction that Bens draws is too nice to be of much practical value in resolving the dilemma. Perhaps one stage in the group's evolution is passed when Oulipians realize that a throw of the dice will never abolish chance; at least one other aspect of their poetics would seem to support such a suspicion: the rehabilitation of the *clinamen*. In Lucretius's account of Epicurean atomic theory, the *clinamen atomorum,* or swerving of the atoms (*De rerum natura* II, 216–93) is an essential part of the model. The random, *aleatory* nature of the swerving of the atoms as they fall is postulated in opposition to the constant, straight fall of the atoms in Democritus's model. Thus, the random is opposed to the deterministic, and the clinamen acquires the status of the locus, and consequently the guarantor, of free will. Stone-dead for nigh on two millennia, the clinamen has been resurrected in the last decade in critical discourse by a surprising variety of people and made to serve a surprising variety of purposes: Harold Bloom has used it extensively, as has Michel Serres, who passes it along to Jeffrey Mehlman; René Thom engendered a polemic articulated around the concept, in which Edgar Morin, Henri Atlan, and Ilya Prigogine participated.[8] (It is both astonishing and perversely rewarding to note a convergence between the Oulipo and Harold Bloom: in both cases, the virus of the clinamen seems to have been transmitted, fittingly enough, by Alfred Jarry.)

Within the Oulipo, it is Georges Perec who has furnished the most lucid explanation of the clinamen. In a discussion of his novel, *La Vie mode d'emploi*—a text elaborated according to several very rigorous systems of formal constraint—Perec notes that a constitutive element (a chapter, in this case) of his otherwise rigidly symmetrical structure has been deliberately omitted, and explains why this must be so:

> More fundamentally, this chapter must disappear in order to break the symmetry, to introduce an error into the system, because when a sys-

tem of constraints is established, there must also be anticonstraint within it. The system of constraints—and this is important—must be destroyed. It must not be rigid; there must be some play in it; it must, as they say, "creak" a bit; it must not be completely coherent; there must be a clinamen—it's from Epicurean atomic theory: "The world functions because from the outset there is a lack of balance." According to Klee, "Genius is the error in the system"; perhaps I'm being too arrogant in saying that, but in Klee's work, it is very important.[9]

How are we to interpret this new "swerve" in Oulipian theory? Is it the flaw in the system, rather than the system itself, that assures creative liberty, just as the clinamen assures free will? Is this the final victory of the aleatory over the motivated? Is it the first note of a tocsin and, if so, for whom tolls the bell? In any case, probably not for the Oulipians: their regenerative powers, one notes with reassurance, are astounding. Italo Calvino, for one, is extraordinarily sanguine; in concluding his essay "Prose and Anticombinatorics," he brings this whole problematic full circle, suggesting that the computer, that scourge of the aleatory, be placed at the service of the clinamen: "This clearly demonstrates, we believe, that the aid of a computer, far from *replacing* the creative act of the artist, permits the latter rather to liberate himself from the slavery of a combinatory search, allowing him also the best chance of concentrating on this 'clinamen' which, alone, can make of the text a true work of art."

Scriptor Ludens, Lector Ludens

Even at its most polemical, even at its most ferociously doctrinaire, the Oulipo's work over the past twenty-five years has consistently been animated by a most refreshing spirit of playfulness. The Oulipian text is quite explicitly offered as a game, as a system of ludic exchange between author and reader. Jacques Bens declares that "a potential work is a work which is not limited to its appearances, which contains secret riches, which willingly lends itself to exploration." Used here to suggest the ideal process of reception, the key word is *exploration,* especially in view of the fact that the Oulipo uses the term to characterize its own efforts in the process of production. The parallelism thus implied privileges the reader, and this is indeed another central concept in Oulipian theory. Says Bens, "For Queneau (I repeat: *for him*), there is no, or very little, literature without a reader." And Queneau himself demands the reader's participation, refusing on behalf of the latter any possibility of passivity toward the literary text: "Why shouldn't one demand a certain effort on the reader's part?

Everything is always explained to him. He must eventually tire of being treated with such contempt." For Queneau, reading must be a *conscious,* a *voluntary* act of decoding. Speaking of his own work, he declares that the novel should resemble an onion, suggesting through this image a hierarchy of hermeticism. This textual hierarchy will necessarily be engaged by a hierarchy of reading in the reception process, and indeed by a hierarchy of readers, "some being content merely to strip away the first layer of skin, while the others, far fewer, strip it layer after layer." What Queneau was calling for, from the point of view at once of the writer and of the reader, is what Roland Barthes would later come to designate as the *texte de jouissance,* or text of ecstasy. Adopting Queneau's aesthetic and broadening it to characterize the Oulipian quest as a whole, Jacques Bens says:

> Potential literature would be that which awaits a reader, which yearns for him, which needs him in order to fully realize itself. Here, we are suddenly plunged into a somber perplexity, for everything that has any claim to be literature presents itself much in this way, from Michel de Saint-Pierre to François Mauriac.
>
> However, if we return to the matter at hand—I mean, to our onion—we will recall that the first postulate of potentiality is the secret, that which is hidden beneath the appearances, and the encouragement for discovery. Nothing prevents us then from deciding that there will be *potential literature* if one disposes of both a resistant work and an explorer.

Thus, to the concept of potential writing corresponds that of potential reading. Faced with this conclusion, some may feel that Oulipian generosity is overshadowed by Oulipian brashness: the radical valorization of the status of the reader, rather than a gift, may seem a dare. And perhaps it is, but it is largely mitigated by the ludic spirit in which it is proposed. For serious and playful intent are not mutually exclusive in the Oulipo's work: they are, on the contrary, insistently and reciprocally implicative. And although this posture leads some to dismiss their work as "mere" play, the Oulipians hold fast to the notion of ludic literature. Addressing this question, Jacques Roubaud argues that Oulipian work, granted its fundamentally innovative nature, "cannot avail itself of any so-called serious finality of any of the criteria serving today in scientific domains to eliminate research that unduly jostles accepted perspectives," and concludes that its categorization as play is thus inevitable. But, he says, "it may be noted that Queneau does not refuse this often intentionally pejorative (in the case of those who distribute the labels) marginalization of the Oulipo." Indeed, far from refusing it, Queneau embraces the notion:

I will insist, however, on the qualifier "amusing." Surely, certain of our labors may appear to be mere pleasantries, or simple witticisms, analogous to certain parlor games.

Let us remember that topology and the theory of numbers sprang in part from that which used to be called "mathematical entertainments," "recreational mathematics." I salute in passing the memory of Bachet de Méziriac, author of *Problèmes plaisants et délectables qui se font par les nombres* (1612—not, as Larousse says, 1613), and one of the first members of the French Academy. Let us also remember that the calculation of probabilities was at first nothing other than an anthology of "diversions," as Bourbaki states in the "Notice Historique" of the twenty-first fascicle on Integration. And likewise game theory until von Neumann.

François Le Lionnais foresaw the same problem and attempted to defuse it in the "First Manifesto," employing a judicious (and entirely characteristic) mixture of humor and polemic: "A word at the end for the benefit of those particularly grave people who condemn without consideration and without appeal all work wherein is manifested any propensity for pleasantry. When they are the work of poets, entertainments, pranks, and hoaxes still fall within the domain of poetry. Potential literature remains thus the most serious thing in the world. Q.E.D."

But this aspect of Oulipian poetics cuts far deeper than either Queneau or Le Lionnais suggests. At its heart is the belief that play is central to literature and, in a broader sense, to the aesthetic experience; in this, Oulipians fervently concur with Johan Huizinga, who asserted that "all poetry is born of play," extending his argument from poetry to culture itself. And play they do, as often as not with the tropes of their own discourse: the forbidding Oulipian "arsenal" of literary structures alluded to previously becomes in Le Lionnais the "Institute for Literary Prosthesis," a charitable institution (and thus an entirely logical annex of the *ouvroir*) devoted to helping congenitally handicapped authors or those unlucky enough to have been maimed in the literary wars. This, then, is the attitude they adopt toward their own enterprise, an attitude whereby, through recourse to irony and humor, the temptations of self-sufficiency are resolutely kept at bay. A definition proposed by the group in its early days illustrates this attitude nicely, and will perhaps serve as a convenient point of conclusion for these introductory remarks:

Oulipians: rats who must build the labyrinth from which they propose to escape.

A Note on the Translations

. . . .

Reading an Oulipian text is challenging; translating it, *a fortiori,* can be very difficult indeed. For translation is a sort of reading, except that the original text may impose its fearful symmetry more immediately upon a translator than upon a reader. My great delight in reading Oulipian work (it would be both foolish and useless to try to hide this bias) is largely engendered by that symmetry, upon which the Oulipo has wagered more heavily than most, and I hope that some of it will survive my translation.

The texts have been chosen from four sources. "Potential Literature" is from Queneau's *Bâtons, chiffres et lettres.* "Rule and Constraint" was published in *Pratiques* 39 (1983). "Lipo: First Manifesto," "Second Manifesto," "Brief History of the Oulipo," "The Collège de Pataphysique and the Oulipo," "History of the Lipogram," "For a Potential Analysis of Combinatory Literature," "The Relation X Takes Y for Z," "A Story as You Like It," and "The Theater Tree: A Combinatory Play" were taken from *La Littérature potentielle.* "Liminal Poem," "Queneau Oulipian," "Raymond Queneau and the Amalgam of Mathematics and Literature," "Mathematics in the Method of Raymond Queneau," "Recurrent Literature," "Mathews's Algorithm," "Computer and Writer: The Centre Pompidou Experiment," and "Prose and Anticombinatorics" are from *Atlas de littérature potentielle,* as is much of the bibliographical material.

These texts present a vertiginous range of style, from the polemical language of the manifestoes to the more conventionally discursive language of, for instance, "History of the Lipogram." I hope that some of this range will be apparent in translation. In those instances where canonical poets (Ronsard, Racine, Mallarmé) are quoted, I have cravenly chosen to use extant authoritative translations, being for my part exceedingly reluctant to incur papal criticism for rushing in where angels fear to tread. I am thus all the more grateful to Harry Mathews for having supplied his own translation of "L'Algorithm de Mathews": that translation is, of course, authoritative in every sense of the word.

Certain passages in the texts presented here assume a familiarity with French culture or literature uncommon outside of France. In others, the author may allude to Oulipian exercises or procedures not included in this collection. And still other references are obscure, perhaps intentionally so. I have tried to attenuate these difficulties in providing notes wherever supplementary information seemed necessary. These are followed by the indication (WM); *all other notes are the authors' own.* The reader should

also be aware that all ellipses in the translated texts are the authors' rather
than mine.

Granted that the purpose of the collection is to acquaint the Anglo-
phonic reader with the principal aspects of Oulipian poetics, most of the
texts herein deal with literary theory. Another consideration conditioning
this choice derives from the Oulipo's own insistence on rigorous form: if
their theory does lead to practical demonstrations, the texts of this sort
resist translation in a way that the theoretical texts do not. Think, for
example, of the problems posed by the translation of Harry Mathews's
"Liminal Poem" from the original English into any other language. Still,
texts like "Prose and Anticombinatorics," "The Relation X Takes Y for
Z," "A Story as You Like It," and "The Theater Tree: A Combinatory
Play" should furnish the reader with some idea of the sort of text that
might result when a given aspect of Oulipian theory is applied.

Finally, and most important, in spite of any eventual infelicities that
might otherwise be remarked, I hope the present collection will preserve
for the reader that which has consistently nourished my own reading of
the Oulipo: the pleasure of the text.

Harry Mathews

· · · · · · · · · ·

Liminal Poem

to Martin Gardner

O
t o
s e e
man's
s t e r n
p o e t i c
t h o u g h t
p u b l i c l y
e s p o u s i n g
r e c k l e s s l y
i m a g i n a t i v e
m a t h e m a t i c a l
i n v e n t i v e n e s s,
o p e n m i n d e d n e s s
u n c o n d i t i o n a l l y
s u p e r f e c u n d a t i n g
n o n a n t a g o n i s t i c a l
h y p e r s o p h i s t i c a t e d
i n t e r d e n o m i n a t i o n a l
i n t e r p e n e t r a b i l i t i e s.
Harry Burchell Mathews
Jacques Denis Roubaud
Albert Marie Schmidt
Paul Lucien Fournel
Jacques Duchateau
Luc Etienne Perin
Marcel M Benabou
Michele Metail
Italo Calvino
Jean Lescure
Noel Arnaud
P Braffort
A Blavier
J Queval
C Berge
Perec
Bens
FLL
RQ

·

25

François Le Lionnais

. . . .

Lipo
First Manifesto

Let's open a dictionary to the words "Potential Literature." We find absolutely nothing. Annoying lacuna. What follows is intended, if not to impose a definition, at least to propose a few remarks, simple hors d'oeuvres meant to assuage the impatience of the starving multitudes until the arrival of the main dish, which will be prepared by people more worthy than myself.

Do you remember the polemic that accompanied the invention of language? Mystification, puerile fantasy, degeneration of the race and decline of the State, treason against Nature, attack on affectivity, criminal neglect of inspiration; language was accused of everything (without, of course, using language) at that time.

And the creation of writing, and grammar—do you think that that happened without a fight? The truth is that the Quarrel of the Ancients and the Moderns is permanent. It began with Zinjanthropus (a million seven hundred and fifty thousand years ago) and will end only with humanity—or perhaps the mutants who succeed us will take up the cause. A Quarrel, by the way, very badly named. Those who are called the Ancients are often the stuffy old descendants of those who in their own day were Moderns; and the latter, if they came back among us, would in many cases take sides with the innovators and renounce their all too faithful imitators.

Potential literature only represents a new rising of the sap in this debate.[1]

Every literary work begins with an inspiration (at least that's what its author suggests) which must accommodate itself as well as possible to a series of constraints and procedures that fit inside each other like Chinese boxes. Constraints of vocabulary and grammar, constraints of the novel

26

(division into chapters, etc.) or of classical tragedy (rule of the three unities), constraints of general versification, constraints of fixed forms (as in the case of the rondeau or the sonnet), etc.

Must one adhere to the old tricks of the trade and obstinately refuse to imagine new possibilities? The partisans of the status quo don't hesitate to answer in the affirmative. Their conviction rests less on reasoned reflection than on force of habit and the impressive series of masterpieces (and also, alas, pieces less masterly) which has been obtained according to the present rules and regulations. The opponents of the invention of language must have argued thus, sensitive as they were to the beauty of shrieks, the expressiveness of sighs, and sidelong glances (and we are certainly not asking lovers to renounce all of this).

Should humanity lie back and be satisfied to watch new thoughts make ancient verses? We don't believe that it should. That which certain writers have introduced with talent (even with genius) in their work, some only occasionally (the forging of new words), others with predilection (counterrhymes), others with insistence but in only one direction (Lettrism),[2] the Ouvroir de Littérature Potentielle (Oulipo) intends to do systematically and scientifically, if need be through recourse to machines that process information.

In the research which the Oulipo proposes to undertake, one may distinguish two principal tendencies, oriented respectively toward Analysis and Synthesis. The analytic tendency investigates works from the past in order to find possibilities that often exceed those their authors had anticipated. This, for example, is the case of the cento, which might be reinvigorated, it seems to me, by a few considerations taken from Markov's chain theory.[3]

The synthetic tendency is more ambitious: it constitutes the essential vocation of the Oulipo. It's a question of developing new possibilities unknown to our predecessors. This is the case, for example, of the *Cent Mille Milliards de poèmes* or the Boolian haikus.[4]

Mathematics—particularly the abstract structures of contemporary mathematics—proposes thousands of possibilities for exploration, both algebraically (recourse to new laws of composition) and topologically (considerations of textual contiguity, openness and closure). We're also thinking of anaglyphic poems, texts that are transformable by projection, etc. Other forays may be imagined, notably into the area of special vocabulary (crows, foxes, dolphins; Algol computer language, etc.).[5] It would take a long article to enumerate the possibilities now foreseen (and in certain cases already sketched out).

It's not easy to discern beforehand, examining only the seed, the taste of a new fruit. Let's take the case of alphabetical constraint. In literature it can result in the acrostic, which has produced truly staggering works (still, Villon and, well before him, the psalmist and author of the *Lamentations* attributed to Jeremiah . . .); in painting it resulted in Herbin, and a good thing too; in music the fugue on the name B.A.C.H.—there we have a respectable piece of work. How could the inventors of the alphabet have imagined all of that?[6]

To conclude, Anoulipism is devoted to discovery, Synthoulipism to invention. From the one to the other there exist many subtle channels.

A word at the end for the benefit of those particularly grave people who condemn without consideration and without appeal all work wherein is manifested any propensity for pleasantry.

When they are the work of poets, entertainments, pranks, and hoaxes still fall within the domain of poetry. Potential literature remains thus the most serious thing in the world. Q.E.D.

François Le Lionnais

· · · · · · · · · · · · · · · ·

Second Manifesto

I am working for people who are primarily intelligent,
rather than serious.   P. Féval

Poetry is a simple art where everything resides in the execution. Such is
the fundamental rule that governs both the critical and the creative activities of the Oulipo. From this point of view, the Second Manifesto does not
intend to modify the principles that presided over the creation of our Association (these principles having been sketched out in the First Manifesto), but rather to amplify and strengthen them. It must however be
remarked that, with increasing ardor (mixed with some anxiety), we have
envisioned in the last few years a new orientation in our research. It consists in the following:

The overwhelming majority of Oulipian works thus far produced inscribe themselves in a SYNTACTIC structurElist perspective (I beg the
reader not to confuse this word—created expressly for this Manifesto—
with structurAlist, a term that many of us consider with circumspection).

Indeed, the creative effort in these works is principally brought to bear
on the formal aspects of literature: alphabetical, consonantal, vocalic, syllabic, phonetic, graphic, prosodic, rhymic, rhythmic, and numerical constraints, structures, or programs. On the other hand, *semantic* aspects
were not dealt with, meaning having been left to the discretion of each
author and excluded from our structural preoccupations.

It seemed desirable to take a step forward, to try to broach the question
of semantics and to try to tame concepts, ideas, images, feelings, and
emotions. The task is arduous, bold, and (precisely because of this) worthy of consideration.[1] If Jean Lescure's history of the Oulipo portrayed us
as we are (and as we were), the ambition described above portrays us as
we should be.

The activity of the Oulipo and the mission it has entrusted to itself raise the problem of the efficacy and the viability of artificial (and, more generally, artistic) literary structures.

The efficacy of a structure—that is, the extent to which it helps a writer—depends primarily on the degree of difficulty imposed by rules that are more or less constraining.

Most writers and readers feel (or pretend to feel) that extremely constraining structures such as the acrostic, spoonerisms, the lipogram, the palindrome, or the holorhyme (to cite only these five) are mere examples of acrobatics and deserve nothing more than a wry grin, since they could never help to engender truly valid works of art. Never? Indeed. People are a little too quick to sneer at acrobatics. Breaking a record in one of these extremely constraining structures can in itself serve to justify the work; the emotion that derives from its semantic aspect constitutes a value which should certainly not be overlooked, but which remains nonetheless secondary.

At the other extreme there's the refusal of all constraint, shriek-literature or eructative literature. This tendency has its gems, and the members of the Oulipo are by no means the least fervent of its admirers . . . during those moments, of course, not devoted to their priestly duties.

Between these two poles exists a whole range of more or less constraining structures which have been the object of numerous experiments since the invention of language. The Oulipo holds very strongly to the conviction that one might envision many, many more of these.

Even when a writer accords the principal importance to the message he intends to deliver (that is, what a text and its translation have in common), he cannot be wholly insensitive to the structures he uses, and it is not at random that he chooses one form rather than another: the (wonderful) thirteen-foot verse rather than the alexandrine, the mingling or separation of genres, etc. Only mildly constraining, these traditional structures offer him a fairly broad choice. That which remains to be seen is whether the Oulipo can create new structures, hardly more and hardly less constraining than traditional ones, and how to go about it. On ancient (or new) thoughts, the poet would be able to make new verses.

But can an artificial structure be viable? Does it have the slightest chance to take root in the cultural tissue of a society and to produce leaf, flower, and fruit? Enthusiastic modernists are convinced of it; diehard traditionalists are persuaded of the contrary. And there we have it, arisen from its ashes: a modern form of the old Quarrel of the Ancients and the Moderns.

One may compare this problem—*mutatis mutandis*—to that of the laboratory synthesis of living matter. That no one has ever succeeded in doing this doesn't prove a priori that it's impossible. The remarkable success of present biochemical syntheses allows room for hope, but nonetheless fails to indicate convincingly that we will be able to fabricate living beings in the very near future. Further discussion of this point would seem otiose. The Oulipo has preferred to put its shoulder to the wheel, recognizing furthermore that the elaboration of artificial literary structures would seem to be infinitely less complicated and less difficult than the creation of life.

Such, in essence, is our project. And perhaps I may be permitted to allude to an apparently (but only *apparently*) modest foundation: the Institute for Literary Prosthesis.

Who has not felt, in reading a text—whatever its quality—the need to improve it through a little judicious retouching? No work is invulnerable to this. The whole of world literature ought to become the object of numerous and discerningly conceived prostheses. Let me offer two examples, both bilingual.

An anecdote embellishes the first. Alexandre Dumas *père* was paying assiduous but vain court to a very beautiful woman who was, alas, both married and virtuous. When she asked him to write a word in her album, he wrote—felicitously enriching Shakespeare—"Tibi or not to be."

In the second example, I may be excused for calling on personal memories. More than a half-century ago, filled with wonder by the poems of John Keats, I was dawdling in the Jardin des Plantes. Stopping in front of the monkey cage, I couldn't help but cry (causing thus not a little astonishment to passers-by): "Un singe de beauté est un jouet pour l'hiver!" [2]

Wasn't Lautréamont approaching this ideal when he wrote: *Plagiarism is necessary. Progress implies it. It embraces an author's words, uses his expressions, rejects false ideas, and replaces them with true ideas.*

And this brings me to the question of plagiarism. Occasionally, we discover that a structure we believed to be entirely new had in fact already been discovered or invented in the past, sometimes even in a distant past. We make it a point of honor to recognize such a state of things in qualifying the text in question as "plagiarism by anticipation." Thus justice is done, and each is rewarded according to his merit.

One may ask what would happen if the Oulipo suddenly ceased to exist. In the short run, people might regret it. In the long run, everything would return to normal, humanity eventually discovering, after much groping and fumbling about, that which the Oulipo has endeavored to promote consciously. There would result however in the fate of civilization a certain delay which we feel it our duty to attenuate.

Jean Lescure

. . . .

Brief History of
the Oulipo

History will never question it: the Oulipo was founded by François Le Lionnais. Queneau said it on the radio. Leaves and writings fade, but words remain. On the same occasion, furthermore, Queneau indicated that he himself was the cofounder. On the cause of this foundation, he expressed himself in the following terms: *I had written five or six of the sonnets of the* Cent Mille Milliards de poèmes, *and I was hesitant to continue; in short, I didn't have the strength to continue; the more I went along, the more difficult it was to do naturally* [here I note that the Gallimard edition, p. 116 of the *Entretiens* with Georges Charbonnier, doesn't punctuate this part of the sentence, whereas one wonders if, when pronouncing it, Raymond Queneau didn't put a comma between *do* and *naturally.* So that we don't know whether the author's intended meaning is *it was difficult to do naturally,* which brings us to the very heart of Oulipian thought, or *it was difficult to do, naturally*]. *But* [I continue to quote] *when I ran into Le Lionnais, who is a friend of mine, he suggested that we start a sort of research group in experimental literature. That encouraged me to continue working on my sonnets.*

It must be admitted: this encouragement, the necessity of which was not evident to everyone, didn't appear sufficient to anyone. We have the proof of this in the minutes of the first meeting, on 24 November 1960, minutes which we owe to the invigorating eagerness of Jacques Bens, named from that day forward, and definitively so, provisional secretary. We read therein: *It would not seem that the composition of poems arising from a vocabulary composed by intersections, inventories, or any other process may constitute an end in itself.*

For the activity of the Oulipo, that goes without saying. As to anyone else's activity, we didn't object that their assigned task be the composition of poems. That day in the basement of the Vrai Gascon, what more nec-

32

essary task brought together Queval Jean, Queneau Raymond, Lescure Jean, Le Lionnais François, Duchateau Jacques, Berge Claude, and Bens Jacques as is noted in the minutes? (With, moreover, the intention to urge Schmidt Albert-Marie, Arnaud Noël, and Latis to attend the next luncheon.)

We asked ourselves that question. We asked ourselves that question the next day in written form: *Considering that we do not meet merely to amuse ourselves (which is in itself appreciable, surely), what can we expect from our work?*

Obviously, if we were asking ourselves this question, the fact was that we had not yet answered it. Allow me to slip a remark into this vacillation of our early days. This is that of the seven persons meeting on the occasion of the first luncheon, six had attended the ten-day conference organized at Cerisy in September, two months earlier, dedicated to Raymond Queneau, entitled *Une nouvelle défense et illustration de la langue française*. Not all of those six had been friends before the meeting at Cerisy. Some of them had never even met. Those six, plus André Blavier, who would later become a corresponding member of the Oulipo, had already met at Cerisy in the little entry pavilion with the intention of forming a group within the Collège de Pataphysique.[1] During that session, Queval was banned several times, for a total of 297 years, and each time readmitted by popular acclaim. Which of course colored his later career as an Oulipian, condemning him to ban himself unceasingly and equally unceasingly to cede to our objections.

At the time of this first meeting in November of 1960, the Oulipo still called itself the S.L.E., short for *sélitex*, or *séminaire de littérature expérimentale*. It wasn't until a month later, on 19 December 1960, and on the happy initiative of Albert-Marie Schmidt, that this S.L.E. became the Oulipo, or rather the Olipo: *ouvroir de littérature potentielle*. One can therefore legitimately say that during a month there was a po oulipo. A potentialoulipo. What important difference did the *oulipo* introduce compared to the stillborn *sélitex,* or S.L.E.? The *li* did not change. Of course, certain people claimed that there was a lot to be said about "li." But our work at Cerisy had convinced us that language only solicited our attention as literature. Thus we kept the *li* of literature. *Séminaire* bothered us in that it conjures up stud farms and artificial insemination; *ouvroir,* on the contrary, flattered the modest taste that we shared for beautiful work and good deeds: out of respect for both fine arts and morals, we consented to join the *ou* to the *li*. There remained the *po,* or the *po* of this *ouli*. The inspiration was general. And the word *expérimental* having seemed to us to base the entire operation on acts and experiments as yet only poorly discernible, we judged it advisable to settle ourselves squarely on an objective notion, on a real fact of every literary being: his potential. (This potential remaining in any case sufficient unto itself, even when the experimental energy of the *littérateurs* would find it lacking.)

It was, finally, the thirteenth of February 1961 that the Private General Secretary to the Baron Vice-Curator of the Collège de Pataphysique, M. Latis, concluded the nomination of this enterprise by suggesting, for the sake of symmetry, that we add the second letter of the word *ouvroir* to the O, which definitely rendered the Olipo the Oulipo.

Our first labors immediately indicated the desire to inscribe the Oulipo within a history. The Oulipo didn't claim to innovate at any price. The first papers dealt with ancient works, works that might serve as ancestors if not as models for the work we wanted to begin. This led us to consider according a good deal of our efforts to an H.L.E., or *Histoire des littératures expérimentales*. Here, we saw the notion of experimentation or exercise reappear; at the same time we were beginning to realize that which distinguished us from the past: potentiality.

But in any case the essential object of our quest was still literature, and François Le Lionnais wrote: *Every literary work begins with an inspiration . . . which must accommodate itself as well as possible to a series of constraints and procedures,* etc. What the Oulipo intended to demonstrate was that these constraints are felicitous, generous, and are in fact literature itself. What it proposed was to discover new ones, under the name of *structures*. But at that time, we didn't formulate this as clearly.

The position of the Oulipo in regard to literature is determined in memorandum #4, minutes of the meeting on 13 February 1961, in the following form: *Jean Queval intervened to ask if we are in favor of literary madmen. To this delicate question, F. Le Lionnais replied very subtly:*

—We are not against them, but the literary vocation interests us above all else.

And R. Queneau stated precisely:

—The only literature is voluntary literature.

If I may refer to the henceforth famous dictum in *Odile,* we can add to this notion the considerable consequences resulting from the fact that: *The really inspired person is never inspired, but always inspired.* What does this mean? What? This thing so rare, inspiration, this gift of the gods which makes the poet, and which this unhappy man never quite deserves in spite of all his heartaches, this enlightenment coming from who knows where, is it possible that it might cease to be capricious, and that any and everybody might find it faithful and compliant to his desires? The serious revolution, the sudden change this simple sentence introduced into a conception of literature still wholly dominated by romantic effusions and the exaltation of subjectivity, has never been fully analyzed. In fact, this sentence implied the revolutionary conception of the objectivity of literature, and from that time forward opened the latter to all possible modes of manipulation. In short, like mathematics, literature could be *explored*.

We know that for Queneau, at Cerisy, the origin of language might be traced back to a man who had a stomachache and wanted to express that fact.[2] But as Queneau stated to Charbonnier, *Of course he didn't succeed in expressing this; never could succeed; nobody will ever succeed.* Since this mysterious origin, the failures of language have little by little led its users to reflect on this strange tool which one could consider, which sometimes commands consideration, without reference to utility.

People noticed that they were language from head to toe. And that when they thought they had a stomachache, it was in fact a language-ache. That all of that was more or less indiscernible. That medicine was fine and dandy, but if we were suffering in our language, medicine wasn't enough, although it itself is a language. We started therefore to explore, or to want to explore, language. We began by relying on its properties. We let it play by itself. Word games became the game of words in Queneau, subject of the excellent Daubercies's doctoral thesis. We directed the games of language, searched, found, and encouraged certain of its capacities. We remained attentive to this nature which it seems to have, or which it constitutes for itself and which, in turn, constitutes us.

This movement became entirely natural. And this is why I underlined Queneau's words a little while ago: *the more difficult it was to do naturally.* It has become so natural that we forget the punctuation and everyone jumps in.

Let me point out that Lévi-Strauss begins the *Pensée sauvage* with a remark on nomination, and the expression of the concrete by the abstract. He quotes two sentences from Chinook, a very useful language for linguists. These two sentences use abstract words to designate properties or qualities of beings or things. Thus, in order to say: *The bad man killed the unfortunate child,* one will say: *The badness of the man killed the misfortune of the child;* and to say: *This woman is using a basket which is too small,* one will say: *She is putting potentilla roots into the smallness of a shell basket.*

It is clear in this case that the notions of abstract and concrete are confused and, as Lévi-Strauss says, that "oak" or "beech" is just as abstract as "tree." But another thing becomes clear to the wise poet who examines this text. This is that *the badness of the man killed the misfortune of the child* is not precisely the same thing as *the bad man killed the unfortunate child.* In fact, it's not the same thing at all. And this difference reveals a new concreteness which is not only that of the thing referred to by the words but also that of the words themselves. Language is a concrete object.

One can therefore operate on it as on other objects of science. Language (literary language) doesn't manipulate notions, as people still believe; it handles verbal objects and maybe even, in the case of poetry (but can one draw a distinction between poetry and literature?), sonorous objects. Just as in painting the dissimulation of the object of reference by grids of non-figuration claimed less to annihilate this object, table, landscape, or face, than to divert attention toward the painting-object, a certain number of sentences written today fix the attention of the observer on the singular object that is literary language, whose significations because of this multiply indefinitely. Unusual designations point to the sign rather than to the signified.

A simple example will clarify this: the beginning of *Le Chiendent*:[3] *A man's silhouette was outlined, simultaneously thousands.* A realist novelist would have written: *Jules came along. There was a crowd.* But in writing this, the realist novelist would only have shown that he was confusing the concreteness of things with literary concreteness, and that he was counting on quashing the latter in favor of the former. He would have claimed to have rendered his sentence wholly transparent to that which it designates. That is literature according to Sartre, and transitive language. In literature, the smallest combination of words secretes perfectly intransitive properties. The recourse to the abstract in Queneau means simply the choice of a system of concreteness at once both very ancient and very new: literature itself.

I don't mean to suggest that this is an absolute discovery. Queneau knows better than anyone that literature existed before us. For example, one finds in *Ange Pitou* a description of a fight that conforms precisely to what we've been saying. Ange Pitou fights with the seminarist who had raised him, if memory serves me, and whom he had just found again. The seminarist throws a punch which, says A. Dumas, *Ange Pitou warded off with an eye.* Everything here is concrete in its terms, but the organization of these various concretes is absurd. It's not the world that's being referred to, but literature. But of course, literature is always the world.

It's because we had the profound feeling that we were not an absolute beginning, but rather that we belonged to a tradition, that the Oulipo decided to devote a large share of its work to bringing together texts for an anthology of experimental literature. For there were not only these naive and aleatory illuminations of Alexandre Dumas's sort: other writers systematically sought to transform the constraints of literary rules into sources of inspiration. Hugo's famous *Je rime à dait*[4] is an example of the energetic virtues of rhyme, if not of the work of the greatest of French poets.

Experimentation was thus reintroduced into the Oulipo, not only in order to establish our genealogical tree, the history of our origins, but also to give direction to our exploration. For most of the experiments that one can conduct on language reveal that the field of meanings extends far beyond the intentions of any author. It's a commonplace today that an author understands only very few of the meanings offered by his work. And one can no longer find a single writer provincial enough to explain: *I intended to say that. . . .* When questioned today, the writer responds: *I wanted to . . .* and the description of a machine producing at the discretion of consumers follows. In short, every literary text is literary because of an indefinite quantity of potential meanings.

That involves the objects of literature, and one notices that, from this point of view, all literature is potential. For which the Oulipo rejoices. But as the equating of potentiality and literature would perhaps cause the Oulipo to lose itself in the totality of language, we had to seek a specific potentiality which we intended to use for our purposes. It's not that of literature already written but that of literature which remains to be written.

It was not an easy thing to accomplish. It was even exceedingly difficult. First, we elaborated the following broad definition. *Oulipo: group which proposes to examine in what manner and by what means, given a scientific theory ultimately concerning language (therefore anthropology), one can introduce aesthetic pleasure (affectivity and fancy) therein.* We will never know exactly who came up with this definition, the definitive secretary having generously attributed it to all in his minutes of the 5 April 1961 meeting.[5]

Things could only get worse. And the same day, the Oulipians "slyly" followed this definition with another: *Oulipians: rats who must build the labyrinth from which they propose to escape.*

The storm broke on the twentieth of April.[6] The word "affectivity" unleashed the tempest that Jacques Bens had been brooding for a month. Appealing to a *method,* and a scientific one, the provisional secretary claimed that we could only work from real things, from existing texts. To Albert-Marie Schmidt, who worried that the treatments to which these texts were subjected in order to actualize their potentialities in fact destroyed the latter as such, transforming them into realities, Arnaud answered that we must begin with the concrete, with the material. Oulipian activity applies systematic and predictable treatments to these materials. That's the experimental method. To which Queneau replied: *Our method could be applied to nonexistent acts.* And Lescure Jean going so far as to suggest that the greatest potentiality is that of nonexistence, Bens cried in an aggressive voice: *That's poetic method, not scientific.* Queneau: *Historically, we may consider that the day when the Carolingians began to count on their fingers 6, 8, and 12 to make verse, they accomplished an Oulipian task. Potential literature is that which doesn't yet exist.* With the worst insincerity in the world, Jacques Bens then affirmed that that was precisely what he had been saying: *To get to the potential (in the future), one must begin with that which exists (in the present)*. Granted that it's he himself who writes the minutes, he didn't interrupt himself, and he gave himself the last word.

It was during the night of 28 August 1961, in the gardens of François Le Lionnais and in the presence of Lady Godiva,[7] that the Oulipians began to understand what they had been trying to do for so long. Le Lionnais expressed himself in these terms: *It is possible to compose texts that have poetic, surrealist, fantastic, or other qualities without having qualities of potential. Now it is these last qualities that are essential for us. They are the only ones that must guide our choice. . . . The goal of potential literature is to furnish future writers with new techniques which can dismiss inspiration from their affectivity. Ergo, the necessity of a certain liberty. Nine or ten centuries ago, when a potential writer proposed the sonnet form, he left, through certain mechanical processes, the possibility of a choice.*

Thus, continues Le Lionnais, *there are two Lipos: an analytic and a synthetic. Analytic lipo seeks possibilities existing in the work of certain authors unbeknownst to them. Synthetic lipo constitutes the principal mission of the Oulipo; it's a question of opening new possibilities previously unknown to authors.*

Finally elaborated, this definition remains the Oulipo's rule. In his conversations with Charbonnier, Queneau returns to it nearly word for word: *The word "potential" concerns the very nature of literature; that is, fundamentally it's less a question of literature strictly speaking than of supplying forms for the good use one can make of literature. We call potential literature the search for new forms and structures that may be used by writers in any way they see fit.*

Finally, and more recently, Le Lionnais: *The Oulipo's goal is to discover new structures and to furnish for each structure a small number of examples.*

As we can see, the rules of the sonnet, which are the Oulipo's bread and butter, remain the perfect example of our aims. But in all of this there is a relatively new way of considering literature, and it is not by chance (and without bad feelings toward the old world) that Queneau writes that we propose to elaborate *a whole arsenal in which the poet may pick and choose, whenever he wishes to escape from that which is called inspiration* (*Entretiens*, p. 154).

History will testify that the Oulipo saved men from the infantile diseases of writers and gave true freedom to the latter, which consists, exercising "their passionate taste for the obstacle,"[8] in finding the springboard of their action in the world itself.

Having understood its mission, the Oulipo happily embarked upon the centuries that awaited it.[9] Barely into the fifth of these, it had astutely mixed the sap which Oulipians were unknowingly making from lipo with the diverse characters of its members. Exercises sometimes illustrated these characters. There were snowballs, isosyntactic, isovocalic, or isoconsonatic poems, anterhymes, lipograms, etc. . . . and numerous proposals for permutations for a combinatory literature.

Bereavements darkened our history. The very dear, very lettered, and very fraternal Albert-Marie Schmidt first, through whose death we lost much of our scholarship, depriving us as well of the most amusing works. Marcel Duchamp, from one of the Americas, became interested in the Oulipo. The Ouvroir flattered itself to count him among its corresponding members. He died an Oulipian.

New ones were born:[10] Georges Perec, Jacques Roubaud, Luc Etienne, Marcel Bénabou, Paul Fournel. And we saw works appear bearing obvious traces of our reflections. By Perec, precisely, *La Disparition*. By Roubaud, whose ε invents constraints that will continue to provoke comment. *Zinga 8* by Jacques Duchateau surprised and even astonished me. Raymond Queneau's *Un Conte à votre façon*, a "programmed" story. *Le Petit Meccano poétique n° 00*, modest exercises for beginners.

Although the goal of the Oulipo is not to give birth to literary works, one ought to mention that the work of the best can draw new force from it—and we are delighted to note from *Le Vol d'Icare* that Raymond Queneau is making very good progress.

Each of our centuries having been celebrated by a conference, it's rather satisfying to realize that we have now youthfully passed our first millennium.

Marcel Bénabou

· · · · · · · · · · · · · ·

Rule and Constraint

Constraint, as everyone knows, often has a bad press. All those who esteem the highest value in literature to be sincerity, emotion, realism, or authenticity mistrust it as a strange and dangerous whim.

Why bridle one's imagination, why browbeat one's liberty through the voluntary imposition of constraints, or by placing obstacles in one's own path? Even the most kindly disposed critics pretend to see in the use of constraint nothing more than a game, rarely innocent but fundamentally vain. The only merit that they might accord to it is that it provides, for a few linguistic acrobats, for a few verbal jugglers, the circus in which they may display their virtuosity. All the while regretting, of course, that so much ingenuity, work, and eagerness had not been placed in the service of a more "serious" literary ambition. *Difficiles nugae*, as was generally said even in the last century of anagrams, palindromes, and lipograms, in order to stigmatize them, these venerable exercises whose antiquity and persistence in the corpus of European literary traditions ought to have preserved them from sarcasm and banter. And even today, there are undoubtedly certain learned dons in whose eyes neither the Alexandrian poets, nor the Grands Rhétoriqueurs, nor the poets of the German Baroque, nor the Russian formalists will ever find grace. In the name, of course, of the sacrosanct liberty of the artist, which nothing must shackle; in the name of the imprescriptible rights of inspiration.

Certain types of constraint, however, seem to have escaped from this discredit. For four centuries, we have been very comfortable, apparently, with the laws of prosody—with the fact, for instance, that an alexandrine has twelve syllables, that a sonnet has fourteen lines, whose rhymes are disposed according to a very precise order. And we do not hesitate to admire in Malherbe or Valéry the scrupulous respect of a demanding canon. In fact, it is rather difficult, except for proponents of "automatic writing," to imagine a poetics that does not rely on rigorous rules and, more generally, a literary production that does not involve the use of cer-

40

tain techniques. Even the most rabid critics of formalism are forced to admit that there are formal demands which a work cannot elude. Responding to those who were trying to confound inspiration, liberty, chance, and the dictates of the unconscious,[1] the terms that Raymond Queneau employed in 1938 are well known: ". . . inspiration which consists in blind obedience to every impulse is in reality a sort of slavery. The classical playwright who writes his tragedy observing a certain number of familiar rules is freer than the poet who writes that which comes into his head and who is the slave of other rules of which he is ignorant" (*Le Voyage en Grèce*, p. 94).

Now it is actually in the passage from the *rule* to the *constraint* that the stumbling block appears: people accept the rule, they tolerate technique, but they refuse constraint. Precisely because it seems like an unnecessary rule, a superfluous redoubling of the exigencies of technique, and consequently no longer belongs—so the argument goes—to the admitted norm but rather to the process, and thus is exaggerative and excessive. It is as if there were a hermetic boundary between two domains: the one wherein the observance of rules is a natural fact, and the one wherein the excess of rules is perceived as shameful artifice.

It is precisely this boundary, wholly arbitrary, that must be challenged in the name of a better knowledge of the functional modes of language and writing. One must first admit that language may be treated as an object in itself, considered in its materiality, and thus freed from its subservience to its significatory obligation. It will then be clear that language is a complex system, in which various elements are at work, whose combinations produce words, sentences, paragraphs, or chapters. Obviously, nothing prevents us from studying the behavior, in every possible circumstance, of each of these elements. On the contrary: it is only in this manner that experimental research into the possibilities of language can proceed. And the role that may be assigned to constraint immediately becomes apparent: to the extent that constraint goes beyond rules which seem natural only to those people who have barely questioned language, it forces the system out of its routine functioning, thereby compelling it to reveal its hidden resources.

Constraint is thus a commodious way of passing from language to writing. If one grants that all writing—in the sense both of the act of writing and of the product of that act—has its autonomy, its coherence, it must be admitted that writing under constraint is superior to other forms insofar as it freely furnishes its own code.

All these obstacles that one creates for oneself—playing, for example, on the nature, the order, the length, or the number of letters, syllables, or words—all these interdictions that one postulates reveal their true function: their final goal is not a mere exhibition of virtuosity but rather an exploration of virtualities.

The work of Georges Perec furnishes an exemplary demonstration of everything that concerns so-called "literal" constraints. As a matter of fact, in Perec one notes a sort of fascination for the letter. Conscious that, to quote J. Roubaud's beautiful expression, "each page is a bed where letters lie," Perec produced several of his texts through diligent work on letters: on their presence, their absence, their repetition, their order of occurrence in words, or even their form. Thus, the exclusion of a vowel engenders an extraordinarily rich novel whose functioning is entirely governed, down to the last detail, by the consequences of this *disappearance*.[2] The inverse constraint, which consists in using *only* the vowel *e*, presides at the birth of exceedingly strange festivities at the bishop's palace in Exeter, involving the derangement of senses and sexes (*Les Revenentes*). And it is on still another literal constraint that are based the vertiginous variations which fill the two collections *La Clôture* and *Alphabets,* that of the heterogram: each verse employs the same set of different letters, whose permutations produce the poem. Not without humor, Perec sees in this play of constraints the beginning of a new poetic art, capable of replacing the rhetorical vestiges still in use in most modern and contemporary poetic production.

It is useful to note in passing, nonetheless, that the petition of bankruptcy of traditional rhetoric had been filed, in less temperate terms, by a contemporary poet: "Rhetoric, why should I recall your name? You are no longer anything but a colonnaded word, the name of a palace which I detest, from which my blood has forever banished itself" (F. Ponge, *Méthodes,* pp. 182–83).

In progressing from the letter to the word, the techniques of Raymond Roussel inevitably come to mind, and his way of exploiting to the limit the evocative power of the word he chooses: sometimes it is the dislocation of an utterance; sometimes the bringing together of a given pair of words that creates an object (imaginary), described with the utmost precision, an event (wholly as imaginary) recounted in minute detail. The unforgettable *rails en mou de veau,* which so impressed the first readers of *Impressions d'Afrique,* is only the most striking example of this aptitude of language in creating myths. Roussel, like Mallarmé, elaborates from the sole lexicon his own universe; and from the arbitrary choice he imposes upon himself, he brings into being a second nature.

This paradoxical effect of constraint, which, rather than stifling the imagination, serves to awaken it, can actually be explained very readily. The choice of a linguistic constraint allows one to skirt, or to ignore, all these other constraints which do not belong to language and which escape from our emprise. Michel Leiris seized this point perfectly, regarding the method used by Raymond Roussel, of whom he said: "His voluntary sub-jugation to a complicated and difficult rule was accompanied, as a corol-lary, by a distraction regarding all the rest, leading to a raising of the censure, the latter being far better skirted by this means than by a process such as automatic writing. . . . Juggling apparently gratuitous elements, in which he himself trusted, he created true myths, insofar as they are all very authentically symbolical" (*Brisées*, pp. 59–60).

Thus, it is not only the virtualities of language that are revealed by constraint, but also the virtualities of him who accepts to submit himself to constraint.

Curious reversal: here, we are far from the wise praise of classicism toward which these few remarks seemed at first to be directed. In fact, one must examine how things really come about.

Rules, so cherished by the classics, were principally used as a means of channeling eventual overflowings of a poorly controlled verbal flood. Va-léry could thus, in his lecture on poetics at the Collège de France on 10 December 1937, say of the rules of traditional prosody that they are "like waves," and that "vague ideas, intuitions, impulsions comb therein."

Linguistic constraints, for their part, granted their arbitrary exigencies, directly create a sort of "great vacuum" into which are sucked and retained whole quantities of elements which, without this violent aspiration, would otherwise remain concealed.

It is thus the paradox of writing under constraint that it possesses a double virtue of liberation, which may one day permit us to supplant the very notion of inspiration. We recall, once again, the fundamental remarks of R. Queneau on this theme: ". . . it must be noted that the poet is never inspired, if by that one means that inspiration is a function of humor, of temperature, of political circumstances, of subjective chance, or of the subconscious. The poet is never inspired, because he is the master of that which appears to others as inspiration. He does not wait for inspiration to fall out of the heavens on him like roasted ortolans. He knows how to hunt, and lives by the incontestable proverb, 'God helps them that help themselves.' He is never inspired because he is unceasingly inspired, be-cause the powers of poetry are always at his disposition, subjected to his will, submissive to his own activity . . ." (*Le Voyage en Grèce*, p. 126).

Since its creation in 1960, the Oulipo has endeavored to explore, to inventory, to analyze the intimate processes and resources of the language of words, of letters. This exploration is naturally based on the use of constraint, either through the use of ancient constraints pushed to the far limit of their possibilities, or through systematic research in new con-straints. Recourse to the axiomatic method, the importance of mathemat-

Table of Elementary Linguistic and Literary Operations

LINGUISTIC OBJECT \ OPERATIONS	DISPLACEMENT	SUBSTITUTION	ADDITION	SUBTRACTION	MULTIPLICATION (repetition)	DIVISION	DEDUCTION	CONTRACTION
LETTER	anagram palindrome pig Latin metathesis	paragram (printer's error) cryptography	prosthesis epenthesis paragoge	abbreviation aphaeresis syncope elision lipogram belle absente constraint of the prisoner	tautogram		acrostic acronym signet chronogram	crasis
PHONEME	phonetic palindrome spoonerism Rrose Sélavy (Desnos) glossary (Leiris)	à-peu-près alphabetical drama	stuttering	lipophoneme	alliteration rhyme homoeoteleuton			
SYLLABLE	syllabic palindrome spoonerism		javanese stuttering gemination echolalia	haplography liposyllable (Precious [con]straint) shortening	stuttering alliteration rhyme	diaeresis	acronym	

WORD	Mathews's Algorithm permutations (Lescure) word palindrome inversion	metonymy S + 7 homosyntaxism L.S.D. translation antonymic translation	redundance pleonasm	liponym La Rien que la Toute la (Le Lionnais)	epanalepsis pleonasm anaphora defective rhyme	"de-portmanteau word" etymology tmesis	haikuization	portmanteau word
SYNTAGM	reversion inversion anastrophe	perverbs (Mathews) proverbs aphorism homophony untraceable locutions	interpolation encasement	ellipsis brachylogia zeugma	reduplication	Roussellian procedure (phonic dislocation) hendiadys	proverbs on rhymes edges of poem	syntagmatic amalgam (Doukipudonktan)
SENTENCE	Mathews's Algorithm	homophony holorhyme	tireur à la ligne larding	coupeur à la ligne	leitmotif refrain	dislocation	citation tireur à la ligne collage	
PARAGRAPH	Mathews's Algorithm		tireur à la ligne	censure			plagiarism anthology	résumé

ical concepts, the utilization of combinatorics are the principal paths of this research.

The Oulipo of course does not seek to impose any thesis; it merely seeks to formulate problems and eventually to offer solutions that allow any and everybody to construct, letter by letter, word by word, a text. To create a structure—Oulipian act *par excellence*—is thus to propose an as yet undiscovered mode of organization for linguistic objects.

The accompanying table offers a systematic and analytic classification of elementary linguistic and literary operations; it is complementary to the table elaborated by R. Queneau in 1974, which appears in *Atlas de littérature potentielle* (pp. 74–77) under the title, "Classification of the Works of the Oulipo."

The intent of my table is to try to assign a place within a given ensemble to as many linguistic manipulations as possible, with neither generic distinction nor hierarchy. Therein are included Oulipian and pre-Oulipian constraints, as well as popular verbal games and figures of classical rhetoric.

In order to elaborate this table, the various linguistic objects susceptible of manipulation first had to be isolated, from the simple to the complex: the letter (or typographic sign), the sound, the syllable, the word, the group of words (or syntagm), the sentence, the paragraph. The table stops at the paragraph, but nothing would prevent us, of course, from working on the page, the chapter, the book, even the library. . . .

Next, the various operations to which the linguistic objects may be submitted had to be identified. For the time being, eight have been isolated: displacement, substitution, addition, subtraction, multiplication, division, deduction, contraction. But it is certain that other means of identifying and naming these sorts of operations are possible. Thus, for example, in his general theory of rhythm, J. Roubaud postulated the following categories: concatenation, imbrication, encasement, encroachment, permutation, effacement, parenthesage.

Granted that the table seeks to account for the thousand and one means of arranging language, there can be no question of giving a concrete illustration for each line here. Definitions and examples may be easily found in consulting, on the one hand, *Atlas de littérature potentielle,* and, on the other, B. Dupriez's dictionary, *Gradus: Les procédés littéraires* (Paris: Union Générale d'Editions, 1984).

General Table: The Three Circles of Lipo[3]

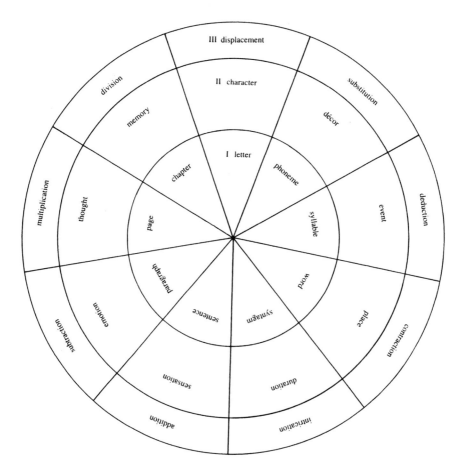

I: Circle of linguistic objects
II: Circle of semantic objects
III: Circle of operations

Collective

. . . .

The Collège de Pataphysique and the Oulipo

Presentation of the Subcommittee's work in Dossier 17 of the Collège de Pataphysique[1]

Faust, disturbed by his antithetical familiar, lends an annoyed but perhaps willing ear to the commonplaces of this representative of culture:

> . . . die Kunst ist lang! Und kurz ist unser Leben.[2]

So sings this welcome *pars negativa*. The researchers meeting under the triple invocation of Potential Literature, Pataphysics, and thus Ethernity do not in the least share this humanistic pessimism. Conforming to the celebrated directives of His Magnificence, "Pataphysics, all Pataphysics," they feel that Art is not long enough even in the shortest of lives. The *Cent Mille Milliards de poèmes* rendered this clear to pataphysicians and to many others as well.

That the "expression" entails something other than itself has been known since the beginnings of language, when people began to relish that "no" which says "yes" and the cruel "yes" which refuses even more categorically than the "no," and so forth. . . . The Word is intimately potential (and thus ontogenetically pataphysical or generator of Imaginary Solutions);[3] precisely because of this, the Word is God. But the time for adoration has passed; that of science, with all its bold ambitions, has arrived. The divine potentiality of the Word, in spite of a few notable fulgurations, had always remained latent and implicit, although ever ready to spring forth. Here, it's a question of going straight to the explicit and putting these forces into play: this is what the creation of the Ouvroir de Littérature Potentielle signified. Thus, the time of *created creations*, which was that of the literary works we know, should cede to the era of *creating*

48

creations, capable of developing from themselves and beyond themselves, in a manner at once predictable and inexhaustibly unforeseen.

Those texts called the masterpieces of the past may perhaps give us some idea of this grandiose procession. Does their density not conceal—through an internal privilege—an indefinite possibility for interpretations, often wildly divergent, whose contradictions, accumulated over centuries, elicit our perplexity? Each generation "renews" them and sees its own preoccupations reflected in them. What hasn't been found "in" Virgil or "in" Rabelais?

And yet—however ironic this may seem—to create Potential Literature it is not sufficient to write "masterpieces." The Oulipo's ambition is both more modest and more pretentious. It resides more in the ordering of the means than in the intuition of the ends. We intend to inventory—or to invent—the procedures by which expression becomes capable of transmuting itself, solely through its verbal craft, into other more or less numerous expressions. It's a question of deliberately provoking that which masterpieces have secondarily produced—produced into the bargain, as it were—and especially to render clear in the very treatment of words and phrases what the mysterious alchemy of masterpieces engenders in the superior spheres of aesthetic meaning and fascination. One can easily believe that Potential Literature is not a recipe for "making masterpieces": its aim is infinitely lower, its efforts are directed toward recovering the same generative faculty that lies beyond, but in the far more elementary and scientific order of the structures of language. When this literature has become conscious and consistent, when it has generated other works, it will be possible (if hierarchies are of any interest) to distinguish between interesting and uninteresting works and, as nonpataphysicians say, between *chefs-d'oeuvre* and *pieds-d'oeuvre*.

For the moment, it's only the twilight of the dawn. In this first Dossier, it's clear that in order to open the eyes of those Members as yet unaccustomed to the Potential Sun, they being citizens of the Dark Lands of the Obvious Word, the Oulipo applied itself to discovering in these shadows the phosphorescent flashes that filter through, either by means of some of the more or less potential endeavors consciously undertaken in the past, or especially in the application of potential therapy to materials unconsciously proposed by previous authors. This exploration in itself is infinite, and our modest preliminary gleaning only begins to suggest the vastness that will be explorable when, for example, thanks to computers we can finally extract an entire given vocabulary (e.g., concerning blows) and even syntactic structures from the work of Corneille or Eugène Sue in order to write original works in "Corneillish" or "Sueian," then to create other works in "Corneillo-Sueian," etc. . . . Or, moreover (as some linguists have already timidly suggested), when these computers begin to reveal the constants of a writer in all sorts of areas, and he will thus himself be made to draw the map of his virtualities . . . (and here we return to Jarry's definition of pataphysics). More abstractly, won't we be tempted by a Topology of Commonplaces, in which one would succeed in abstracting commonplaces from the structures of commonplaces—and then a "squared" topology of these places, and so forth until one attains, in a rigorous analysis of this *regressus* itself, the absolute, the Absolute "whose armature," according to Jarry, "is made of clichés"?

But that's only half of our program, and the less fruitful half at that. As soon as he is broken in to this research and sensitized to this intellection to the *n*th degree, the potentialpotent literator (we certainly do not dare to say the present Members of the Oulipo Subcommittee) will be in a position to play his own fugue on this organ with multiple keyboards, mathematically labyrinthine combinations of register, "mixtures" arising from infinitely subtle and irridescent harmonics. And what music? We have no idea. Do we actually believe in it? The only example we can offer to distantly evoke these intimations of the future is not part of our present deposition: the Transcendent Satrap Queneau's *Cent Mille Milliards de poèmes*. This text's effect is one of mystification (and this word is by no means pejorative for us). And being, like Swift, skeptical prophets, we entertain these prospects pataphysically.

But is there any other canonical way of viewing the future (whether one calls oneself serious in the profane or pataphysical sense of the word), than as a bouquet of Imaginary Solutions—that is, of potentialities?

Raymond Queneau

. . . .

Potential Literature

What is potential literature? First, I would say that it is the object of a group founded three years ago by François Le Lionnais. It includes ten members and calls itself the Ouvroir de Littérature Potentielle:

Ouvroir because it intends to work.

Littérature because it is a question of literature.

Potentielle—the word must be taken to mean various things which will be made clear, I hope, in the course of this lecture.

In short: OU. LI. PO.

What is the objective of our work? To propose new "structures" to writers, mathematical in nature, or to invent new artificial or mechanical procedures that will contribute to literary activity: props for inspiration as it were, or rather, in a way, aids for creativity.

What is the Oulipo *not?*

(1) It is not a movement or a literary school. We place ourselves beyond aesthetic value, which does not mean that we despise it.

(2) Nor is it a scientific seminar, a so-called "serious" work group, although a professor of literature and a professor of science at the university are both members. Moreover, it is in all modesty that I submit our work to the present audience.

Finally, (3) We are not concerned with experimental or aleatory literature (as it is practiced, for example, by Max Bense's group in Stuttgart).

I will now say what the Oulipo *is*—or rather what it believes itself to be. Our research is:

(1) *Naive:* I use the work "naive" in its perimathematical sense, as one speaks of the naive theory of sets. We forge ahead without undue refinement. We try to prove motion by walking.

(2) *Craftsmanlike*—but this is not essential. We regret having no access to machines: this is a constant *lamento* during our meetings.

(3) *Amusing:* at least for us. Certain people find our work "sordidly

51

boring," which ought not to frighten you, because you are not here to amuse yourselves.

I will insist, however, on the qualifier "amusing." Surely, certain of our labors may appear to be mere pleasantries, or simple witticisms, analogous to certain parlor games.

Let us remember that topology and the theory of numbers sprang in part from that which used to be called "mathematical entertainments," "recreational mathematics." I salute in passing the memory of Bachet de Méziriac, author of *Problèmes plaisants et délectables qui se font par les nombres* (1612—not, as Larousse says, 1613), and one of the first members of the French Academy. Let us also remember that the calculation of probabilities was at first nothing other than an anthology of "diversions," as Bourbaki[1] states in the "Notice Historique" of the twenty-first fascicle on Integration. And likewise game theory until von Neumann.

Since we as yet have no Kolmogoroff, I will now present our diversions to you, or, rather, furnish you with some examples of them. We have already determined roughly sixty points of interest. I will therefore limit my choice. First of all, our research on our precursors (for we have had many).

A part of our activity is historical; that is, it consists in tracking down work analogous to our own in the past. It is a huge subject, and I will give only two examples of it.

The first is lipogrammatic—not oulipogrammatic—from λείπω, to lack, and γράμμα, letter. The word λιπογράμματοσ is found in Bailly.

Here is G. Peignot's definition from his *Poétique curieuse* (which appears in his *Amusements philologiques ou Variétés en tous genres* [again, this word "amusement"], 2d ed., 1825; 3rd ed., 1842): "Lipogrammatics is the art of writing in prose or in verse, imposing on oneself the rule of excluding a letter of the alphabet."

One may exclude several, but we will limit ourselves to the case of $n = 1$. One deprives oneself, then, of the use of one letter.

Naturally, the text must be long enough to render the exercise difficult.

G. Peignot himself composed twenty-six quatrains in alexandrines: in the first, he excluded the letter A, in the second, the letter B, etc.

Nestor of Laranda, in the third or fourth century, wrote a lipogrammatic *Iliad:* the letter A is absent from the first canto, etc. Fulgence, in the sixth century, in his *De aetatibus mundi et hominis,* did the same "in a singularly puerile pursuit," as the old Larousse says, an opinion we do not share. One might be led to believe that only anthologists and small-minded people have written lipogrammatic texts. Far from it. Like his mentor Lasus of Hermione, Pindar wrote an ode without the S, and Lope de Vega wrote five stories, one without the A, the others without E, I, O, and U, respectively.[2]

Are these "puerile" literary acrobatics, as the old Larousse would have it, or "bagatelles," as Peignot says? After all, wouldn't it be comparable to the activity of a logician who tries to avoid certain logical signs, and who experiences great satisfaction when he has eliminated them all in favor of Sheffer's stroke?[3]

If we examine the question from a slightly more modern point of view, we may attempt to measure the "lipogrammatic difficulty" of a text by multiplying the frequency of the omitted letter by the number of words in the text under consideration.

The lipogrammatic difficulty is obviously zero if one uses all the letters of the alphabet. The frequency of W being 0.02 (in English), writing a text of 100 words without using the letter W would thus be of difficulty 2. The frequency of E being 0.13, writing a text of 100 words without using the letter E would be of difficulty 13.

To write a typed page of 300 words without E would already be of difficulty 39. But to write a text of difficulty 10,413?

This is, nonetheless, the result achieved by Ernest Vincent Wright, who, in 1939, published a novel of 267 pages entitled *Gadsby,* in which he used the E not at all (see J. R. Pierce, *Symbols, Signals and Noise,* p. 48, who cites other examples of lipogrammatic texts).

We have not been able to procure this work, but the passage cited by Pierce does not give a massive impression of artificiality: "It is a story about a small town. It is not a gossipy yarn; nor is it a dry, monotonous account, full of such customary 'fill-ins' as 'romantic moonlight casting murky shadows down a long, winding country road.' Nor will it say anything about tinklings lulling distant folds, robins caroling at twilight nor any 'warm glow of lamplight' from a cabin window, no."

Obviously, he could not have said *yes.*

In Cantor's day, there were surely some geometricians who deemed puerile Cantor's curve, filling a two-dimensional continuum or its triadic ensemble.[4] Like Bourbaki, who in his early career devoted himself to teratopology, perhaps linguists would profit from a more attentive study of these examples of potential literature . . . prepotential literature. It is interesting to see just where the possibilities (potentialities) of a language may lead.

Another domain of literature that is particularly Oulipian is fixed-form poetry, which must be scrupulously distinguished from limited-form poetry such as the epigram and the epitaph—Boileau fails to make this distinction in the second canto of his *Art poétique,* a small error that does not at all diminish one of the greatest masterpieces of the French language.

In limited-form poetry, like the madrigal, to cite another example, only the number of verses and the nature of the subject are predetermined.

Fixed-form poetry obeys strict rules concerning the length of its verses, the order, alternation, or repetition of rhymes, of words, or even of entire verses.

The most familiar are the triolet, the virelay, the rondel, the villanelle, etc. Almost all of them have fallen out of use—out of poetic use—with the exception of the sonnet, the only one still practiced in our day. Why has the sonnet alone survived? This is perhaps a problem for literary sociology or, rather, a problem for mathematics and linguistics, the sonnet furnishing an optimal solution to the poet's demand for a well-defined form that responds to conscious or unconscious aesthetic exigencies.

The structure of the triolet does not lack for charm:

> A
> B
> A'
> A
>
> A"
> B'
> A
> B

Verse A is repeated thrice, verse B twice. Rhyme *a* is repeated five times, rhyme *b* thrice.

The triolet, which is very appropriately named, goes back to the Middle Ages. The Parnassians tried to revive it; a triolet by Alphonse Daudet is frequently cited. Among contemporary poets, even those interested in fixed forms, I am not aware of anyone who has attempted to restore the triolet to its place of honor.

Naturally, I did not come here to eulogize fixed-form poetry; this is far from my intentions and from Oulipian preoccupations. Now, therefore, I must present something slightly more potential than the triolet and even the sonnet—whose rules everyone professes to know. In fact, few sonnets are regular. The sonnet, "whose invention is less scholarly than pleasant," as du Bellay said (just as Bachet de Méziriac's problems are "pleasant and delectable"), comprises *two* rules, the first concerning the alternation of rhymes:

```
F M M F        M F F M
F M M F        M F F M
          or
M' M' F'       F' F' M'
M" F' M"       F" M' F"
```

The other rule demands that no word be repeated. But a sonnet is not necessarily written in alexandrines. (Parenthetically, allow me to note here a simple intervention of arithmetic. The poet, however refractory toward mathematics he may be, is nonetheless obliged to count up to twelve in order to compose an alexandrine.) Yes, the sonnet is not necessarily alexandrine; it may be monosyllabic. In this case, one of us has discovered that it may be called Asiatic, because, until further notice, it reads from top to bottom like Chinese.

The *sestina* seems to me to be particularly potential, It is composed of six stanzas of six lines each and a half-stanza of three lines; I will not insist on the latter: that would be dealt with in a master's course on potential literature.

The sestina, preferably, is written in alexandrines.

The first stanza is composed of six lines with, for example, the following rhyme scheme:

Feuillages	1
Soleil	2
Volages	3
Rivages	4
Vermeil	5
Sommeil[5]	6

I have taken the example cited by Théodore de Banville, in his *Petit Traité de poésie française*. The rhymes may seem mediocre, but the use which is made of them is not. Each of the five other stanzas is constructed using the same rhymes, and each time one proceeds to the same permutation.

The second is:

Sommeil	6
Feuillages	1
Vermeil	5
Soleil	2
Rivages	4
Volages	3

and so forth; the seventh stanza would duplicate the order of the first. For, as everyone has realized, it is a case of an element of the sixth degree of the symmetrical group of the same degree, and therefore of order 720.

The sestina goes back, it seems, to Arnaut Daniel (1180?–1210). Petrarch (1304–74) used it. It was put back into service by Ferdinand de Gramont (1815–97); after having translated Petrarch (in 1842), he published some sestinas in *Chant du Passé* in 1854, a collection noted already by Théodore de Banville as being extremely rare, and in *Olim* in 1882.

This Ferdinand de Gramont is not wholly unknown in literary history; he collaborated on the early works of Balzac, notably on *Don Gigadas* (1840), and it was he who composed the coats of arms for the noble characters in the *Comédie humaine;* this armorial was published by Ferdinand Lotte last year at Garnier.

Let us return to the sestina. We have seen that it is based on the successive powers of a permutation.

$$1\,2\,3\,4\,5\,6$$
$$6\,1\,5\,2\,4\,3$$
$$3\,6\,4\,1\,2\,5$$
$$5\,3\,2\,6\,1\,4$$
$$4\,5\,1\,3\,6\,2$$
$$2\,4\,6\,5\,3\,1$$
$$\overline{}$$
$$1\,2\,3\,4\,5\,6$$

It will also be remarked that:

$$E = \begin{pmatrix} 134\ 256 \\ 134\ 256 \end{pmatrix} \quad A^3 = \begin{pmatrix} 134\ 256 \\ 526\ 314 \end{pmatrix}$$

$$A = \begin{pmatrix} 134\ 256 \\ 652\ 143 \end{pmatrix} \quad A^4 = \begin{pmatrix} 134\ 256 \\ 413\ 562 \end{pmatrix}$$

$$A^2 = \begin{pmatrix} 134\ 256 \\ 341\ 625 \end{pmatrix} \quad A^5 = \begin{pmatrix} 134\ 256 \\ 265\ 431 \end{pmatrix}$$

Thus, there are two systems of imprimitivity. It is thus an imprimitive subgroup of the symmetrical group. There are 36 possible permutations with two imprimitive groups, of which 6 are of the 2nd degree (that is, there could only be two stanzas), 18 of the 4th degree, and 12 of the 6th degree.

There were thus 12 possible types of sestinas. Why did Count de Gramont adopt this one? Perhaps, it is again a case of the optimal solution. Did the Count de Gramont have a particular taste for mathematics? I do not know,[6] and we shall undoubtedly never know, as the archives of the Gramont family disappeared during the Second World War. You see that one could also create *octinas*.

For example:

1347	2568
8652	1743
3471	8256
6528	3174
4713	6825
5286	4317
7134	5682
2865	7431
1347	2568

but is this in fact the optimal permutation?

You see the immensity of the field of work offered to us. Group theory can thus furnish an indefinite series of fixed-form poetic structures.

I cannot leave the domain of fixed-form poetry without speaking of the *pantoum*. Of Malaysian origin, it appears in a note to the *Orientales* (1828). It was cultivated—as they say—by Charles Asselineau, Théodore de Banville, and Siefert.

It is composed of an *ad libitum* number of quatrains, in the following manner (the letters denoting entire lines and the same letter with or without prime indicating the same rhyme):

A
B
A'
B'

B
C
B'
C'

C
D
C'
D'

• • •

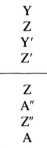

Finally, for the pantoum to be perfect, "from beginning to end of the poem, two meanings must be pursued in parallel," the first in the first two lines of each stanza, the second in the last two. That is, the A at the end of the poem must change its semantic domain. There, again, is an indication of numerous potentialities.

We shall now move on to the work of the Oulipo. I shall choose three examples of it, the third of which oversteps the domain of potential literature to enter that of quantitative linguistics—which is, after all, why we are here.

I shall choose three examples from among forty-odd possible ones; I can only allude in passing here to the anterhyme, the antirhyme, the intersective novel, tangency between sonnets, etc., and will limit my discussion to:

(1) redundancy in Mallarmé

(2) the S + 7 Method (of Jean Lescure)

(3) isomorphisms (whose general theory was elaborated by François Le Lionnais).

1. Redundancy in Mallarmé

Take a sonnet by Mallarmé:

> Le vierge, le vivace et le bel aujourd'hui
> Va-t-il nous déchirer avec un coup d'aile ivre
> Ce lac dur que hante sous le givre
> Le transparent glacier des vols qui n'ont pas fui!
>
> Un cygne d'autrefois se souvient que c'est lui
> Magnifique, mais qui sans espoir se délivre
> Pour n'avoir pas chanté la région où vivre
> Quand du stérile hiver a resplendi l'ennui.
>
> Tout son col secouera cette blanche agonie
> Par l'espace infligée à l'oiseau qui le nie,
> Mais non l'horreur du sol où le plumage est pris.

Fantôme qu'à ce lieu son pur éclat assigne,
Il s'immobilise au songe froid de mépris
Que vêt parmi l'exil inutile le Cygne.[7]

I shall proceed to a haikuization of this sonnet; that is, I will erase it, preserving only the rhyming sections; or, rather, to use mathematical language, I shall consider a restriction of this poem to its rhyming sections. (I shall permit myself to add subjective punctuation):

Aujourd'hui
Ivre,
le givre
pas fui!

Lui
se délivre . . .
où vivre?
L'ennui . . .

Agonie
le nie,
pris,

assigne
mépris
le Cygne.

What is the point of this? *Primo,* I obtain a new poem which, upon my word, is not bad, and one should never complain if one finds beautiful poems. *Secundo,* one has the impression that there is almost as much in the restriction as in the entire poem; that is why I spoke of redundancy. *Tertio:* without going to the far limits of sacrilege, one can at least say that this restriction sheds light on the original poem; it is not wholly without exegetical value and may contribute to interpretation.

The example is perhaps clearer with:

Ses purs ongles très haut dédiant leur onyx
L'Angoisse, ce minuit, soutient, lampadophore
Maint rêve vespéral brûlé par le Phénix
Que ne recueille pas de cinéraire amphore.

Sur les crédences, au salon vide: nul ptyx,
Aboli bibelot d'inanité sonore
(Car le Maître est allé puiser dans des pleurs au Styx
Avec ce seul objet dont le Néant s'honore).

> Mais proche de la croisée au nord vacante, un or
> Agonise selon peut-être le décor
> Des licornes ruant du feu contre une nixe,
>
> Elle, défunte nue en le miroir, encor
> Que, dans l'oubli fermé par le cadre, se fixe,
> De scintillations sitôt le septuor.[8]

Which gives

> Onyx?
> Lampadophore . . .
> Phénix?
> Amphore . . .
>
> Nul Ptyx
> sonore
> au Styx
> s'honore
>
> Un or?
> le décor . . .
> Une Nixe
>
> encor
> se fixe:
> septuor

The *angoisse* is *lampadophore*, but also the *onyx*, just as the *amphore* also takes the shape of *Phénix*. Finally, one can guess, in this fashion, what the *septuor* may be; most exegetes have seen in it the seven stars of Ursa Major, but it may also be the seven rare rhymes of the sonnet.

Not every poem may be haikuized; that is, not all poems let themselves be treated—or mistreated—thus. Not every poem withstands such a treatment. The reason for this is simple, I believe: in Mallarmé, and particularly in Mallarmé's sonnets, each line is a little world, a unity whose meaning accumulates, as it were, in the rhyming section, whereas in Racine or Victor Hugo, still more in Molière or Lamartine, meaning runs through rhymes without stopping, so to speak, and one cannot cull it there. Even so, Athalie's dream can be haikuized:

> Nuit
> montrée . . .
> Parée
> fierté . . .
> Emprunté

visage:
outrage.
Moi,
toi:
redoutables,
épouvantables.
Se baisser,
embrasser,
mélange
fange:
affreux. . . .[9]

One will notice that if haikuization is a restriction, the extension of the "haiku" is nothing other than a set rhyme.

2. The S + 7 Method

It consists in taking a text and replacing each substantive with the seventh following it in a given dictionary. The result obviously depends on the dictionary one chooses. Naturally, the number seven is arbitrary. Of course, if one takes, for example, a 2,000-word dictionary and uses the S + 2,000 Method, one ends up with the original text. One can also use the V (verb) + n, Adj. + p, etc. methods, and combine them; finally, n, p . . . are not necessarily constants.

A certain number of examples may be found in dossier 17 of the Collège de Pataphysique. The results are not always very interesting; sometimes, on the other hand, they are striking. It seems that only *good* texts give good results. The reasons for the qualitative relation between the original text and the terminal text are still rather mysterious, and the question remains open.

One will notice that if the inverse of haikuization is the set rhyme, the inverse of S + 7 is cryptography (or, at the least, a chapter of cryptography): given a text treated by this method, find the original.

3. Isomorphisms

Given a text, write another one using the same phonemes (isovocalism or isoconsonantism or, even better, isophonientism and isosymphonism) or the same grammatical pattern (isosyntaxism). One sees that the S + 7 Method is a numerical and lexicographical variant of isosyntaxism.

Here is an example of isovocalism:

Le liège, le titane et le sel aujourd'hui
Vont-ils nous repiquer avec un bout d'aine ivre
Ce mac pur oublié que tente sous le givre
Le cancanant gravier des coqs qui n'ont pas fui

Un singe d'ocre loi me soutient que c'est lui
Satirique qui sans versoir se délivre
Pour n'avoir pas planté la lésion où vivre
Quand du puéril pivert a retenti l'ennui

Tout ce porc tatouera cette grande agonie
Par l'escale intimée au poireau qui le nie
Mais non l'odeur du corps où le curare est pris

Grand pôle qu'à ce pieu son dur ébat assigne
Il cintre, ô cytise, un bonze droit de mépris
Que met parmi le style obnubilé le Cygne[10]

The original text is again taken from Mallarmé: as we can see, Mallarmé's sonnets are very high-grade material, like the fruit fly in genetics.

I conserved the last word of the poem in order to recall the original text, much like the early Cubists, who sometimes painted a nail in the corner of their canvas, for example, as a *trompe l'oeil*.

From isosyntaxism, we move naturally to what I have called (perhaps abusively) the matrical analysis of language. Here, we leave the work in pure potential literature behind in order to broach the borders of quantitative linguistics.

The formation of a sentence may be compared to the product of two matrices whose elements are words, the first (those of the matrix on the left) being all formers; the others (those of the matrix on the right) being all signifiers. Of course, I am supposing that the notions *sentence, former,* and *signifier* are well defined. By *sentence,* I mean that which is usually concluded with a punctuation mark, including at least a period. By *signifiers,* I mean substantives, adjectives, and verbs, and by *former,* all the other words, including the forms of the verbs *to be* and *to have*. The words in the French language are thus divided into two discrete sets. The product of two matrices of words gives thus a matrix composed of sentences, conforming to the classic rules of matrix multiplication.

Example:

the	has	the		cat	rat	lion	
a	has	a	×	eaten	devoured	degusted	=
the	had	a		fish	cheese	tourist	

the cat has eaten	the rat has devoured	the lion has degusted
the fish	the cheese	the tourist
a cat has eaten	a rat has devoured	a lion has degusted
a fish	a cheese	a tourist
the cat had eaten	the rat had devoured	the lion had degusted
a fish	a cheese	a tourist

For this to "work," the two matrices (on the left of the "equals" sign) must be associated, such that:

(1) In the left matrix:

(a) the elements of the first and third columns are articles or possessive pronouns in the masculine singular;

(b) the elements of the second column are forms of the verb *to have* in the third person singular.

(2) In the right matrix:

(a) the elements of the first and third line are masculine substantives in the singular, beginning with consonants:

(b) the elements of the second line are masculine singular past participles of transitive verbs.

To the elements of 1a may be added *ce, certain, maint, quelque,* etc. (*cet,* etc., being limited). On the other hand, the right matrix may be indefinitely prolonged toward the right by adding triads, conformant to rules 2a and 2b.

For simplicity's sake, let us restrict our consideration to the product of a matrix-line by a matrix-column:

$$\| \text{ the has the } \| \times \begin{Vmatrix} \text{gastronomist} \\ \text{degusted} \\ \text{caviar} \end{Vmatrix} = \begin{matrix} \text{the} \times \text{gastronomist} \\ + \text{ has} \times \text{degusted} \\ + \text{ the} \times \text{caviar.} \end{matrix}$$

We see that this "works" only if formers and signifiers alternate regularly.

If our matrical calculation is to be applicable in every case, we must add to the set of formers (respectively, signifiers) a unity-element that we shall call 1f (respectively, 1s), or, more simply, 1, when it will not lead to confusion.

Example:

$$\| \text{ the } 1 \text{ the } \| \times \begin{Vmatrix} \text{gastrono-} \\ \text{mist} \\ \text{degusts} \\ \text{caviar} \end{Vmatrix} = \begin{matrix} \text{the} \times \text{gastronomist} + 1 \times \\ \text{degusts} + \text{the} \times \text{caviar.} \end{matrix}$$

Following Le Lionnais's suggestion, we shall call the product of former × signifier *bimot;* one or the other may be equal to one (but not both at the same time, in order to avoid redundancy in notation).

The addition of "unity-elements" allows us to postulate a theorem which is now trivial: *In any sentence, there are as many formers as signifiers.*

We shall call the result of a first abstraction, considering only the grammatical functions of each word in a sentence, a *g-diagram*. In a second abstraction (*diagram*), we shall consider only the number and the alternation of formers and signifiers.

The example above will be written (on a single line for more convenience):

$$\| \ X \quad 1 \quad X \ \| \qquad \times \qquad \| \ X \quad X \quad X \ \|$$

(Let us remark in passing the analogy of this writing and, on the one hand, the sentence structure of certain American languages like Chinook, all formers being placed in initial position, and, on the other hand, "Polish" notation in logic.)

For the diagram to be correct, *primo,* as I have said, the two unities must not correspond; *secundo,* and for the same reason, one must not have:

$$\| \ \ldots\ldots\ldots\ldots x_n 1 \ldots\ldots\ldots\ldots \ \| \quad \times \quad \| \ \ldots\ldots\ldots 1y_n + 1\ldots\ldots\ldots \ \|$$

These rules of good construction once having been accepted, the number of possible diagrams of *n* elements (equal to the index term $n + 2$ of Fibonacci's sequence)[11] or of *n* words (equal to 2 to the *n*th power) may be determined, as well as some simple formulas on constants and variations, and the different types of diagrams and their proportions. Then, these will be compared to concrete data from literary texts (or other sorts of texts), which will furnish us with possibly interesting stylistic indices, for they are not the products of the conscious will of an author, and depend undoubtedly on several hidden parameters.

I must limit myself to allusion to these different problems (likewise to that of determining whether a given sentence corresponds fully to a given diagram and . . . what is a sentence?). I will note, however, the "potential" character of linguistic criteria overlooked by a writer's clear conscience. After Flaubert, the latter will avoid repetition and unrhymed verse (in Latin, he would have searched for metrical clausulae), he will (or not) be attentive to the length of his sentences, the choice of his vocabulary; but he will not seek to disobey Estoup-Zipf's law[12] or to use such and such a diagram following such and such a percentage.

Until now, that is. Perhaps we shall change that. I shall end on a pedagogical conclusion: granted that there is no longer any hope of reviving the translation into Latin, this marvelous exercise which bridged the gap between the composition in French and the geometry problem, perhaps this function could be fulfilled by Oulipian work on potential literature.[13]

Jacques Bens

. . . .

Queneau Oulipian

The little research group in experimental literature that formed in 1960 around François Le Lionnais and Raymond Queneau, under the ambiguous name of *Ouvroir de Littérature Potentielle,* has until now confined itself to a modest but essential technical role. Its first definitions, its first declarations of faith stated, for example:

There are two potential literatures: an analytic and a synthetic. Analytic lipo seeks possibilities existing in the work of certain authors unbeknownst to them. Synthetic lipo constitutes the principal mission of the Oulipo; it is a question of opening new possibilities previously unknown to authors (François Le Lionnais).

And Raymond Queneau stated explicitly, in order to remove all dubitation of an "artistic" nature:

The Oulipo is not a movement or a literary school. We place ourselves beyond aesthetic value, which does not mean that we despise it.

Everything had begun with the *Cent Millie Milliards de poèmes,* which Raymond Queneau was in the process of composing. When this composition was finished, the work was hailed by the Oulipians as the first work of potential literature. It was just that, and doubly so.

Indeed, if the Oulipo, because of lack of time, has been able to define potential literature only through recourse to *technical* criteria, it is nonetheless true that the notion of "potentiality" brims over amply from the rather thin frame of these definitions. One can state, without for the moment any attempt to delve more deeply, that a potential work is a work which is not limited to its appearances, which contains secret riches, which willingly lends itself to exploration.

One sees, then, all that makes for the potentiality of the *Cent Mille Milliards de poèmes:* it is not only the example, the archetype they constitute, but also the ninety-nine trillion nine hundred ninety-nine billion nine hundred ninety-nine thousand nine hundred ninety sonnets that are found, inexpressed but *in potential,* in the ten others.

Still, it must be noted that it was incorrect to consider Queneau's combinatory poems as "the first work of potential literature," for potential literature existed before the Oulipo was founded (that is precisely what we intend to demonstrate here). On the other hand, one can state with little risk of error that they constitute the first work of *conscious* potential literature. Or rather: *concerted*.

Concerted, yes, I prefer that term, for Raymond Queneau is not known for letting "the unconscious" dominate his writing. I believe, actually, that the foundation of the Oulipo was merely the public flowering of a long series of unformulated but perfectly clairvoyant experiments.

Twenty-five years ago, Queneau had already declared that the novel must resemble an onion, "*some being content merely to strip away the first layer of skin, while the others, far fewer, strip it layer after layer*" (*Volontés*, 11 November 1938). These interior layers constitute, without a doubt, a novel, or an episode, or a fragment, all of which are equally *potential*.

Here, a first question suggests itself, relative to the existence of literature and consequently thorny, but it would be of no use to dodge it. For Queneau (I repeat: *for him*), there is no, or very little, literature without a reader. This was remarked by Claude Simonnet, who writes in his shrewd and knowing book: "It is essential that certain aspects of the content be merely evoked, allusively, that they exist only within the book, like horizons which anyone can investigate in his own manner. The important thing is that the text exists, imposes itself through its presence, and resists the reader. This resistance is a fundamental element in Queneau's novelistic art, one of the factors contributing toward the objectivity of the text, toward its density, and thus toward its beauty . . . A disguise is amusing only if someone is there to discover it. The role of the reader is thus capitally important . . . Queneau makes him play the game, demands his collaboration. The experimental character of his conception of literature demands a witness."[1]

It is clear that the words "horizon," "resistance," "disguise," "experimental character" hide another word, which Simonnet did not use, because it had not yet been invented, but you can guess what it is now: it's the word *potentiality*. Potential literature would be that which awaits a reader, which yearns for him, which needs him in order to fully realize itself. Here, we are suddenly plunged into a somber perplexity, for everything that has any claim to be literature presents itself much in this way, from Michel de Saint-Pierre to François Mauriac.

However, if we come back to the matter at hand—I mean, to our onion—we will recall that the first postulate of potentiality is the secret, that which is hidden beneath the appearances, and the encouragement for discovery. Nothing prevents us then from deciding that there will be *potential literature* if one disposes of both a resistant work and an explorer. And we will immediately abandon the second member of this duo, because we have no power over him, in order to consider the first: the province, the domain, the share of the conscious writer.

The adjectival epithet "conscious" did not recur at the end of the preceding sentence by chance. It is intended to eliminate obscure or vague authors, hermetics and literary madmen. For the members of the Oulipo have never hidden their abhorrence of the aleatory, of bogus fortunetellers and penny-ante lotteries: "The Oulipo is anti-chance," the Oulipian Claude Berge affirmed one day with a straight face, which leaves no doubt about our aversion to the dice shaker.

Make no mistake about it: potentiality is uncertain, but not a matter of chance. We know perfectly well everything that can happen, but we don't know whether it will happen. Here as elsewhere, we shall ask the reader to understand what we shall talk about. (And that is not all: he will encounter later the terms of another apparent contradiction.)

Raymond Queneau's theoretical texts are not numerous, and generally confine themselves to discreet and modest technical considerations: so many chapters here, so many characters there, elements that reveal nothing, compromise nobody. One must dig a little deeper in order to discover a suggestion of intention.

Already in 1934, the notes on the jacket of *Gueule de Pierre* declared: "*Why shouldn't one demand a certain effort on the reader's part? Everything is always explained to him. He must eventually tire of being treated with such contempt.*"

Other notes, those to *Pierrot mon ami* (1942), claimed: "*A great savant said it: 'There is a certain pleasure in ignorance, because the imagination works' (Claude Bernard).*"

All these considerations suggest that it will be useful to read between the lines, to fill up the margins, and to scribble in the indentations. Thus, taking the sorcerer's-apprentice writer at his word, one might be curious to go and examine on the site, through his essential works, what sorts of floods are born of his awkward and sulfureous invocations.

In *Le Chiendent*, several subjects of perplexity will be found. Claude Simonnet[2] enumerates some of them, among which the existence of Pierre le Grand, the meditations of Etienne and Saturnin, the avatars of Madame Cloche, and the *Discours de la Méthode* are the most famous and the most obvious. One cannot help noticing that a sort of "second novel" unfurls in parallel with the first, a novel whose essential traits do not coincide with the general plot of the other (this is what constitutes the parallelism), and whose action is precipitated and made explicit by the outbreak of the war against the Etruscans: this is altogether natural, moreover, since all belligerency shuffles both cards and territories, mixes guts and destinies. Ruptures in space and time can then occur, leaps may be realized: the characters of a novel discover, with impotent and resigned stupor, their state as characters, as well as the probable existence of another life, in the sky or under their feet:

"*It's nonetheless a weird story, said Saturnin. We eventually create ourselves and the book gobbles us up immediately with its little fly-legs. Yeah, we're all like that, and everyone around us is too, oh queen my sister, your cowardly generals, your logwooden soldiers, and the fish in the pond next door who can't get to sleep. Double life, double knots. Hou ya ya.*"

Ten years later, in the epilogue of *Pierrot mon ami*, the notion of the potential novel is rendered explicit, this time with no ambiguity whatever:

"*. . . he clearly saw how all the elements that constitute it might have thickened into an adventure that would have developed mysteriously, to resolve itself afterward like an algebra problem where there are as many equations as unknowns, and how it had not been thus,—he saw the novel which that might have made, a detective novel with a crime, a criminal, and a detective, and the necessary meshing of the different asperities of the demonstration, and he saw the novel which that had made, a novel so stripped of artifice that it was impossible to know if there was a mystery to solve or not, a novel wherein everything could have been linked together according to police plans and, indeed, wholly depleted of the pleasures which the spectacle of this sort of activity provokes.*"

It must not be forgotten, in order to appreciate the conditionals which precede, that all the elements of the equations, the adventures, the mysteries, the meshings, and the asperities *exist* in the novel that became *Pierrot mon ami*. The other novel (the detective novel) would have arisen only from the manner in which these elements were presented, ordered, and described. There is thus *potentiality* as we have defined it, since the second novel is expressly included in the first, although unformulated, since any reasonably perspicacious reader can discover it and, with closed eyes or pen in hand, nicely narrate it to himself.

With *Loin de Rueil*, the process multiplies, engendering infinite ramifications: it is no longer a potential novel that we shall encounter but ten, twenty, or thirty fragments scattered in an amazing, enraptured bursting forth. The frontier between Jacques L'Aumône's dreams and reality is hazy: a shady area exists that may not be resolved in satisfactory fashion. For if he dreams that he becomes Middleweight Boxing Champion of the

World, it would seem that he is in reality "Amateur Champion of Paris"; he is probably a chemist, and a distinguished one (but where did he learn?); he undoubtedly becomes a sort of cruddy and inoffensive saint; it is almost certain that he explores the inhospitable territory of the Borgeiros Indians, and that he finally becomes a film star in Hollywood under the name of James Charity. *Almost.*

It is clear that the story keeps slipping toward innumerable possibilities, that from time to time the author backs off (and we tell ourselves that it was a dream), that sometimes he lets things run their course (and they become, thus, reality). The reader's imagination is perpetually solicited: that which seemed imaginary here is suddenly authenticated thirty pages further on; he hesitates (the reader), he gropes, he no longer knows very well, he must, whether he wants to or not, bring his pawn and play the game.

In *Le Dimanche de la vie* there is another process or, if one prefers, another purpose. The potential action is no longer exercised on the events but rather on the inward life of the principal character: who is Valentin Brû? Put this question to ten different people, and you will receive ten different answers. The fact is that the ex-soldier Brû wields silence admirably. It remains to be seen what the vacuity of his conversation (and, often, of his thought) hides: his being, or nothingness? Appearances, surely, tell against him, but then this is the case of almost all appearances. That which he is deep inside himself, definitively, we shall never discover. Let us take Madagascar, for instance, where he claims to have fought against the Hain-Tenys; let us take Madagascar and see what Paul Gayot thinks of it:

"It is Madagascar that Valentin Brû remembers most often, throughout *Le Dimanche de la vie,* in a curiously imprecise fashion, in the form of questions sometimes left unanswered. That is how Brû skirts the question when his brother-in-law asks him about the flora in Madagascar . . . When Paul asks him what plants he saw in Madagascar, Brû merely responds: 'Many are exotic.' The flora and the fauna of that huge island are nevertheless tolerably odd, as is its language, wherein the spoken differs from the written almost as much as in Ireland."[3]

And as to his trip to Bruges, Gayot has this to say:

"Brû's trips (Madagascar, Bruges, Germany) are never described. All that we know about them is that which he deigns to say. Now, Brû is exceedingly discreet, or rather very mysterious concerning these periods during which he literally disappears. The trip to Bruges, for example, seems highly suspect. Would Brû be beginning to lie?"[4]

It is not exactly a question of lying, but rather of dissimulation. If it may be said that Valentin Brû becomes cunning, if not intelligent, during

the course of the novel in which he serves as the hero, it is to all intents
and purposes impossible to say precisely when he acquires this cunning,
how it appears, develops, evolves. All the interpretations this authorizes,
all the "virtualities," in a word, of his behavior define precisely, following
the rules we have adopted, a *literary potentiality*.

Before soliciting any other sort of potentiality, I would like to respond
to an objection that came to my mind as we went along. "It is well
known," one might object, "that Raymond Queneau constructs his novels
with obstinate and laborious rigor, and cannot tolerate leaving anything to
chance (he himself says it). How can one reconcile such rigor with the
vagueness, the incertitude, the approximations that necessarily accompany potentiality?"
I believe, actually, that the contradictions exist solely in appearance. Or
rather that there is no contradiction: it is the problem that is ill-formulated.
For the writer never claimed that he detested incertitude itself but merely
that incertitude born of chance, which is not at all the same thing. It is
probable that he permits multiple solutions, granted that he himself has
put the machine in motion, that he proposes them, that he directs them.
Finally, if it happens that a given layer of the onion fails to appear immediately (or never appears) to a given casual reader, the latter should not
accuse fate but rather himself: the layers of the onion do not hide each
other fortuitously; it is the author himself who disposes them thus, such
that they may be discovered only one by one, and after careful searching.

We will find another sort of potentiality in what is commonly called
"parody." Parody may take two forms, and only two forms: *heteroparody,*
which imitates the works of others, and *autoparody,* wherein the author
refers to his own works. Each has its merits, of course, and Raymond
Queneau, being a well-rounded literary athlete, practices both.
The goal and result of heteroparody is to enlarge the dimensions of a
work, or rather to inscribe it within a vaster creative ensemble. The par-
odic elements function then as references, tokens, and passwords. If they
are not too obvious, a beginning of potential operation will result.
There is no doubt, for example, that the modernization, in *Le Chiendent,* of the *Discours de la Méthode* and the Platonic meditations is by
nature potential. The same is true of the Hegelian developments in *Le
Dimanche de la vie,* and of the (rather frequent) allusions to Hamlet in
Les Derniers jours, Un Rude Hiver, Pierrot mon ami, and *Zazie dans le
métro.*
Autoparody plays an analogous role. But instead of attempting to situate a work within, and in relation to, a creation both foreign and collective

(in short, *literature*), it will constitute, let us say, the cement intended to, umm, to join together the, the little stones of one's previous works, in order to make a whole. Yep.

This enterprise is both more difficult and more meritorious. More difficult, for after all, that which one has previously spawned does not necessarily have the audience and the clout of *to be or not to be*. Thus, the finest allusion, the most delicate quotation may very well go wholly unnoticed. More meritorious, since, if it is only of secondary interest to shout from the rooftops that one has read Plato and Master Shakes-Pear, it is essential, on the contrary, to prove to the ignorant and uncaring population that one has direction in one's thought: this is not overwhelmingly frequent in these days of wide diffusion of ideas.

One finds this sort of parody rather often in Raymond Queneau's novels. To restrict ourselves to the last, *Les Fleurs bleues,* whose profundities we have not had the time to sound entirely, we shall cite:

Page 19, Cidrolin's brief monologue: *Hardly had they left than I hardly remembered them* . . . recalls Gabriel's monologue in *Zazie* (p. 120), and notably: *And now they are almost dead, because they are absent.*

Page 23, the Duke of Auge has just admired *the Sainte-Chapelle, jewel of Gothic art,* leitmotif from *Zazie.*

Page 35, a Canadian female camper tells Cidrolin: *How mistaken you are, Sir! How mistaken you are!*

Page 43, the exclamation, *Tape recorder, my nostrils!* has the allure of a Zazic refrain.

Page 130, the speech of the guide who conducts the visit, in 1614, of the site of the Arcueil Viaduct resembles certain of Fédor Balanovitch's touristico-lyrical flights of oratory (*Zazie*).

Page 166, the Duke of Auge is meditating by a tomb; nearby, two gravediggers unearth bones. This scene from Hamlet has been used so frequently by Queneau that we may henceforth consider it as forming a part of the Quenellian universe.

Pages 193 to 196, and 226, 249, 250, the obstinate efforts of the keeper of the camping-ground toward thought take up once again the theme of Descartes's *cogito,* developed at length in *Le Chiendent* and already reused in *Pierrot mon ami.*

Pages 201 and following, the visit to the grottoes in the Périgord is not wholly unrelated to the descent into the gutters and the halls of the subway that closes *Zazie.*

Page 210, *France with its new parapets* parodies *Gibraltar with its ancient parapets* (*Zazie*, p. 222).

(Let us leave aside, for it would lead us too far away, autoparody of inner meaning: dream, the central theme of *Les Fleurs bleues,* is also that of *Loin de Rueil;* the final flood recalls the interminable rain of *Saint-Glinglin,* etc.)

Are not the links thus established essentially potential? If one has read the preceding with care, the answer is obviously yes.

Thus, there remains only one question for us to pose.

Here is the last question: is that phenomenon of which we have been speaking, the potential layers of the novelistic onion, exceptional? Why allude to it when speaking of Raymond Queneau?

No, let's be frank, this phenomenon is not absolutely exceptional. One may find it (to limit ourselves to simple examples) in Flaubert, Jarry, Proust, Joyce, Faulkner. I am sure that you could, upon reflection, quote ten more modern authors. But it is not extremely widespread, either. And moreover, in how many cases is it a question not of "conscious" potentiality (that is the least of things), but of *concerted* potentiality? This is a condition that we imposed in the beginning, and one can now see the importance it assumes.

For it is the clear will of the utterance that determines its value as potential; if this were not the case, any *unfinished* work would take on this character. Thus, Pascal's *Pensées?* Mallarmé's *Le Livre?* Of course not.

I do not know, however, whether one ought not to give the benefit of the doubt, gratuitously, to a certain number of famous ancestors, some of whom are considered by the Oulipo to be "plagiarizers by anticipation," a rare compliment: we shall cite here Rabelais, the Villon, and maybe Marot. We shall add the Grands Rhétoriqueurs. And we shall not forget that there existed in their time an eminently potential type of literature, the *commedia dell'arte,* which acquired really definite form only at the very moment of its staging.

And now, if one began to reflect that *potentiality,* more than a technique of composition, is a certain means of conceiving literature, one would perhaps admit that it opens onto a perfectly authentic modern realism. For reality never shows more than a part of itself, authorizing a thousand interpretations, significations, and solutions, all equally probable. Thus, attention to the potential will save the writer from both the hermeticism of the literary salon and the populism of the suburbs, phenomena which, in our day, must corrupt his pen and his inspiration.

As to Raymond Queneau, he is, among all contemporary French writers, the one who has been the most attracted by the notion of potentiality. The proof is that he writes very erudite and still secret studies on this subject.

But he who will read him with the eyes of second sight will need no further proof. For here are works that grow richer with each reading, that swell, that expand; for here are people and cities that come to life, begin to move, to spread out; for here are irises where your dreams will easily engender, if you have even a shadow of a taste for horticulture, a handful of blue flowers.[5]

François Le Lionnais

. . . .

Raymond Queneau and
the Amalgam of Mathematics
and Literature

At the time of the outbreak of the Second World War, I had read everything that Raymond Queneau had published: his novels, filled with sly
winks and laced with mathematical digressions, and his poems, among
which "L'Explication des métaphores" dazzled me most; more than anything else, I wanted to meet him. The preparation of the *Grands Courants
de la pensée mathématique* gave me the occasion to do so. Immediately
falling into step, Raymond Queneau gave me "La Place des mathématiques dans la classification des sciences."

   When I returned from deportation, we began to meet more and more
often, for no other reason than to wallow together in that which interested
us so passionately. Imperceptibly, as we gradually became conscious of
belonging to a sort of knighthood of the heteroclite, the affinity we felt in
the beginning was transformed into profound friendship. We indulged de-
lightedly in slaloms that led us, in a couple of hours (with neither effort
nor incoherence), from, for example, Goldbach's Conjecture to the Erlanger Program,[1] passing along the way the *Franfreluches antidotées,* Clovis
Trouille, the respiration of tunicates, Lady Beltham, the Mormons, and
Sei Shônagon. These moments *à deux* were sometimes expanded during
the "Boulogne Luncheons."[2] We proceeded then rather in the manner of a
potluck supper: Raymond introduced me to Georg Kreisel; I arranged for
him to meet René Thom and Stan Ulam, and I secured an invitation for
him to a luncheon with Pierre Deligne and several leading mathematicians
at the Institut des Hautes Etudes Scientifiques, in Bures-sur-Yvette.

   Beginning with a solid basic education in mathematics, Raymond Queneau never ceased to increase and extend his knowledge, so that finally—
wholly outside university channels and in sacrificing aspects that are,

properly speaking, technical—he attained a more than respectable level. He had been since 1948 a member of the Société Mathématique de France. Apart from the *Bulletin de la Société Mathématique de France* (whose content we in general only partly seized, when it wasn't frankly over our heads), Raymond subscribed to the *Bulletin of the American Society of Mathematics*, the *Journal of Combinatorial Theory*, the *Journal of Symbolic Logic*, and *Mathematical Reviews* (whose abundance is discouraging, but one can—if one knows how to peruse them fast and well—extract a few gems from these monthly accumulations). Both of us were faithful readers of Martin Gardner's exciting column in *Scientific American*, "Mathematical Games." The first one of us to receive, or otherwise procure, the new issue never waited until the next day to announce the good news by telephone and comment upon it to the other.

But this expert amateur was not merely a consumer of mathematics; he was also an authentic mathematician. Not a great one (the pomposity of this adjective would have displeased him) but a real one (this appraisal would have gratified him), whose work was considered by the best to be both valid and interesting. Fascinated by the strange union of implacable rigor and raving fantasy that animates the theory of numbers,[3] he had invented and studied a new notion, that of "Queneau's Series." These are series of whole numbers; the idea was probably suggested to him by the famous Fibonacci Series (of which he was very fond). They are constituted by successions of whole numbers, each greater than the one that precedes it and less than the one that follows, such that, beginning with a certain point (the preceding numbers constituting the "base" of the series), each term is the sum of exactly s different modes[4] of two previous terms. All possible sequences of whole numbers are not necessarily capable of furnishing a base that can engender an s-additive series; when this condition is filled, the s-additive that is engendered can comport, according to the case, a finite or infinite number of terms. Children of their bases, s-additive sequences may possess very different properties. Arithmetical progressions are very particular, elementary cases of this. Other series have been independently discovered by Ulam.

Raymond Queneau not only discovered this new domain but also studied it and demonstrated that it was governed, aside from the value of s, by two other parameters, U and V, of which we shall not speak here. His work was the object of two publications: a résumé presented to the Académie des Sciences by André Lichnerowicz (6 May 1968), and a detailed presentation published in the *Journal of Combinatorial Theory* (12, no.1, January 1972). In 1972, Paul Braffort and his colleagues J. de Meulenaar and W. Lebrun produced and analyzed finite Queneau Series with the help of computers.

The *s*-additive series constitute the principal but not the only original mathematical work of Raymond Queneau. A fan of whole numbers cannot help but yearn to confront the horrors and delights of those rebel angels, the prime numbers. Raymond had imagined a category of the latter which he baptized *hyperprime numbers*. A right hyperprime number (respectively, left) is a prime number written in decimal numeration (but one quickly sees that all even numbers are excluded), such that if one strikes one or several consecutive numbers beginning from the right (respectively, from the left), the part left intact is still a prime number. (We consider, by convention, that 1 is a prime number). Here is the biggest right hyperprime: 1,979,339,339; the largest known left hyperprime is 12,953. It is not known whether left hyperprime numbers necessarily have a finite number of numerals. Finally, there exist hyperprime numbers that are simultaneously left and right: the largest one of these is 3,137.

History, philosophy, and popularization naturally take their places beside mathematical activity and creation proper. Raymond Queneau dealt with the former more than once. Let us cite: "Sur la cinématique des jeux" (*Le Sphinx,* 1935); "La Place des mathématiques dans la classification des sciences" (*Les Grands Courants de la pensée mathématique,* 1948); "Bourbaki et les mathématiques de demain" (*Critique,* 1962); "La Dialectique des mathématiques chez Engels" (Bordas, 1963), an article on Hilbert in volume 9 of *Die Grössen der Weltgeschichte* (Zurich: Kindler Verlag, 1971); and the film *Arithmétique* (directed by Pierre Kast, 1951).

The history of mathematics is a road lined with sphinxes, with celebrated conjectures and problems; several have been wholly or partially solved, whereas others still await their Oedipus. Certain among them are characterized by simple and elementary terms that may be easily understood, even by grade-schoolers, but over which the best mathematicians from antiquity to the present have nonetheless racked their brains. Some of these problems are lyrically evoked and correctly described in two of Queneau's novels: the partition of any whole number into at the most nine cubes (this is a particular case of Waring's Conjecture),[5] theoretically resolved in *Odile;* the impossibility of solution by radicals of the algebraic equation of the fifth degree, also in *Odile;* the Quadrature of the Circle, in the delicious encyclopedia of inexact sciences in *Les Enfants du Limon.*

Visited by mathematical grace, a small minority of writers and artists (small, but weighty) have written intelligently and enthusiastically about "the queen of sciences."[6] Infinitely rarer are those who—like Pascal and d'Alembert—possessed double nationality and distinguished themselves both as writers (or artists) and as mathematicians. Outside, perhaps, of Lewis Carroll and some Oulipians, I know of only Raymond Queneau who has brought about in his work, to such a fine degree, the intimate amalgam of poetical inspiration and mathematical sense of structure.

How did he do it? I would undoubtedly never have known—when we were together, we never spoke of ourselves—if Janine Queneau had not asked me, on a certain October third[7] (circa 1968), how I had had the idea for the Oulipo, which led Raymond to compliment my confidences with his. We discovered that our routes had been rather similar, and that the idea of injecting original mathematical notions into novelistic or poetic creation had come to us at about the same time, after secondary school, during our university studies. First vaguely, then more and more clearly, and finally with a blinding force.

From our first conversations, in 1942 and 1943, we had discussed the *Exercices de style,* even before he had given the manuscript to Gallimard. My sonnet without substantive, verb, or adjective, "La rien que la toute la," published in *Messages* in 1946, was dedicated to him. I had submitted my *Poèmes booléens*[8] (intersection and symmetric difference of Corneille and Brébeuf) to him before publishing them in dossier 17 of the Collège de Pataphysique in 1961. He asked me to write a postface for his *Cent Mille Milliards de poèmes* in 1961. It was during this period that the fruit, having ripened, fell off the tree. During luncheon in a little bistro where one could talk peacefully, I decided to propose to Raymond the creation of a workshop or seminar of experimental literature, which would address in a scientific manner that which the troubadours, the Rhétoriqueurs, Raymond Roussel, the Russian formalists and a few others had merely adumbrated. He would never have approved this project had we not been viscerally in agreement about radically warding off any group activity that might engender fulminations, excommunications, or any other form of terror.[9] This axiom being solidly posed, Raymond agreed to my proposition with enthusiasm. The Oulipo (baptized thus by one of its members, Albert-Marie Schmidt) was to be born at the conclusion of the *Décade Queneau* at Cerisy-la-Salle in 1960, and permit itself to be affiliated with the Collège de Pataphysique.

Queneau's contribution to the Oulipo's work was major. The evidence one will find in the first volume of the Oulipo's works does not do justice to the richness of his erudition, the intelligence of his analyses, and the pertinence of his remarks in the one hundred fifty–odd meetings, where he generally arrived first and of which he missed less than a dozen. Apart from the combinatory structure of the *Cent Mille Milliards de poèmes,* whose meaning has not been fully understood,[10] Queneau brought two original creations—both with a great future, I am certain: "The Relation X Takes Y for Z," which encourages one to imagine and cultivate other binary, ternary, n-ary relations; and a few months before his death, the introduction of hypergraphs, a notion whose great specialist is an eminent mathematician and member of the Oulipo, our friend Claude Berge.

We owe to Queneau a fine example of anastomosis between the mathematical analysis of a traditional literary fixed form and the potentialities that one can deduce from it. Conceived by the Provençal troubadour Arnaut Daniel in the thirteenth century, and after having enjoyed a great success in Italy with Dante, Petrarch, and Tasso, the *sestina* returned to France where it elicited the attention of two members of the Oulipo, Harry Mathews and Jacques Roubaud, the latter drawing along in his wake the Centre de Poétique Comparée.

A sestina is a series of stanzas, each of which is composed of six verses ending in six different words. The structure of each stanza is deduced through permutation of that of the preceding stanza, and dictates that of the following stanza, such that the poem can contain only six stanzas, as a seventh stanza would merely repeat the structure of the first. Raymond Queneau asked himself whether it was always possible to construct n-inas when n is a number other than six. It is a problem that belongs to the theory of groups of permutations. It has not yet been wholly solved, but Queneau began to dismantle the fortress in demonstrating that, for two types of value of n, n-inas are impossible ("Sextines," *Subsidea Pataphysica* 1, 29 December 1965). A new chapter of applied mathematics, n-inology, had just been born.[11]

Where, among all that, may we classify the fourteen delicious pages of *Les Fondements de la littérature d'après David Hilbert* (Bibliothèque Oulipienne, no. 3)? Let us not classify them at all.

During the third of a century when we knew each other, and certainly before that, not a day passed without Raymond being visited by mathematics. In the last years, we had developed the habit of telephoning ritually to each other, speaking sometimes for an hour each Saturday and/or each Sunday, above all about math but also about other sciences, artists who pleased us, strange writers (and, sometimes, about my "easy-going" dictatorship over the Oulipo). It was by telephone that he informed me of the discovery, if not of the general formula of prime numbers, at least of an excellent approach to this Grail of the Theory of Numbers. A few weeks before his end, I brought him joy and amazement in telling him that Wolfgang Haken and Kenneth Appel (their demonstration having been improved by David Cohen) had just solved the "Problem of the Four Colors."[12]

Jacques Roubaud

. . . .

Mathematics in the Method of
Raymond Queneau

It is curious to note that among the sciences which Bouvard and
Pécuchet undertake to study, mathematics is almost the only one
that is absent.

Preface to *Bouvard et Pécuchet*, in *Bâtons, chiffres et lettres*

1. READING. Queneau was never a beginner in mathematics. He had
always practiced it, always gratuitously, and often under the cloak of literature. ". . . *The idea of injecting original mathematical notions into
novelistic or poetic creation had come to us at about the same time, after
secondary school, during our university studies. First vaguely, then more
and more clearly, and, finally, with blinding force.*"[1]
To be a mathematician, first one must be a reader of mathematics: its
games (Martin Gardner's column in *Scientific American*); its history (the
origin of conjectures; famous errors;[2] the historic notes of Nicolas Bourbaki's *Eléments de Mathématique*); its anecdotes (in 1770 a schoolteacher
in eastern Prussia kneels before the young Gauss, then seven years old,
whose slate is proof of a prodigious mathematical gift; G. H. Hardy visits
Ramanujan on his deathbed and "*tells him—a subject of conversation like
any other—'to come here, I took a taxi bearing the number 1729. That,
it would seem to me, is a singularly uninteresting number.' 'Not at all,'
replied Ramanujan after a few instants of thought. 'It is the smallest number which may be broken up in two different ways into the sum of two
cubes'*");[3] its madmen (among others, Léopold Hugo, Victor's nephew,
who in 1877—a centenary!—publishes his "*hugodecimal theory or the
definitive and scientific basis for universal arithmologistics which contains
. . . panimaginary geometry in 1/m dimensions, arithmetic in 1/m figures,*

79

an Ecumenical Presidential Decree relative to the hugodefinitive basis of decimal notation").[4]
Such readings stimulate the imagination.

2. All the more so since this manner of reading remains neither in the memory nor in the surroundings. Presenting right here in 1962 "Bourbaki et les mathématiques de demain,"[5] Queneau noted, *"a good mathematician who finished his studies around 1930 and who has not followed the development of modern mathematics is even more baffled in opening Bourbaki's treatise than someone who is entirely ignorant of the subject."*[6] This remark reveals an experience. It would seem probable, however, that he had early on encountered this provocative and avant-gardist treatise which, after an enigmatic first publication in 1939, became a real model for young French mathematicians only at the end of the 1940s: a sort of mathematical surrealism, but altogether foreign to literature. The provocation of the *"directions for use,"* which he quotes—*"the treatise takes mathematics at its beginning and gives complete demonstrations. Thus, it does not in principle require any particular knowledge of mathematics, but merely a certain practice of mathematical reasoning and a certain capacity for abstraction"*—could not have left him, granted its demoniacal character, indifferent. Which also explains why, being aware of the usual trajectory of the avant-garde, of the jolt to the establishment, he noted at the end the then brand-new first volume of Grothendieck's *Eléments de géométrie algébrique* with the following final thrust: ". . . *our sons wonder how Bourbaki will found the notion of category after his Book I."*[7] A prophetic remark in many ways.

Proposition 1: To be a mathematician, for Queneau, is to be a reader of mathematics.

3. AMATEURISM. *Proposition 2:* To be a mathematician, for Queneau, is to be an amateur of mathematics.

Never having wanted to fall into "an excessive and useless generality" nor "to legislate for eternity," he was in mathematics, in accordance with a broader attitude, an amateur. Which implies neither offhandedness nor technical insufficiency, but rather the refusal of a career; and positively, an exactingness in understanding as well as in discovery. This conception may appear, if one considers general practice and the organization of this practice in today's society, both anachronistic and archaic. Perhaps we might consider it as anticipatory as well.

4. *S*-ADDITIVE SERIES. Nevertheless, Queneau on at least one occasion pushed his research as far as the public statement (i.e., within the mathe-

matical community) of a problem and its (partial) solution. This arithmetic problem was the object of a paper[8] and of an article in the internationally-known review the *Journal of Combinatorial Theory*.

Sur les suites s-additives
RAYMOND QUENEAU
9, rue Casimir-Pinel, 92 Neuilly-sur-Seine, France
Communicated by Gian-Carlo Rota
Received 23 June 1969[9]

An example: the four whole numbers 1, 2, 3, 4 being the *base* of the series, the following term will be the smallest whole number that may be expressed in two ways and in two ways only as the sum of two distinct whole numbers in the base. It is 5. To find the next one, one uses the whole numbers already obtained (1, 2, 3, 4, 5) in the same manner. Which gives 6. The next term will not be seven, because $7 = 4 + 3 = 2 + 5 = 6 + 1$ and may thus be expressed in *three* different ways. *S*-additive sequences are important for us in the present case (apart from their technical interest and their use in the outline of the article)[10] as illustrations of our

Proposition 3: The privileged domain of Queneau, producer of mathematics, is combinatorics. More precisely,

(a) particularly the combinatorics of natural numbers, of whole numbers,

(b) not problems of enumeration, but those of recursive generation of series by means of procedures both finite and simple, whose complexity is created in their application.

And *proposition 4:* These combinatorics are part of a tradition that is almost as old as Western mathematics.[11]

5. THE MATRICAL ANALYSIS OF LANGUAGE. An article in the *Cahiers de Linguistique Quantitative* from 1963 (corresponding to research that is obviously much older)[12] presents an embryonic effort toward the algebraization of the construction of sentences through the use of matrices. *"The formation of a sentence may be compared to the product of two matrices whose elements are words, the first (those of the matrix on the left) being all formers; the others (those of the matrix on the right) being all signifiers."*[13]

This analysis, contemporary with the explosive development of generative grammar, has not been amplified, to my knowledge, beyond its rather elementary first presentation; perhaps provisionally, for even though its formalism be insufficiently sophisticated when compared to the great machines now operating, the basic idea is fairly close to another contemporary effort (which, although more sophisticated, also remained in embryonic form), that of J. P. Benzécri's *combs and ladders;* it is an idea that does not lack for pertinence:

Proposition 5: The nature of sentences is lacunary, and the combinatorics of their construction are more of the order of intrication than of concatenation, the substitution and permutation of indivisible elements.

Behind all this, one finds a more general preoccupation on the part of Queneau, which is expressed by

Proposition 6: To comport oneself toward language as if the latter could be mathematized; and language can be mathematized, moreover, in a very specific fashion.

Proposition 7: If language may be manipulated by the mathematician, this is because it may be arithmeticized.

It is therefore discrete (fragmentary), nonaleatory (disguised continuum), without topological stigmata; and it may be mastered piece by piece.

6. MECCANO. Immediately putting words into action,[14] Queneau converted, in his 1955 *Meccano*,[15] the algebraic hypothesis into text.

Example:

On the of the	×	end	summit	edge	side
was the 1		1	1	1	1
of (the)		highway	Annapurna	ocean	fencer
		rising	standing	bathing	standing
		black	Tibetan	mystical	passionate
		sun	Sherpa	masseur	bully
		1	1	1	1
		melancholy	team	Trinidad	Marquise

the resultant "product" would give a semantic (thus trivial) translation of the text:

"On the end of the highway was rising the black sun of melancholy."[16]

7. The simultaneous *existence* of *meccano* and *matrical analysis* leads us to suspect, concerning the Quenellian relations of mathematics and language, the verisimilitude of two conjectures:

Conjecture 1: Arithmetic applied to language gives rise to texts.

Conjecture 2: Language producing texts gives rise to arithmetic.

Undoubtedly, for the verification of *conjectures 1 and 2*, *s*-additive series (see 4) pose several problems. If it is true, however, as indeed it would seem to be, that Queneau's work on the series is just about as old as his novelistic work, this would suggest hypotheses whose verification is now being undertaken.[17]

8. FROM THE SESTINA TO THE QUENINA. The sestina of the troubadour Arnaut Daniel fascinated Dante, in his *rhymes of stone*, before Petrarch and Pound. Each stanza of the poem ends its six verses in echo-words without rhyme, which turn, from one *cobla* to the other, according to a spiral permutation:

$$1\ 2\ 3\ 4\ 5\ 6$$
$$6\ 1\ 5\ 2\ 4\ 3$$

A seventh stanza would offer the same structure as the first, but as in a helix, higher than the rest of the poem. In the *Subsidia Pataphysica,*[18] Queneau generalized the sestina as an *n*-ina (or quenina in present terminology) thus:

"'*Spiral mutation' defines a permutation such that to each element numbered 2p + 1 corresponds the element n − p, and to each element numbered 2p corresponds the element p.*"

If this permutation is of order *n*—that is, if it comes back to initial order after *n* "mutations"—the problem of the *n*-ina is solvable. An infinity of poems with distinct stanzas but analogous mechanisms becomes possible (provided that the set of *n*s, the solutions of the problems, be infinite, which is of course the case); all of these poems will be, potentially, "*like the thin flame that furls and then unfurls" (Pound);*[19] apart from the trivial cases 1, 2, 3, one has the choice between the whole numbers 5, 9, 11, 14, 18, 23, 26, 29, 30, 33, 35, 39, and 41, to restrict ourselves to those whose choice would engender a poem no longer than a Racine tragedy.

9. The problem of the quenina may be arithmetically solved (and has been, by two American scholars and one French), or at least led back to a more traditional problem. G. Guilbaud, who demonstrated the similarity of the problem with that of the "card shuffling" formerly discussed by Monge, proposed a very promising interpretation of its "combinatory direction," introducing the notion of *tropical permutation:* these "mutations" are at the antipodes of, or at least at a very great distance (the greatest possible) from, the static; that is, they guarantee a radical upsetting of the order.

In the domain of practical accomplishments, after Dante's celebrated double sestinas, Barnaby Barnes's triple sestinas, and that of Harry Mathews (wherein, according to a particularly efficient "double helix" principle, Daniel's permutation structures the ends of verses and Monge's permutation, the inverse, structures the beginnings),[20] it would seem that there are for the time being only noninas[21] and undicinas,[22] a few unpublished quattordicinas, and a diciottina which is in the process of being composed.

10. THE RELATION "X TAKES Y FOR Z." This is a second example illustrating *Conjecture 2*.

If its apparent starting point is vaudeville,[23] this mode of presentation of relations among characters functioning like a literature machine is evident in many other domains. Algebraic presentation, as the table of a law of composition, gives (if one is interested in the particularly important case of groups) the following "theorem":

"The multiplication table of a group corresponds to the following situation: nobody takes himself for what he is, nor takes the others for what they are, with the exception of the unity element, which takes itself for what it is and takes the others for what they are." [24]

11. The examples cited as testimony to the functioning of the relation resulted essentially from the analysis of texts existing prior to the formulation; one may take an additional step in choosing the table itself as the mechanism of construction rather than elucidation; the relation "X takes Y for Z" is only, moreover, a possible realization of the table; the predicate "to take an object for another" may be replaced by any other new predicate. Which was tested in a story,[25] with the relation "X schemes with Y against Z"; therein, the associativity of the group structure is entrusted to the care of Saint Benedict. It should be noted that this route is exactly the inverse of that taken, historically, by algebra, making clear with Viète the notation of the linguistic designation of its object; this method might admit rather varied generalizations.

12. QUENEAU IN THE OULIPO. And so we get to the creation (in 1960) of the Oulipo, where the strategy previously described becomes explicit, systematic, and collective. Queneau's role in the formation and activities of the group is known.[26] We will limit ourselves here to three propositions, stated in very nearly the same terms in a paper presented in 1964.[27] Let us remember that "Oulipo" is an acronym for *"ouvroir de littérature potentielle"*; the adjective "Oulipian" may also be used.

13. *Proposition 8:* Oulipian work is naive. Queneau's commentary on this proposition says: *"I use the word 'naive' in its perimathematical sense, as one speaks of the naive theory of sets."* [28]

The explicit reference to Bourbaki's *theory of sets* surely indicates that

Oulipian practice is understood here as being preformalized, though admitting of a descriptive systematic; but at the same time the possibility of a formal syntax is foreseen, of a "foundation" from which the practical, thus "naive," procedure would be shifted toward an activity of "models."

14. *Proposition 9:* Oulipian work is amusing. Here again the reference is obviously of mathematical order: "*Let us remember that topology and theory of numbers sprang in part from that which used to be called 'mathematical entertainments,' 'recreational mathematics'* . . . *that the calculation of probabilities was at first nothing other than an anthology of 'diversions,' as Bourbaki states in the 'Notice Historique' of the twenty-first fascicle on Integration.*"[29]

This means that Oulipian work is regarded as fundamentally innovative, as being situated on the cutting-edge, that it cannot avail itself of any so-called serious finality of any of the criteria serving today in scientific domains to eliminate research that unduly jostles accepted perspectives, this on behalf of existing smoothly functioning machines. Where the criteria are: What good is it? Who guarantees it? What problem does it solve? That it enters thus inevitably into the category of "play." It may be noted that Queneau does not refuse this often intentionally pejorative (in the case of those who distribute the labels) marginalization of the Oulipo.

Indeed, it is clear that one cannot respond to the question of "utility" or to that of "seriousness" if one is not already both useful and serious (and thus incapable of posing oneself that question); that at the same time it is not necessary to affirm this seriousness, this utility, as an unverifiable postulate.

15. *Proposition 10:* Oulipian work is craftsmanlike. Queneau's commentary seems here to mask something: "*. . . this is not essential. We regret having no access to machines.*" I would take it in a slightly different manner, and machines would be irrelevant. It seems to me, according to the status implied by propositions 9 and 10 (and Queneau's own positions, enumerated in propositions 1 to 7), that it is a case of a trait which is, on the contrary, essential. The claim to craftsmanship reflects an affirmation of amateurism; it is a voluntary archaism (and perhaps, here again, an anticipation).

16. One will not be surprised to find, then, that the Oulipians, in their Oulipian work, whether they be mathematicians or not (or "and not"), very generally satisfy the conditions of propositions 8, 9, 10: this is *proposition 11*.

17. CONSTRAINT. The Oulipo's first manifesto introduces, in opposition to "inspiration," the Oulipian operative concept of constraint—*"Every literary work begins with an inspiration (at least that's what its author suggests) which must accommodate itself as well as possible to a series of constraints and procedures that fit inside each other like Chinese boxes. Constraints of vocabulary and grammar, constraints of the novel . . . or of classical tragedy . . . constraints of general versification, constraints of fixed forms (as in the case of the sonnet), etc."*[30]—and proposes as one of the Oulipo's goals the search for constraints in ancient or in contemporary, though non-Oulipian, works (anticipatory or synchronous plagiarisms): this is *anoulipism;* the putting into play of these or new constraints in Oulipian works is *synthoulipism*. The status of constraint is thus fundamental. It should be noted that it is not posed as being a priori different from that of constraints elaborated by tradition, as the first manifesto clearly demonstrates.

18. *Let us choose, for example* (Queneau himself, who alludes to it first in his paper on potential literature,[31] invites us to do so), *the lipogram:* a lipogrammatic text is a text wherein is lacking, for whatever reason, one or more letters of the alphabet used to write it (generally, letters of alphabets *not* used in writing the text will be lacking also). This constraint, which goes back to most ancient antiquity, presents most rigorously the qualities Queneau insisted on for the Oulipian text, which we presented above (propositions 8, 9, 10 of sections 13 to 15): it is naive, amusing, craftsmanlike; most important, a great Oulipian virtue:

Proposition 12: A good Oulipian constraint is a simple constraint.

"The suppression of the letter, of the typographical sign, of the basic prop, is a purer, more objective, more decisive operation, something like constraint degree zero, after which everything becomes possible."[32]

19. *The lipogram,* abundantly pre-Oulipian (and undoubtedly peri-) through various plagiarists, became Oulipian with the publication of *La Disparition,* a novel by G. Perec:[33] *"qui, d'abord, a l'air d'un roman jadis fait où il s'agissait d'un individu qui dormait tout son saoul."*[34]

In what does the Oulipization of this constraint, as old or almost as old as the alphabet, consist? In this, which is a fundamental trait: that, as opposed to the different plagiarists who use the lipogram as a process of translation (Nestor of Laranda and the *Iliad*),[35] process of mnemotechnics, moral or metaphysical formulary . . . the constraint therein is at once principle of the writing of the text, its developmental mechanism, and at the same time the meaning of the text: *La Disparition* is a novel about a disappearance, the disappearance of the *e;* it is thus both the story of what it recounts and the story of the constraint which creates that which is recounted. This highly involuted aspect of constraint (which is undoubtedly not proper to Oulipian constraint, but which is in this case practically pure) is a direct consequence of the axiom of the Oulipian constraints, which may be formulated in the following manner:

Axiom: Constraint is a principle, not a means.

(This axiom has a corollary which we shall evoke further on: see 27.)

Moreover, *La Disparition* incorporates several e-lipogrammatic texts written by other Oulipians—in particular, this one (a- and e-lipogrammatic) by Queneau:

"*Ondoyons un poupon, dit Orgon, fils d'Ubu. Bouffons choux, bijoux, poux, puis du mou, du confit; buvons, non point un grog: un punch. . . .*"[36]

20. A methodical organization of constraints, resembling that which classifies the chemical elements (Mendelejeff's Table), and known as Quenelejeff's Table, has recently been elaborated by Queneau.[37]

The columns of the table classify the constraints, the lines classify the elements upon which they operate (the lipogram appears in column IV, line a).[38] This systematic classification brings out, as is only natural, several blank spaces, which must, through some sort of Oulipian alchemy, be filled. On the other hand, the table, prolonged by transquenellian elements, is in the process of being enlarged, and the new table will undoubtedly have an enumerable infinity of lines and columns.

21. ANTI-CHANCE. *Proposition 13:* The Oulipo's work is anti-chance.

Presenting *potential literature,* Queneau takes great pains to specify: "*we are not concerned with . . . aleatory literature.*"[39]

The intentional, voluntary character of constraint to which he insistently alludes time and again is for him indissolubly linked to this lively refusal of chance, and even more so to the refusal of the frequent equation of chance and freedom.

"*Another entirely false idea in fashion nowadays is the equivalence which is established between inspiration, exploration of the subconscious, and liberation; between chance, automatism, and freedom. Now the inspiration that consists in blind obedience to every impulse is in reality a sort of slavery. The classical playwright who writes his tragedy observing a certain number of familiar rules is freer than the poet who writes that which comes into his head and who is the slave of other rules of which he is ignorant.*"[40]

In this fundamental text (from 1938), the attack, of course, is on surrealism; for all of that, it is hardly less of current interest. This constant attitude must be directly related, it seems to me, to the fascination always exercised on him by arithmetical series that imitate chance while obeying a law. In the article on *s*-additive series already cited,[41] he remarks, about a series of this type previously studied by Ulam, "*it gives the impression of great 'irregularity'*"; the finest example of this is obviously the series of prime numbers.[42] The exemplary value of such series lay for him in the fact that it is a case of exorcised chance, since recognized as such, thus mastered insofar as possible. The refusal of "automatism" is thus for him in no way the rejection of mechanical procedures, but only of those that are mechanical merely through ignorance. Moreover, to the extent that all literature (like language) is subject to automatisms, he is irritated by the illusion of thinking that they may be avoided by simply deciding to act as if they did not exist: jamming, etc.; proposition 13 thus means the rejection of the mystical belief according to which freedom may be born from the random elimination of constraints.[43]

22. I will now take two Oulipian examples that are situated in this perspective: the *Sonnets irrationnels* by Jacques Bens,[44] and *Mezura*.[45]

In each case the sequence of the decimals of the number π, an example of this acknowledged and thus tamed chance, is given as constraint, on the one hand to determine the division into stanzas of that which is still called a sonnet, on the other hand to govern the disposition in segments within that which is still called a verse of a poem. That there results a nonregularity disavowing that of the reference (fixed form on the one hand, metric on the other) is undeniable, but this reference to chance does not change the fact that the nonregularity is not accidental: it results from the decision to use it, thus is predetermined, thus is constrained. It is furthermore supremely difficult, as any computer will tell you, to extract spontaneously from one's head nonregular series, and even series that are non-grossly-regular. Rigid mechanisms, very poor from the combinatoric point of view, will appear: the gesture of freedom will lead to stuttering.

23. THE AXIOMATIC METHOD. The Oulipo's constraint method leads one inexorably to think of another, particularly in favor during the 1940s to the 1960s (the Oulipo's incubation years), the axiomatic method. Let us listen to Bourbaki:[46]

"*Strictly speaking, the axiomatic method is nothing other than the art of drafting texts whose formalization is easy to conceive. This is by no means a new invention, but its systematic use as an instrument of discovery is one of the original traits of contemporary mathematics. It matters little whether the formalized text is to be written or read, whether one attaches such and such a meaning to the words or signs of this text or rather none at all; only the correct observation of the rules of syntax matters. It is thus that the same algebraic calculation may, as everyone knows, serve to solve problems involving kilograms or francs, parabolas or uniformly accelerated movements. The same advantage, and for the same reasons, accrues to any text drafted according to the axiomatic method. . . ."*

One might say that the Oulipian method *imitates* the axiomatic method, that the former is a transposition of the latter, a transfer to the field of literature.

Proposition 14: A constraint is an axiom of a text.

Proposition 15: Writing under Oulipian constraint is the literary equivalent of the drafting of a mathematical text, which may be formalized according to the axiomatic method.

Undoubtedly this is only an ideal situation, for two reasons. First, in spite of the undeniable classification progress represented by Quenelejeff's Table, it is clear that the domain of the formulation of constraints, as opposed to that of axioms (inscribable in the "unique source" of sets, for example), remains strongly unhomogeneous, its heterogeneity easily surpassing that which existed in the nineteenth century between the "obvious truths" of geometry (syntactic and semantic "truths" of ordinary language) and the even then "freer" (as Bourbaki notes) formulations of algebra (versificative "rules," for example). Second, and still more important, even if the "axioms" of an Oulipian constraint may be established with sufficient precision (as in the case of the lipogram), what will play the rather primordial role of deduction in mathematics? What is an Oulipian demonstration?

One may think that a text composed according to a given constraint (or several constraints) will be the equivalent of a theorem. It is a fairly interesting hypothesis. It is nonetheless true that the foreseeable means of passage from the statement of the constraint to its "consequences," the texts, remain in a profound metaphorical vagueness.

This question never ceased to preoccupy Queneau; clearly, if the historical possibility (a question of relative chronology) of disposing early on of current developments in the logic of the theory of categories and linguistics (multiple deductions: according to a formal system, according to the language) had been given to him, he would have furnished decisive progress in the effort to answer this question. In spite of everything, we have two indirect testimonies to this preoccupation.

24. First (see 28 for the second), the constant fascination exercised on him (and partly because of him on the Oulipo) by a form, that of the sonnet:

the writing of sonnets,[47] the hundred thousand billion poems, whose basic element is the sonnet,[48] and certain manipulations and transformations brought to these "most sonnetlike of all sonnets," the sonnets of Mallarmé,[49] are all proof of this, among other proofs.

Now it is well known that the form and the practice of the sonnet in many languages make it appear as a poetic model of deduction, as "poetic reasoning"; this is true not only of the articulation of the discourse of what a sonnet says, but also, simultaneously, of the formal, rhythmic organization itself.[50] The Oulipian exploration of the sonnet constitutes for Queneau a practical means of approaching the problem of "demonstration" according to constraints.[51]

25. An Oulipian work has come close to a possible answer: I am referring to G. Perec and M. Bénabou's A.P.F.L. (Automatic Production of French Literature).[52]

"Method: *One chooses two utterances that are as different as possible. In each of these two utterances, one replaces the significant words with their definition to obtain a quotation 'à la manière de. . . .' After a series of transformations, the two original utterances result in a single text.*" The example (partially) treated would result in an Oulipian *demonstration* of the equivalence of the following two utterances:

"*Utterance 1: The presbytery has lost none of its charm, nor the garden its brilliance.*

"*Utterance 2: Workers of the world, unite.*"

It has been conjectured that, according to this method, any two utterances in a language are always equivalent, that is, that according to this mode of deduction, language is tautological.

26. The *Oulipian method*, like the *axiomatic method*, runs into a wholly natural, if insidious, difficulty, that of the relation between arbitrariness and tradition. Let us listen again to Bourbaki, in the presentation of his book on topology:

"*The choice of the axioms to be imposed on the surroundings is obviously rather arbitrary, and historically it has caused long gropings . . . the system of axioms finally chosen responds to a considerable extent to the present needs of Analysis, without falling into an excessive and vain generality.*"[53]

And still again: "*The first efforts to define that which the properties of sets of points and of functions have in common were carried out by Fréchet and F. Riecz, but the former, beginning with the notion of enumerable infinity, did not succeed in constructing a commodious and fertile system of axioms. . . .*"[54]

Underneath the good-natured, pragmatic certitude, one sees the difficulty arise. Between systems of axioms, considered purely from the formal point of view, there is hardly a reason to choose. The reasons for the choice: "commodity, utility, fertility, beauty . . ." which vary according to the needs of the mathematical schools, are, finally, solidly anchored in the historical situation and the state of the tradition. Queneau's attitude (and that of the Oulipo) toward traditional constraints, if it is less bold and naive than Bourbaki's, reflects nonetheless the inherent ambiguity of the procedure: on the one hand, the eminently arbitrary character of constraints is revindicated; at the same time traditional constraints are marked as arbitrary, but, precisely because they are traditional and solidly anchored in history, they guard a power of fascination that situates them elsewhere, beyond the arbitrary . . . it is difficult to get out of this; and considerations outside the problem, the valorizing justifications of the type developed "innocently" by Bourbaki in the passages quoted, threaten.

27. It is undoubtedly the necessity of situating oneself, of distinguishing oneself from tradition, which explains one of the strange characteristics of the Oulipian method: the tendency—not really explicit but strongly encouraged, as far as I can judge, by Queneau—toward *unicity*. It works like this: a constraint having been defined, a small number of texts (only one, in some cases) are composed by deduction from this axiom, which then ceases to preoccupy the Oulipo; the former then enter either into the public domain or into that of the "applied Oulipo" (whose status is but ill-defined).

Proposition 16: The ideal constraint gives rise to one text only. (In fact, there even exists a tendency, which might be qualified as *ultra,* for which *every* text deduced from a constraint must be classed in the "applied" domain, the only admissible text, for the Oulipian method being the text that formulates the constraint and, in so doing, exhausts it. This, it seems to me, is to omit the deductive aspect of the method. *Proposition 16a:* A constraint must "prove" at least one text.)[55]

Here, we are at the very antipodes of the functioning of traditional constraint. The latter presupposes multiplication, and even demands it. To return to the (very typical) example of the sonnet, *a* sonnet is something that does not exist. The first sonnet, at the moment of becoming a sonnet, is not a sonnet but a Sicilian variant of the Provençal *cobla*. It is only with the thousandth sonnet (or more or less—in any case after many sonnets) that the sonnet appears. Moreover, an efficient traditional constraint tends toward imperialism: when the alexandrine triumphs in French prosody, it invades everything. French tends to become alexandrine (and non-alexandrine, to organize itself in relation to the alexandrine). Oulipian constraint, on the contrary, can tend toward multiplicity (toward which, seemingly, it is tending) only in ceasing to be Oulipian.

28. THE "FOUNDATIONS OF LITERATURE." To use in Oulipian fashion the Oulipian method in order to compose a system of axioms for literature: that is Queneau's project in one of his very last texts, published in the Bibliothèque Oulipienne in March 1976:[56]

*Les Fondements de la littérature
d'après David Hilbert*

29. *The model is in fact* one of the fundamental texts of the axiomatic method, the famous *Grundlagen der Geometrie*, the first edition of which dates from 1899. In this work, whose impact was very great, Hilbert described for the first time in a detailed, rather than circular, manner the properties of a "geometry," beginning with an explicit system of axioms. Queneau in his introduction speaks of Hilbert's starting point:

"After having listened at Halle to a paper presented by Wiener . . . David Hilbert, waiting for the Königsberg train in the Berlin station, murmured pensively: 'Rather than points, lines, and planes, one might just as well use the words tables, chairs, and drinking glasses.'"[57]

30. The principle adopted by Queneau, after Hilbert, is the following: *"Taking my inspiration from this famous example, I present here a system of axioms for literature, replacing in Hilbert's propositions the words 'points,' 'lines,' and 'planes' with, respectively, 'words,' 'sentences,' and 'paragraphs.'"*[58]

The result, armed with all the unshakable coherence furnished by Hilbert's text, is consistently surprising in its linguistic intuition.

The following axiom: *"A sentence having been given, and a word not belonging to this sentence, in the paragraph determined by the sentence and this word, there exists at the most one sentence including this word which has no other word in common with the first given sentence"*[59] may be merely the Quenellian translation of an obvious truth, "Euclid's Postulate"; nevertheless, its "literary" pertinence causes some perplexity.

But certain consequences impose themselves. Thus, this corollary to "Theorem 7":

"Every sentence includes an infinity of words; one perceives only a very few of them, the others being in the infinite or being imaginary."[60]

31. *Why? What for?*

32. THE RUIN OF RULES. The "what for" is clear: recourse to mathematics according to the modalities we have just described in a few propo-

sitions (propositions 1 to 16, conjectures 1 and 2, the axiom about constraint) has a sole finality: literature. It remains to furnish some hypothesis about the "why," in order to better elucidate the "how."

The solution, undoubtedly, is not unique. We shall choose this one: a sentence in *Bâtons, chiffres et lettres,* from 1937.[61]

Proposition 17: There are no rules after the moment when they outlive their value.

The exhaustion of tradition, represented by rules, is the starting point in the search for a *second foundation,* that of mathematics.

Proposition 18: Mathematics repairs the ruin of rules.

The problem of "value" is to be put in parentheses.

33. Once the "shift" has been made, from the rule to the constraint by axiom, mathematics then furnishes another concept of substitution: for replacing "form." After the 1937 statement that we used for proposition 17, Queneau wrote:

"But forms subsist eternally."

The notion then substituted for this "eternity," leaving the question of "eternity" in darkness, is of course the keystone of the Bourbakian edifice, the notion of *structure.*

34. STRUCTURES. Structure, in its Quenellian and Oulipian sense, has only a minimal relation to "Structuralism." Ideally (like constraint in respect to axiom), it refers to the Bourbakian structure: the object in the mathematical case is a (or several) set(s) with something "on it" (one or several algebraic laws, proximities in topology . . .); in the case of the Oulipo, the object is linguistic,[62] and its structure is a mode of organization. This structure will satisfy one or many conditions: axioms in one case, constraint in another. Thus, a set armed with a law of composition will have a monoid structure if this law obeys the axiom of associativity; a text will have a lipogrammatic structure if it obeys the constraint of the same name. It is clear, and this is an important point, that the Oulipian notion of structure is not entirely distinct from that of constraint, many structures (traditionally) remaining implicit: must a lipogrammatic sonnet be examined in the same manner as a lipogrammatic novel? A topological group is, certainly, a group and a topological space, but its operation and its topology are not indifferent one to the other. How may we approach, in Oulipian fashion, this link in the case of the lipogram, for example, and in that of the sonnet? The neutrality of the conventionality of the props (texts, poems, stories . . .) is without doubt an obstacle in the development of the Oulipian notion of structure. In this sense, one understands why Queneau never wrote an "Oulipian novel."

35. For the present, the most efficient method seems to be that of "structure transport": a set, armed with a given structure, is "interpreted" in a text; the elements of the set become the data of the text; the structures existing in the set are converted into procedures for composing the text, with constraints: a privileged experiment is that of Georges Perec's work-in-progress, written *from* a Latin bi-square.[63]

36. An examination, in this perspective, of the celebrated *Cent Mille Milliards de poèmes* will permit us to shed some light on this book's place in the passage from mathematics to its literalization.

Let us remember this principle: ten sonnets are written, using the same rhymes. The grammatical structure is such that every verse of every "base" sonnet may be smoothly interchanged with any other situated in the same position within the sonnet. Thus, each verse of a new sonnet has ten possible independent choices. There are fourteen verses; there exist thus, virtually, 10^{14} or one hundred thousand billion sonnets.

What does this in fact signify? Let us proceed by analogy: let us take ten letters; let us then take certain letters among these, any ones, and put them one after the other; let us call the result of this a *word*. We do not impose upon the "words" thus constituted the necessity of figuring in any dictionary whatever. The "procedure" works freely and furnishes, according to the number of letters which one accepts in a "word," a more or less considerable quantity of such words. One thus has a more or less extensive piece of the "free monoid" constructed on the given letters, a "free object" of monoid structure.

Let us then consider the "hundred thousand billion" as "free object" of sonnet structure, as the book, metaphorically, of free structure.

Whence for this reason also its importance: for let us try, in analogous fashion, something very similar with *a* sonnet by Baudelaire, for instance: to substitute one verse for another therein (in this same sonnet or elsewhere) all the while respecting that which makes it a sonnet (its "structure"). One will run up against what Queneau parried in advance (and that is why his "structure" is "free"), difficulties whose nature is principally syntactic. *But*—and this is what the "hundred thousand billion" really teach us—*against* the constraints of semantic verisimilitude, the sonnet structure makes from (virtually) a single sonnet all possible sonnets through all the substitutions that respect it. *The* proposed sonnet, if it imposes a choice, or rather proposes to impose one, does not eliminate the other possibilities, which expand it: confrontation of structural "freedom" with the constraints of the milieu (linguistic or other) in which it inscribes itself.[64]

37. We may now situate this key concept of Quenellian work, which ap-

pears in the Oulipo's very name: *potentiality*. The Oulipo is potential literature because the givens of a structure are those of all the virtualities of free objects, if they exist, of all the virtualities of the texts that realize it, necessarily multiple; the unicity of the Oulipian text actualizing a constraint (Proposition 16) being then envisaged only on the condition that this text contain all the *possibilities* of the constraint—texts and virtual, potential readings: multiplicity again but, unlike that which traditionally results from the multiplication of examples, implicit and, at the outside, imaginary multiplicity (Proposition 16a), exhausted by the very gesture that announces or writes the structure.

38. An explicit trajectory leads thus from mathematics, as reading and practice in writing of this practiced mathematics: this, in great part, is the creation and the advance of the Oulipo. We shall not go any further here, that is, to search for the invisible mathematics in the more visible part of Queneau's work: novels, poems—not that it cannot be found (at least partially),[65] but because its dissimulation is a necessary part of Queneau's project and of his method. Let us leave this unmasking to others, and until later. Let us merely try to elucidate its meaning.

39. THE MEANING OF COMBINATORICS. We have, above, justified the "recourse" to mathematics as a consequence of the "collapse of rules." Granted this, it remains to understand the why of the combinatoric choice, of the arithmetical bias. Why, anywhere one looks, does one almost always find whole numbers in Queneau?

40. A piece of evidence: "*It was intolerable to me to leave to chance the number of chapters in these novels.*[66] *Thus,* Le Chiendent *is composed of 91 (7 × 13) sections, 91 being the sum of the first thirteen numbers and its 'sum' being 1, it is thus both the number of the death of beings and that of their return to existence, return which I then imagined merely as the irresoluble perpetuity of hopeless grief. At that time, I saw in 13 a beneficent number, because it denied happiness; as to 7, I took it, and may still take it, as a numerical image of myself, since my last name and my first and middle names are each composed of seven letters, and I was born on a 21st (3 × 7).*"
Another piece:
"—*Look here, that is awfully idealistic, what you're telling me.*
—*Realistic, you mean: numbers are realities. They exist, numbers do! They exist as much as this table, sempiternal example of philosophers, infinitely more than this table! Bang!*
—*Couldn't you make a little less noise, said the waiter.*"[67]

41. The obvious intensity of this numerical, or rather numerological, identification of personal identity, the suggestion of the extraterrestrial or historical intrinsic reality of numbers: all that evokes[68] a specter which already made an insidious appearance in section 4 in connection with
s-additive series: indeed, let us remember the following remark, already
quoted above:[69] *"For 1' = 1, we discover with pleasure Fibonacci's numbers"*; now Fibonacci's numbers, which are constructed (as Queneau gra-
ciously points out) according to a procedure analogous to that on which
he is working, have, it is well known, the particularity of being at the
center of very honorable and ever-resurgent old esthetico-metaphysical
speculations, since the relation between two consecutive numbers in the
series tends toward a limit, called *golden number*. One may then allow
oneself to suppose that, somewhere in the study or the project of the *s*-
additive series, something "additional to" their production intervenes, different from the secrets of their enumeration: the search for a new multiplicity of limits (or of non-limits, when the series is interrupted), each the
founder of a remarkable and perfect proposition, a number no longer
golden, but made of some other precious element, "rare earth" of esthet-
ics: an eminently ironical multiplication of the truth of beauty.

42. This, still: *"There are forms of the novel that impose all the virtues of
the Number on the material proposed and, springing from the very expression and from the various aspects of the story, connatural with the guiding
principle, daughter and mother of all the elements it polarizes, a structure
develops that transmits to the works the last rays of universal light and
the last echoes of the Music of the Spheres."*[70]

43. CONTEMPLATING THIS, WE SHALL PART.[71]

Georges Perec

· · · · · · · · · · · · · ·

History of the Lipogram

Of the 21 groups defined by Scholem, which in their entirety compose the 5 books of the Zohar, the 16th is a monologue by Rabbi Simeon on the letters that form the name of God; he gives 70 interpretations of the first word of the Torah: Berechit.

In his *Praise of the Cabala,* Borges speaks of "this prodigious idea of a book wholly impervious to contingency." If it is true that in the beginning there was the Word, and that the Work of God is called Writing, each word, each letter is motivated: the Book is an infinite network constantly traversed by Meaning; the Spirit merges with the Letter; the Secret (Knowledge, Wisdom) is a hidden letter, an unspoken word: the Book is a cryptogram whose code is the Alphabet.

The exegetical fever of the Cabalists seems to have been oriented in three principal directions. The first, *Gematry,* concerns the numerical value of letters (aleph = 1, beth = 2, gimel = 3, etc.) and compares words of identical totals. Its nearest rhetorical equivalent would be the chronogram, where the roman numerals contained in a verse reflect a significant date; this was one of the specialties of Belgian convents in the seventeenth and eighteenth centuries; André de Solre enshrined 1670 in one, and an *Art of the Chronogram* was published in Brussels in 1718.

The second direction, *Notarikon,* treats each word of the Book as an acronym; Agla would mean Atha Gibor Leolam Adonaï. Each letter of the Book is merely the first letter of a word, and the Bible thus becomes a gigantic inverted acrostic.

For the third, *Temurah,* the Book is an anagram that encodes (I suppose something like a hundred thousand billion times)[1] the name of God. . . .

A considerably diminished echo of these vertiginous preoccupations seems to me to resound still in the case of the lipogram.

Littré defines the lipogram as a "work in which one affects to exclude a particular letter of the alphabet"; Larousse says, more precisely: "literary work in which one compels oneself strictly to exclude one or several letters of the alphabet." An appreciation of the nuance between "one affects" and "one compels oneself" might have constituted one of the purposes of this article.

"Lipogram" (not the hypogram, whose meaning is close but without a doubt more ambiguous) does not mean "greasy letter," nor still less "a gram of grease." The radical *lipo* comes from *leipo*, "I leave"; apart from the derivatives of "lipogram" ("lipogrammatic," "lipogrammatist"), there exists to my knowledge only one other French word with this root: *lipothymie:* loss of consciousness with respiration and circulation remaining normal; lipothymy is the first symptom of syncope.

The Germans say *Leipogram* or *Lipogram,* the Spanish *lipogramacia* or *lipograma,* the English *lipogram* or, occasionally, *letter-dropping.* This, of course, when they do say it, for most of the time they do not say it at all.

Absent from Furetière and from the first edition of the *Dictionnaire de l'Académie* (1694), the word appears in the *Dictionnaire de Trévoux* (1704). The Academy admits it in 1762, then suppresses it in 1878.

The *Robert* (which gives, let us note in passing, a *false* definition of *haiku,* volume 3, page 436, or, in the abridged version, page 822) ignores the word, as does Henri Morier's *Dictionnaire de poétique et de rhétorique.*

This lexicographical ignorance is accompanied by a critical misappreciation as tenacious as it is contemptuous. Exclusively preoccupied with its great capitals (Work, Style, Inspiration, World-Vision, Fundamental Options, Genius, Creation, etc.), literary history seems deliberately to ignore writing as practice, as work, as play. Systematic artifices, formal mannerisms (that which, in the final analysis, constitutes Rabelais, Sterne, Roussel . . .) are relegated to the registers of asylums for literary madmen, the "Curiosities": "Amusing Library," "Treasury of Singularities," "Philological Entertainments," "Literary Frivolities," compilations of a maniacal erudition where rhetorical "exploits" are described with suspect complaisance, useless exaggeration, and cretinous ignorance. Constraints are treated therein as aberrations, as pathological monstrosities of language and of writing; the works resulting from them are not even worthy to be called "works": locked away, once and for all and without appeal, and often by their authors themselves, these works, in their prowess and their skillfulness, remain paraliterary monsters justiciable only to a symptomology whose enumeration and classification order a dictionary of literary madness.

Without wishing to distinguish between that which, in writing, is madness, and that which is not (is platitude a form of wisdom?), one might at least recall that formal mannerisms have existed since time immemorial and not only, as some feign to believe, during so-called "decadent periods"; they have traversed all of Western literature (we shall not speak of the others here) and have left their trace on every genre. The list that the Oulipo intends to elaborate of its "plagiarists by anticipation" might very well constitute in the end a new Universal Dictionary of Letters.

We do not pretend that systematic artifices are identical to writing, but only that they constitute a dimension of writing which must not be ignored. Rather than harrying the ineffable to who knows where, shouldn't we first examine the reasons for the persistence of the sonnet? And why should we forget that the most beautiful line of poetry in the French language is composed of monosyllables?[2]

Lexicographers, bibliophiles, historians—the majority of those who have spoken of the lipogram—have generally described it as "a puerile game," "an inept tour de force," "foolish playing-around," "a sad example of silliness," "misplaced ingenuity," "witless foolery."

The severity of these appreciations leaves one reeling. Even without going as far as Dinaux, who speaks of "these monuments to human foolishness," one will learn, in perusing these anthologies, that it is "vain and frivolous to enumerate such twaddle" (Gausseron), that a lipogrammatist has, in truth, "nothing to say" (Raby), that their works have no merit apart from their bibliophilic rarity (Canel), that one must be a dolt to write lipograms (Fournier *fils*), and that only a pedant could admire such ineptitudes (Boissonade).

One must either turn toward German literary history (6, 10, 12, 13, 18 [these numbers are keyed to works listed in the bibliography following this article]) or wait for the Oulipo (1, 17) or the information theorists (9, 16) to find this quasi-unanimous depreciation that dismisses the lipogram with a line from Martial:

> Turpe est difficiles habere nugas
> Et stultus labor est ineptiarum[3]

gradually giving way to a slightly more positive interest, justified, it seems to me, by the following three elementary observations:
—the principle of the lipogram is childishly simple;
—its application can prove to be excessively difficult;
—its result is not necessarily spectacular.

The history of the lipogram is difficult to reconstitute: its sources are disparate and dispersed; numerous works have disappeared or are unlocatable for an amateur researcher; pillages and plagiarisms pullulate, whence a sometimes problematical identification of authors; three Italians wrote different texts that share the same title, *L'R sbandita;* Navarette's *Los dos hermanos incognitos* becomes *Los dos hermanos* in Zurita and *Los tres hermanos* in Velez de Guevara; Alcala y Herrera's *Varios effectos de amor* is often attributed to Isidro de Robles (who merely copied it), or to Lope de Vega, to Calderon, or even to Cervantes!

Moreover, any sentence of any author in any language has every chance of being lipogrammatic: one of the verses of the seven psalms of the penitence *Beati Quorum* doesn't have any A; the second sentence of *Rocambole* lacks, among other letters, both P and V; the first quatrain of Corneille's *Stances à la Marquise* does without the B and the C; one of Ingres's *pensées* has no I, etc. Lipogrammatic probability (which is one of the bases of cryptography) easily explains the existence of an inverse art: pangrammatic art, at least one example of which is familiar to anyone who has taken a typing course—"The quick brown fox jumps over the lazy dog." The difficulty of this art seems such that six pangrammatic verses by a Greek author of the twelfth century sufficed to preserve his name for us: Jean Tzetzes.

The most ancient lipogrammatist would be Lasus of Hermione (certain people have claimed that he was one of the Seven Wise Men, but I do not believe a word of it), who lived during the second half of the sixth century (B.C.), which would make the lipogram, according to Curtius, the most ancient systematic artifice of Western literature. Lasus did not like the sigma; he excluded it in an *Ode to the Centaurs,* of which nothing remains, and in a *Hymn to Demeter,* of which the first verse remains, such as it was passed down to us by Athenaeus:

Δήμητρα μέλπω Κόραν τε Κλυμένοιο ἄλοχον.[4]

Abbé Barthélemy, whose opinion we have no reason to doubt, considers that Lasus, who was above all a musician, wanted to avoid in this manner "the unpleasant hissing of the Sigma," which on the contrary was so sought after by Euripides. The interested reader will find several examples of Euripides' Sigmatism in Boissonade (3).

Pindar, Lasus's student, who also stigmatized the sigma, also wrote an ode without the sigma (not without the zeta, as Gausseron claims in the article "lipogramme" of Berthelot's *Encyclopédie*). Nothing remains of it, but Eustathius confirms it, after Clearchus, who had it from Athenaeus.

These first two examples (if one can call them examples) seem in any case to spring more from a sort of euphonical purism, a form of counter-alliteration, than from a real taste for constraint.

After Pindar, did the Greeks lose interest in their alphabet? One must wait several centuries (neglecting in passing the dubious lipogrammatic *Metamorphoses* of Parthenius of Nicaea) until the appearance, in the third century A.D., of a new lipogrammatist, Nestor of Laranda, whose ambition was grandiose: like so many others, Nester rewrote the *Iliad*, but he denied himself the alpha in the first canto, the beta in the second, the gamma in the third, and so forth until the mutual exhaustion of both the alphabet and the work. One can measure the difficulty of the enterprise in reflecting on the role of redundance and on the weight of Homeric epithets; one can minimize it by remembering that no letter is irreplaceable and that only two or three are really essential.

Less than two hundred years later, Tryphiodorus of Sicily, an Egyptian Greek, complemented Nestor's effort in addressing himself, using the same procedure, to the *Odyssey*. Twelve centuries later, more precisely on Tuesday, 8 May 1711, he incurred the ironic reprobation of Addison: it must have been amusing, Addison's argument ran, to see the most useful and most elegant word of the language rejected like "a diamond with a flaw in it" if it was tainted by the proscribed letter. It is difficult to understand why Addison attacks Tryphiodorus in particular, whom he had never read, for his work was lost. Nothing remains either of Nestor's *Iliad* or of the much earlier but far more dubious *Metamorphoses* by Parthenius. The existence of these works (about which Leonicenus said that they were the result of "much work, an ingenious mind, and an inestimable industry") is confirmed in a fragment of Eustathius of Thessalonica, quoted five centuries later in the colossal and fastidious compilation attributed to Suidas, fictive author if there ever was one! All of which does not prevent Nestor and Tryphiodorus from being the best-known, the most cited of lipogrammatists.

The first attested lipogram is the *De Aetatibus Mundi & Hominis,* by a Latin grammarian residing in Egypt in the sixth century, Fabius Planciades Fulgentius, also known as Fabius Claudius Gordianus Fulgentius (or Gordien Fulgence). Saint Fulgentius is not the man in question here.

The *De Aetatibus* is a treatise treating diverse uninteresting subjects. It is divided into twenty-three chapters. The first is without A, the second without B, etc. The first fourteen chapters have been preserved; an Augustinian, Jacques Hommey, published them in Paris in 1696 under the title, *Liber absque litteris historia. De Aetatibus . . . absque a, absque z. Opus mirificum.* A second edition was published in Leipzig in 1898 by Rudolph Helm.

Toward the middle of the eleventh century, Pierre de Riga, canon of Sainte-Marie-de-Reims, translated the Bible in verse under the Leirisian title, *Aurora* (because the obscurities of the scriptures are dissipated therein). Each canto is followed by a "repetitio priorum sub compendio," or résumé, in lipogrammatic verse; the résumé of the first canto has no A, the second has no B, etc. The work was remarkably successful, for today there still remain two hundred and fifty manuscripts of it. Polycarp Leyser published an edition of it at Halle in 1721.

During approximately the same period, the Arab poet and grammarian Hariri also tried his hand at lipograms but, it must be admitted, in an amateurish fashion.

Here ends what one might call the first tradition of the lipogram, in which are produced continuous works, most often taken from a master-work (the *Iliad*, the *Odyssey*, the Bible), divided into as many chapters as there are letters in the alphabet used, each chapter excluding one letter.

This tradition, which I propose to call totalitarian, is henceforth pro-longed only in degraded form: sets of distinct pieces whose union forms an alphabet, but without continuity from one piece to another. Let us cite, so as to be done with them, Cardone's *Alfabeto distrutto*, F. A. C. Key-ser's *Unterhaltende Geduldsproben*, Gabriel Peignot's twenty-six qua-trains, where the brevity of the pieces renders the constraint practically null, the sixty-six sonnets (three alphabets) of Salomon Certon (Sedan, 1620), of whom it shall be remembered that (a) as an intimate friend of Admiral de Coligny, he owed his escape from the Saint Bartholomew Massacre to a miracle; (b) he was an esteemed translator of Homer; and (c) he also wrote sestinas.

The second tradition of the lipogram describes a history of the non-letter R. This tradition, remarkably stable from the beginning of the seventeenth century to our day, characterizes almost exclusively German and Italian lipograms. Some authors rarely if occasionally excluded other letters (Frey the C, Müllner the M and the O, Harsdörffer the L and the M, Caroline W. or Otto Nebel from nine to twelve consonants), but it is the R and the R alone that guarantees the continuity of the tradition; this may be explained by the fact that the R, even if it is not the most frequently used letter, has, in German at least, an essential "grammatical" role; its ab-sence, as Schulz-Besser (18) shows, prevents any use of a masculine rel-ative (*er, der, dieser, jener, welcher, usw.*), which constitutes a relatively strong constraint.

The tradition first develops in sermons and theological dissertations in Latin: Adreas Prolaeus Pomeranus's *Xenium* (1616), a Panegyric by Janus Caecilius Frey, who excludes both the R and the S (1616), an anonymous sermon on the birth of Christ (Strasbourg, 1666). German-speaking preachers and theologians continue to nourish the tradition: Joachim Müll-ner, Erdmann Uhse, Johann Conrad Bonorand. In the eighteenth century, the letter R was renounced by poets, first by Brockes, whose poem "Auf ein starckes Ungewitter erfolgten Stille" contains a sequence of seventy lines without an R, then by Gottlob Wilhelm Burmann who, less parsimonious, wrote three whole collections. One still finds a piece without the R in the poetry of Kempner (1903).

In the nineteenth century, one finds mostly prose writers: Franz Rittler (1813), Leopold Kolbe (1816), Paul von Schonathan (1883), and even Hariri's translator.

Of all these projects, the most ambitious was undoubtedly that of Franz Rittler, who wrote a novel of 198 pages, *Die Zwillinge* (*The Twins*).[5] The very principle of the lipogram undoubtedly fascinated Rittler, for on the back cover of the third edition of his novel (1820), he proposed a subscription to a work entitled *Ottilie von Riesenstein,* which he proposed to write with the aid of neither the A, the B, the C, the CH, nor the CK—a courageous enterprise which, alas, failed to produce any concrete result.

The whole of the Italian school evinced a profound distaste for the letter R, and most often for that letter only. In addition to several minor works (a tale by Riccoboni, a treatise by Luigi Casolini, an anonymous play produced in Genoa in 1826), one finds a poem of 1,700 lines by Orazio Fidele, *L'R sbandita sopra la potenza d'amore nella quale si leggono mille e settecento versi senze la lettera R* (Turin, 1633), whose title borrows that of an earlier and much shorter poem by the Dominican Giovanni Nicole Ciminello Cardone (Naples, 1619); a third *R sbandita,* a treatise by Gregorio Leti, was published in Bologna twenty years later (1653).

Some stupid scorners claim that Orazio Fidele's poem has no value whatever, that it suffices merely to say *Cupido* for *Amore* and *Cintia* for *Venere;* they slyly remark that the poem has 1,541 lines, and not 1,700. Nevertheless, one finds therein a magnificent line without the E: "D'Apollo fulmino l'incanto figlio."[6] And in a superb preface, Orazio Fidele reminds us that: "E pure l'R è lettera dell'alfabeto, lettera che per tre, quattro parole que diciamo molte volte s'interviene. Lettera che ancor che si passano tutte l'altre ella non può sfugirli. Hor si, che può dirsi qu'elle antico, & divulgato motto NATURA VINCITUR ARTE."[7] The capitalization is the author's own.

The third tradition of the lipogram is the vocalic tradition, which banishes the vowels. It is not necessarily the most difficult one; writing without the A is simple in French, perilous in Spanish; it's the contrary for the E. The vocalic tradition developed principally in Spain, accessorily in France and England.

The Spanish tradition is principally based on a Portuguese author, Alonso de Alcala y Herrera (12 September 1599–21 November 1682), who published at Lisbon in 1641 a charming octavo entitled *Varios efetos de amor, en cinco novelas exemplares, y nuevo artificio para escrivir prosa y versos sin una de las letras vocales.*[8] One finds therein: *Los dos soles de Toledo,* without the A; *La carroza con las damas,* without the E; *La perla de Portugal,* without the I; *La peregrina ermintaña,* without the O; and *La serrana de Cintra,* without the U.

The work was pillaged by Isidro de Robles under the title *Varios effectos de Amor* (or sometimes *Varios Prodigios de Amor*), an anthology that includes eleven stories by diverse authors; only Alcala y Herrera's stories are lipogrammatic. The work was published in Madrid in 1666; I have located thirteen editions, ten in Madrid and three in Barcelona, the last dating from 1871. Several authors, among them Peignot (15), attribute this work to Lope de Vega, undoubtedly because he is the author of one of the six other stories in the anthology. Joseph T. Shipley (*Playing With Words,* 1960) attributes it to Cervantes.

It is not impossible that before Isidro de Robles, Alcala y Herrera had already been plundered by Manuel Lorenzo de Lizarazu y Berbuizana, who published in Saragossa in 1654 *Triumphos de Amor, dos novelas singulares.*

Castillo Solorzano's *La Quinta de Laura* (Madrid, 1649) excludes the Y. One finds a *Chanson* with no U in one of the very last picaresque novels, *Estebanillo Gonzales* (1646), especially valuable because of the description of the Spanish soldiery in Flanders.

In Francisco Navarette y Ribera's *Flor des Sainetes* (Madrid, 1640), one finds the *Novela de los tres hermanos, escrita sin el uso de la A,* which was reprinted by itself in Seville in 1665 under the title *Los dos hermanos incognitos. Novela singular escrita sin usar en toda ella de la letra A.* In the meantime, Fernando Jacinto de Zurita y Haro, too, signed *Los dos hermanos* (without the A) in Madrid in 1654. And in the third edition of Luis Velez de Guevara's *El Diabolo coxuelo* (Madrid, 1733), one finds a story without the A entitled, as if one couldn't guess, *Los tres hermanos.* No satisfactory explanation has ever been offered concerning the disappearance or reappearance of the third brother from one edition to another. Borges also wrote *Los dos hermanos,* but his is a song, more precisely a *milonga,* from which all lipogrammatic preoccupation seems absent.

In France, the avocalic tradition was above all epistolary. P. H. M. Le Carpentier, "former military man," published at Dentu in Paris in 1858 *Essais lipogrammatiques et lettres originales familières et badines.* This work is actually a collection of his correspondence, consisting mostly of dinner invitations and New Year's greeting cards. In his preface, the author notes that "la voyelle e se rencontre dans la majeure partie des mots les plus usuels de la langue, tels que . . . père, mère, bienveillance . . . légèreté . . . jeune, agréable, excellent . . . néanmoins . . . hélas . . . zest!"[9] His eight letters without the E are for the most part short notes, sometimes traversed by real inspiration, however. In the third, one finds, notably: "Nous bivouaquons dans Malakoff, ou plutôt, ni vu ni connu, Malakoff a disparu rasibus, nous bivouaquons là où il surgissait jadis, si insultant (Vanitas vanitatum, omnia vanitas!)"[10] On the other hand, the letter of 30 August 1857 copies almost word for word the letter without the E signed by François Martin Frappart, which Simon Blocquel had just published in his *Trésor des Singularités* (1857) (2), and which had already appeared in Gabriel Peignot's *Amusements philologiques* (1842) (15).

Peignot also cites some "letters without vowels" by a certain M. Marchant, published in an *Encyclopédie méthodique,* which I have not been able to locate.

The only (vocalic) lipogrammatic endeavor of any consistency was the work of a writer of the late seventeenth century, the Abbé de Court (1658–1732), author of *Variétés ingénieuses* (Paris, 1725), wherein one finds letters in monosyllables, monorhyme poetry, letters in double meaning, set rhymes, acrostics, very pretty tautograms ("Mazarin, ministre malade, méditait même moribond malicieusement mille maltôtes"), and five letters with four vowels, thus introduced:

In the society of very noble Ladies, the author of the following letters was dared to make an uninterrupted speech without the letter E. The same challenge had previously been posed at the Court, where nobody could respond to it. The author composed these speeches to please his companions, who were assembled in the country, where one seeks to entertain onself through a myriad of innocent and recreational occupations.

The letter without the E tells the edifying story of a "courtisan qui passait à la cour pour un saint." Preoccupied by the idea of death ("n'oublions jamais l'instant fatal qui doit finir nos jours," says he in a troubling anticipation of Queneau),[11] he devotes himself to abstinence ("quand il dînait, on lui apportait du pain fort noir") and to devotion ("la nuit il faisait trois fois l'oraison"); finally, having given away all his earthly goods, "il garda pour lui un crucifix qu'il porta aux Capucins où il prit l'habit, mais il mourut au bout d'un an sans avoir fini son noviciat."

Jacques Arago wrote a very weak résumé of his *Voyage autour du Monde* without the A. Joseph Raoul Ronden produced a play, *La Pièce sans a,* on 18 September 1816. The play was interrupted before the epilogue. And yet the author's motives were patriotic: stung by the fact that English journalists unceasingly ridiculed the French language, calling it poor under the pretext that each day brings new Frenchifications of Albionish expressions, this heir to Etiemble decided to prove the richness of his native tongue by amputating a third of it! Contemporary critics immediately detected in this explanation a pure phenomenon of rationalization and accused the author of "publicly proclaiming himself an enemy, the proscriber of the letter which figures so happily in our most beautiful words."

The Anglo-Saxon school numbers few authors, but all of them demonstrate a remarkable virtuosity. Here are two anonymous examples published in almanacks: the first is a quatrain without the E which is also a pangram, for it contains all the other letters of the alphabet:

> Quixotic boys who look for joys
> Quixotic hazards run
> A lass annoying with trivial toys
> Opposing man for fun

The second is a quadruple vocalic lipogram: the author permits himself only one vowel; here are a few isolated verses from the poems he wrote:

> War harms all ranks, all arts, all crafts appal!

> Idling, I sit in this mild twilight dim
> Whilst birds, in wild swift vigils, circling skim.

> Bold Ostrogoths show no horror of ghosts.

> Lucullus snuffs up musk, Mundungus shuns.

Henry Richard Vassal-Fox Holland, third Lord Holland, nephew of Fox and author of a life of Lope de Vega and of Guillen de Castro, published in the *Keepsake* of 1836 a three-page text, *Eve's Legend,* where the only vowel used is the E. On the contrary, but on a much larger scale, Ernest Vincent Wright (1872–1939), an American sailor, published in Los Angeles in the year of his death *Gadsby: A Story of Over 50,000 Words without Using the Letter E.*

That's about it for the history of the lipogram. It's astonishing to realize that none of the Grands Rhétoriqueurs participate in it; one might explain this in recalling that acrostics, set rhymes, and tautograms are always spectacular, whereas a lipogram may not be remarked; most of the time the omission must be announced in its title. A lipogram that did not advertise itself as such (but can we conceive of this?) would have every chance of being overlooked.

This property, which accords a special place among systematic artifices to the lipogram, would justify a more profound study of the lipogram's qualities: what it entails and what it produces. Of course, this is not my object here. At the most, permit me in conclusion to postulate a definition of the lipogram that excludes two forms which are, to my way of thinking, heretical.

The first excludes not the letter, but the sound. Joseph Weinheber published a poem "without the E" which begins superbly: "Sprachmacht alt, im Atta unsar braust,"[12] but in the second line one finds "dein," "Ur-Teil," then "die," "frei," "wie," "bleicht," "Heil," and finally "Reich." One wonders why this is supposed to be a poem "without the E"; perhaps he could not say "Hitler"?

The second heresy is liponymy: it forbids the use of a given word. It's a classic form of purism: Gomberville, Coeffeteau, and Béroalde de Verville avoided the conjunction *car* like the plague; Henri de Chenevières wrote *Contes sans qui ni que*. Liponymy may, of course, become constraining: we know that Conrad compelled himself to write an entire novel about love without using the word "love" a single time; a contemporary English female novelist, in analogous fashion, refused to use the diverse forms and derivatives of the verb "to be." One can see that the proscribed words are heavy with meaning and that their omission will merely be the pretext for paraphrases and obstinately oriented metaphors.[13]

In this sense, the suppression of the letter, of the typographical sign, of the basic prop, is a purer, more objective, more decisive operation, something like constraint degree zero, after which everything becomes possible.

Bibliography

1. Bens, J. *Guide des jeux d'esprit*. Paris: Albin Michel, 1967.
2. Blocquel, S. *Trésor des singularités en tous genres et de philologie amusante*. Paris: Delorme, 1857.
3. Boissonade, J. F. *Sur les poésies figurées et autres ouvrages singuliers des Anciens*, II. *Journal de l'Empire*, 27-XII-1806.
4. Canel, A. *Recherches sur les jeux d'esprit, les singularités et les bizarreries littéraires principalement en France*. 2 vols. Evreux: Aug. Hérissey, 1867.
5. Chalon, R. *Nugae difficiles*. Brussels: A. Van Dale, 1844.
6. Curtius, E. R. *Europaïsche Literatur und Lateinisches Mittelalter*. Berne, 1948.
7. D'Iraeli, I. *Curiosities of Literature*. Paris: Baudry, 1835.
8. Dobson, W. T. *Literary frivolities, fancies, follies and frolics*. London: Chatto & Windus, 1880.

9. Friedman, W. F., and Friedman, E. S. *The Shakespearian Ciphers examined*. Cambridge: Cambridge University Press, 1957.
10. Hocke, G. R. *Manierismus in der Literatur. Sprach-Alchimie und esoterische Kombinationskunst*. Hamburg: Rowohlt, 1959.
11. Lalanne, L. *Curiosités littéraires*. Paris: Paulin, 1845.
12. Lausberg, H. *Handbuch der literarische Rhetorik*. 2 vols. Munich: M. Hueber, 1960.
13. Liede, A. *Dichtung als Spiel. Studien zur Unsinnspoesie an den Grenzen der Sprache*. 2 vols. Berlin: W. de Gruyter, 1963.
14. Niceron, J. P. *Bibliothèque amusante*. Paris, 1753.
15. Peignot, G. *Amusements philologiques*. Dijon: Lagier, 1842.
16. Pierce, J. R. *Symboles, Signaux et Bruits*. Paris: Masson, 1965.
17. Queneau, R. *Bâtons, chiffres et lettres*. Paris: Gallimard, 1965.
18. Schulz-Besser, E. *Deutsche Dictungen ohne den Buchstaben R*. Ztschr. f. Bücherfreund. 1909–1910; n. f. I: 382–389.
19. Walsh, W. S. *Handy Book of Literary Curiosities*. London: W. W. Gibbings, 1893.

Jacques Bens, Claude Berge, and Paul Braffort

· · · · · · · · · · · · · · · · · · · ·

Recurrent Literature

I. The Concept of Recurrence in Literature[1]

The word "recurrence" evokes a movement of eternal return, of unlimited repetition. We would like, under the title "recurrent literature," to enlarge this theme through reference to the mathematical connotation that appears in notions like "demonstration through recurrence," "recursive functions," etc.

We will thus classify under the heading of "recurrent literature" any text that contains, explicitly or implicitly, generative rules that invite the reader (or the teller, or the singer) to pursue the production of the text to infinity (or until the exhaustion of interest or attention).

The definition we propose implies, for the recurrent text, the existence of a statement about generation, of an algorithm. This is what immediately places recurrent literature in the category of potential literature. But, of course, many anticipatory plagiarisms become apparent when one examines the various possible forms of this new literature.

All classification being obviously arbitrary in this case, we have adopted a system of incremental complexity, in the mathematical sense of the word. We shall thus examine successively:

—*repetitive* literature,
—*iterative* literature,
—*recursive* literature.

II. Repetitive Literature

This is the simplest form of recurrent literature, and for this reason it abounds in anticipatory plagiarisms. We shall distinguish two subclasses:

—*Explicit repetition* (or extensional repetition), which will necessarily be limited, in its written or oral presentation, to an initial finite segment.

A well-known anticipatory plagiarism is the song:

> *Je demande à un joueur d'orgue*
> *s'il connaît la Chaussée d'Antin,* etc.

This example puts an essential semantic constraint into play: the possibility of an unlimited cycle of requests for information and efforts of orientation on the part of the hero, who translates the topological possibility of circuits in an itinerary on a graph. One may easily foresee the possibilities of more difficult constraints which a more rigorous consideration of the properties of the graph in question would raise.

In another well-known plagiarism which is also a song:

> *Lundi matin,*
> *l'empereur,*
> *sa femme et le petit prince . . .*

the repetitiveness is linked to the unlimited return of the days of the week, etc.

—*Implicit repetition* (or extensional repetition) poses delicate semantic problems.

The most elementary form is that of the story in which the first and last sentences are identical (innumerable anticipatory plagiarisms, the dearest to our heart being of course Raymond Queneau's *Le Chiendent*).

The elaborate form is that of the auto-encased, or "nested" story, which fantastic literature is so fond of (Jean Ray furnished a fine illustration of this in *Malpertuis*).

The constraint—eminently semantic—is the following: at the end of the story, the circumstances are such that all the parameters have regained the value they had in the beginning, and the reader is thus led to imagine that the story is about to begin again in identical fashion—most often, this happens in adventures during which the hero finds himself on the horns of the most horrible dilemmas.

Two versions are then possible. In the first, the repetition is apparent: the first version is a dream and the second (the last) is reality. The dream was premonitory and the reality in general leads to the hero's death.

The second version—the only one that concerns us—contradicts the Second Principle of Thermodynamics, because the "time" parameter cannot be reinitialized.

This permits us to illustrate here what one of us means by "theoretical literature" (by analogy to theoretical physics or chemistry). An utterance of theoretical literature might in fact be:

Theorem: Every nondegenerate, intentionally repetitive story necessarily develops in the fantastic genre.

Among the rarely explored avenues of intentionally repetitive literature, let us point out "cross-nested" stories: story A contains the evocation of story B, which itself contains the evocation of story A.

III. Iterative Literature

A purely repetitive story is a generator of texts producing—efficiently or not—an infinite series of identical texts.

If we replace the identity requirement with a weaker requirement of similitude (on the condition that the notion of similitude be beyond all question), we obtain a richer literature that we call "iterative."

Here again, popular songs furnish us with a wide choice of anticipatory plagiarisms:

> *Alouette, gentille alouette . . .*
> *J'ai le foie qu'est pas droit . . . ,* etc.

In most instances, it is a case of enumerations that are too long to be exhaustive. The numerable infinity they sometimes evoke appears clearly with:

> *Y a qu'un cheveu sur la tête à Mathieu . . .*

which uses moreover a process of iteration followed by a mirror.

Iteration can also imply a spiral, as in the theme of Schnitzler's *La Ronde*.

In fact, amorous passion (the propagation of venereal diseases) and the great Auger Showers of cosmic radiation evoke, for the mathematician, arborescent situations that already put recursive procedures and structures into play.

Many structures and constraints may be generalized by iteration. It is thus that the general Lescurian structure $C_i + N_i$,[2] where C_i denotes grammatical categories and N_i the whole numbers associated with them, may be generalized as

$$C_i + N_i + M_i$$

where M_i is the "step" associated with the category C_i.

For example, { S + 7 + 1, V + 5 + 2 } engenders, beginning from an initial text, a series of texts which is, in principle, unlimited, through replacing first the substantives (respectively, the verbs) with the substantives (respectively, the verbs) situated 7 (respectively, 5) steps further along in a dictionary chosen in advance. The second text will be engendered by taking 8 (respectively, 7) as the intersubstantive (respectively, interverb) distance, the third by taking 9 (respectively, 9), etc.

IV. Recursive Literature

As repetitive literature is a particular category of iterative literature (when the increment is null), so the latter is a particular category of recursive literature—so the "constant" and "following" functions are "elementary" recursive functions.

This is to say that the domain of the recursive, properly so called, is highly receptive to potentiality.

We shall confine ourselves here to presenting three examples with a view toward future meditations and suggestions.

The Lescurian with variable arithmetic

First, one chooses the syntactic category or categories that engender the lexical transference. The length of the transference is then determined with the help of a simple (recursive) arithmetical function of one or several parameters of the word to be transferred: number of syllables, length, etc.

Regarding constraints of this sort, one may pose interesting inverse problems: given two texts, a source and a target, let us determine a set of morphological parameters and (recursive) functions on these parameters permitting the passage from one text to the other, applying the corresponding Lescurian. It will be noted that the two texts must be homosyntactic.

Let us suppose, for instance, that one determined the set permitting the passage from Latis's to Duchateau's texts in the homosyntactic exercises of *Oulipo 1* (p. 176).[3]

It would be interesting to apply this particular Lescurian again to Duchateau's text (or to Queneau's, etc.).

This leads us to evoke another theme from theoretical literature (as one of us understands it) in the form of a problem:

Problem: What condition must be imposed on the choice of the parameters and the functions on these parameters, in a generalized Lescurian, in order for all the Lescurians that satisfy the condition to form a group? Is this group Abelian? (This problem is known, in the literature, as Braffort's Lescurian "Problem.")

Cellular prosody

This is a system of constraints inspired by the English mathematician Conway's "the game of life," a particularly simple and elegant variant of the notion of the cellular automaton developed by Von Neumann and Ulam.

The general idea is the following: one defines an "organism" by a configuration of points on a grid. Then, one specifies the metabolism of the organism with the help of a set of rules determining:

—the conditions for the death of an existing point;

—the conditions for the appearance of a point on a vacant node of the grid.

In the case of "the game of life," a point *dies* of isolation if it has 0 or 1 neighbor, of suffocation if it has more than 3 neighbors. A point is *born* on a node of the grid if this node has exactly 3 neighbors occupied by points.

It may be demonstrated that certain organisms survive indefinitely, that others engender configurations which repeat themselves with a certain periodicity, etc.

One can easily imagine the possibilities offered by the application of an algorithm of this sort to prosody.

Indeed, let us consider a fixed form: a sonnet, an ode, a virelay, etc.: the words therein constitute a certain configuration that we shall consider as the initial organism. One may then imagine innumerable laws of evolution that cause words to appear and disappear in function of the relations they bear to their neighbors: alphabetical, lexical, syntactic, or semantic relations.

Two attitudes are then possible:

—"direct" research, where one postulates in advance the laws of metabolism and seeks to define a poem which, through the application of these laws, will give birth to an infinite series of poems possessing given properties;

—"inverse" research, where one postulates in advance a series of poems, and seeks laws of metabolism that permit the engendering (respecting or not the given order) of this series. For instance, one might pose the following (difficult) problem.

Problem: Find the metabolism which, when applied to the first poem of *La Légende des siècles*, engenders, in order, the other poems in this work.

Metapragmatic program literature

The division between the syntactic, semantic, and pragmatic aspects of language (traditional since Morris) is well known.

—Syntax is concerned with the relations that linguistic objects maintain among themselves.

—Semantics is concerned with the relations that linguistic objects maintain with the "exterior" universe they are supposed to represent.

—Pragmatics specifies the relations that linguistic objects maintain with the users of the language, the "locutors."

The pragmatic aspect of semiotic studies is relatively impoverished. In literature, it appears only very episodically and allusively in texts of theater such as pragmatic dialogue:

CHARACTER—I'm leaving! *He leaves.*

Or, better:

CHARACTER—I'm leaving! *He does as he says.*

Anglo-Saxon analytic philosophy and contemporary linguists have identified, in the universe of discourse, a certain number of situations wherein the pragmatic aspect becomes preponderant. This is the case, in particular, of "illocutionary acts," where the utterance of a proposition is the affirmation itself, as in the sentence:

"I promise it to you"

which both states and *is* a promise.

The reader is probably already thinking of several possibilities of opening new domains for recurrent literature offered by the systematic explanation of the pragmatic aspect of natural language.

Let us thus imagine a text A which contains a rule for generating text B; we may represent this formally with the expression:

$$B \leftarrow \phi A$$

(text B is the result of the execution of instructions given by text A).

If the generative rules and text B have been properly chosen, text B may well be of the sort ϕC, and so forth.

One may imagine the power and depth of such an approach in reflecting on the behavior of the most elementary text constructed in this spirit, the text

$$A \leftarrow \phi \text{ 'A'}$$

(text A is confined to the order: execute the text whose only name is "A"). For the algorithm expressed by this text obviously leads the author wishing to conform to it to impose upon himself an unlimited silent meditation.

It is thus preeminently the formula of all potential literature.

Claude Berge

· · · · · · · · · · · · ·

For a Potential Analysis
of Combinatory Literature

When, at twenty years of age, Leibniz published his *Dissertatio de Arte Combinatoria*,[1] he claimed to have discovered a new branch of mathematics with ramifications in logic, history, ethics, and metaphysics. He treated all sorts of combinations therein: syllogisms, juridical forms, colors, sounds; and he announced two-by-two, three-by-three, etc., combinations, which he wrote: com2natio, com3natio, etc. . . .

In the field of plastic arts, the idea was not entirely new, since Breughel the Elder several years before had numbered the colors of his characters in order to determine their distribution by a roll of the dice; in the field of music, people were beginning to glimpse new possibilities, which were to inspire Mozart in his "Musical Game," a sort of card index that allows anyone to achieve the aleatory composition of waltzes, rondos, and minuets. But what about literature?

One has to wait until 1961 for the expression *combinatory literature* to be used, undoubtedly for the first time, by François Le Lionnais, in the postface to Raymond Queneau's *Cent Mille Milliards de poèmes*. Literature is a known quantity, but combinatorics? Makers of dictionaries and encyclopedias manifest an extreme degree of cowardice when it comes to giving a definition of the latter; one can hardly blame their insipid imprecision, since traditional mathematicians who "feel" that problems are of combinatory nature very seldom are inclined to engage in systematic and independent study of the methods of resolving them.

In an attempt to furnish a more precise definition, we shall rely on the concept of *configuration;* one looks for a configuration each time one disposes a finite number of objects, and one wishes to dispose them according to certain constraints postulated in advance; Latin squares and finite geometries are configurations, but so is the arrangement of packages of different sizes in a drawer that is too small, or the disposition of words or sentences given in advance (on the condition that the given constraints be sufficiently "crafty" for the problem to be real).[2] Just as arithmetic studies whole numbers (along with the traditional operations), as algebra studies operations in general, as analysis studies functions, as geometry studies forms that are rigid and topology those that are not, so combinatorics, for its part, studies configurations. It attempts to demonstrate the existence of configurations of a certain type. And if this existence is no longer open to doubt, it undertakes to count them (equalities or inequalities of counting), or to list them ("listing"), or to extract an "optimal" example from them (the problem of optimization).

It is thus not surprising to learn that a systematic study of these problems revealed a large number of new mathematical concepts, easily transposable into the realm of language, and that the pruritus of combinatorics has wrought its worst on the Oulipian breast.

Although the first complete literary work of frankly combinatory nature is the *Cent Mille Milliards de poèmes,* and although Raymond Queneau and François Le Lionnais are the cofounders of the Oulipo, created simultaneously, it should not be deduced that combinatory literature *is* the Oulipo.

If one dissects Oulipian tendencies with a sharp enough scalpel, three currents become apparent: the first Oulipian vocation is undoubtedly "the search for new structures, which may be used by writers in any way they see fit," which means that we wish to replace traditional *constraints* like the "sonnet" with other linguistic constraints: alphabetical (Georges Perec's poems without e), phonetic (Noël Arnaud's heterosexual rhymes), syntactic (J. Queval's isosyntactic novels), numerical (J. Bens's irrational sonnets), even semantic.

The second Oulipian vocation, apparently unrelated to the first, is research into *methods of automatic transformation* of texts: for example, J. Lescure's S + 7 method.

Finally, the third vocation, the one that perhaps interests us most, is the *transposition* of concepts existing in different branches of mathematics into the realm of words: geometry (Le Lionnais's poems which are tangential among themselves), Boolean algebra (intersection of two novels by J. Duchateau), matrical algebra (R. Queneau's multiplication of texts), etc. . . .

It is within this last current that combinatory literature is situated. Let us sharpen our scalpel a little bit more and cut up a few specimens.

The roughest form, the Stone Age of combinatory literature, it must be noted, is *factorial poetry,* in which certain elements of the text may be permuted *in all possible ways* as the reader (or chance) sees fit; the meaning changes, but syntactic correctness is preserved.

As early as the seventeenth century, Harsdörffer published in his *Récréations* factorial couplets like:

> *Ehr, Kunst, Geld, Guth, Lob, Weib* und *Kind*
> *Man* hat, *sucht, fehlt,* hofft und verschwind[3]

The ten words in *italics* may be permuted in all possible ways by the speaker without altering the rhythm (for they are all monosyllabic); whence 3,628,800 poems, different and grammatically correct (if one changes *sucht* to *Sucht, fehlt* to *Fehl, man* to *Mann*). With *n* words to permute, the number of possibilities would be "*n* factorial," that is, the number:

$$n! = 1 \times 2 \times \ldots \times n$$

This form of poetry seems moreover to have been common during the period when it was called "Protean Poetry" (*Poetices Proteos*), following Julius Caesar Scaliger, who supposedly invented it. Leibniz, in his *Dissertatio,* cites numerous examples in monosyllabic Latin, from Bernhardus Bauhusius, Thomas Lansius, Johan Philippus Ebelius, Johan Baptistus Ricciolus, etc. . . .

And, as nothing is invented, we must wait until 1965 for Saporta to write and publish a "factorial" novel, whose pages, unbound, may be read in any order, according to the whim of the reader.[4]

Finally, in 1967, the Oulipo stated that it no longer expected any good to come from pure, unbridled chance, and Jacques Roubaud published his collection of poems, ∈ (Gallimard, 1967), wherein the author proposes the reading of the 361 texts that compose it in four different but well-determined orders.

Another more elaborate form of combinatory poetry: Fibonaccian poems. We call thus a text which has been split into elements (sentences, verses, words), and which one recites using only elements that were not juxtaposed in the original text.

This type of poetry is called Fibonaccian because, with *n* elements, the number of poems one can engender is none other than "Fibonacci's Number":

$$F_n = 1 + \frac{n!}{1!(n-1)} + \frac{(n-1)!}{2!(n-3)!} + \frac{(n-2)!}{3!(n-5)!} + \frac{(n-3)!}{4!(n-7)!} + \ldots$$

Here is an example, whose origin is easily recognizable:

> Feu filant,
> déjà sommeillant,

bénissez votre
os
je prendrai
une vieille accroupie
vivez les roses de la vie![5]

Unfortunately, it is difficult to invent texts that lend themselves to such manipulations or rules for intervals that permit the conservation of literary quality.

In the *Cent Mille Milliards de poèmes,* Raymond Queneau introduces ten sonnets, of fourteen verses each, in such a way that the reader may replace as he wishes each verse by one of the nine others that correspond to it. The reader himself may thus compose $10^{14} = 100,000,000,000,000$ different poems, all of which respect all the immutable rules of the sonnet. This type of poetry could be called "exponential," for the number of poems of n verses one can obtain with Queneau's method is given by the exponential function, 10^n. However, each of the hundred thousand billion poems may also be considered as a line drawn in a graph of the sort indicated in figure 1. According to this point of view, it should be noted that the reader advances in a graph *without circuits;* that is, he can never encounter the same verse twice in a reading respecting the direction of the arrows.

For this reason, in 1966 we proposed the dual form, the antipode: that is, poems on graphs *without cocircuits.* Without wishing to define a cocircuit here, let us say that these graphs are characterized by the property that, beginning from a given point, one can always end up at a point determined in advance.

Let us consider the simplified example of figure 2.

Other pathway procedures were proposed by Paul Braffort and François Le Lionnais at the 79th meeting of the Oulipo. This principle is also behind Raymond Queneau's "A Story as You Like It." This text, submitted at the Oulipo's 83rd working meeting, draws its inspiration from the instructions given to computers, the reader at each moment disposing of two continuations, according to whether the adventures of the "three alert peas" suit him or not. Presented in the form of a bifurcating graph (figure 3), imbrication of circuits becomes apparent, as do converging paths, etc. . . . whose properties might be analyzed in terms of the Theory of Graphs. [See figure 4 for additional Queneau graphs.]

Finally, it should be noted that in his *Drailles* (Gallimard, 1968), Jean Lescure travels pleasantly through a graph of order 4:

Feuille de rose porte d'ombre
Ombre de feuille porte rose

Figure 1

Principle of the graph of the Cent Mille Milliards de poèmes *(not all of the arcs and vertices have been drawn)*

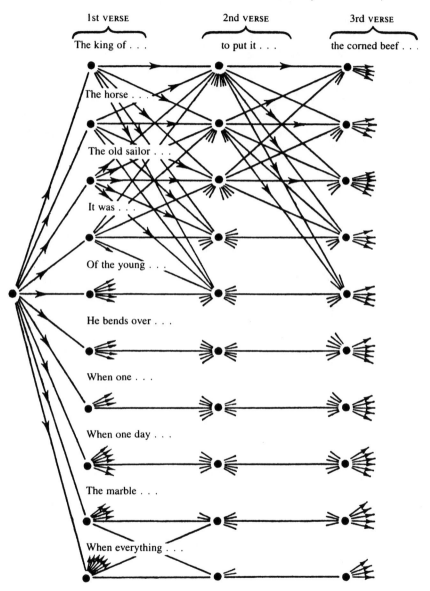

Feuille, porte l'ombre d'une rose
Feuille rose à l'ombre d'une porte
Toute rose ombre une porte de feuille

. . .

Another form of literature, which may lend itself to schemas rich in combinatory properties, is what has come to be called the *episodic story*. Since Potocki's famous novel, *Un Manuscrit trouvé à Saragosse*, especially since the episodic novels of Eugène Sue, certain authors have imagined characters who relate adventures in which figure other garrulous heroes who in turn relate other adventures, which leads to a whole series of stories embedded one in the other. In his poems, Raymond Roussel[6] went so far as to embed progressively six sets of parentheses [see figure 5].

Figure 2

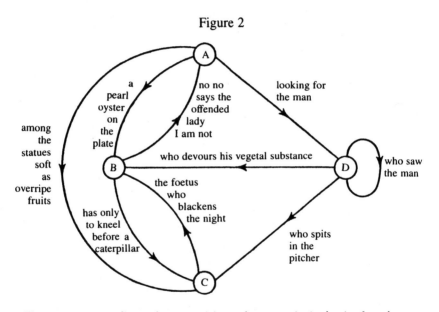

The verses corresponding to the arcs arriving at the same point (or leaving from the same point) were chosen in function of a very precise constraint; for example, those that end up at point D contain the word "man"; those leaving from point D have the same grammatical structure, etc. . . . Using this figure, the reader may choose a priori the point of departure and the point of arrival, and look for "the shortest path." He can also construct "Hamiltonian Poems," which correspond to an itinerary in which each point is encountered once and only once. Thus, the Hamiltonian Path BADC gives:
    "No no says the offended lady I am not looking for the man who spits in the pitcher."
    One can even construct quasi-Eulerian poems, traveling through the figure without passing twice by the same arc, and in maximizing the number of arcs used; fundamental, purely mathematical concepts from the Theory of Graphs furnish thus so many constraints . . . and the number of texts that may be constructed using the same figure is infinite!

Figure 3

Bifurcating graph representing the structure of Raymond Queneau's "A Story as You Like It," Lettres Nouvelles, *July–September 1967. (We owe this sagittal representation to Queneau)*

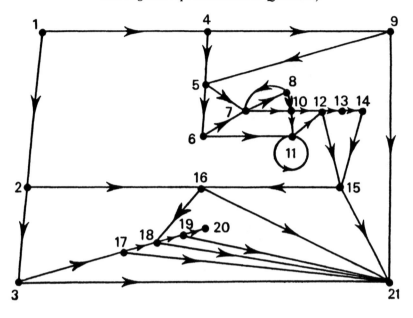

In order to describe or count the agglomerations of parentheses in a monoid, the Polish logician Łukasiewicz established the bases of a mathematical theory; it is to this theory that we refer in figure 6, where we represent the structure of the first canto of Raymond Roussel's *Nouvelles Impressions d'Afrique* by a bifurcating arborescence. It may be remarked that this arborescence is much less complex than that of figure 7, for instance . . . which seems to open the door to a new field of research for the Oulipo.

We could not conclude this little inventory without mentioning bi-Latin literature and the work begun within the Oulipo by the author with Jacques Roubaud and Georges Perec. Since Euler, combinatorics has been interested in Latin bi-squares; a *Latin bi-square of order n* is a table of $n \times n$ squares, filled with *n* different letters and *n* different numbers, each square containing a letter and a number, each letter figuring only once in each line and each column, each number figuring only once in each line and each column.

Figure 4

Graphs of the Ternary Relation: X Takes Y for Z (paper delivered by Raymond Queneau at the 26 December 1965 meeting of the Oulipo)

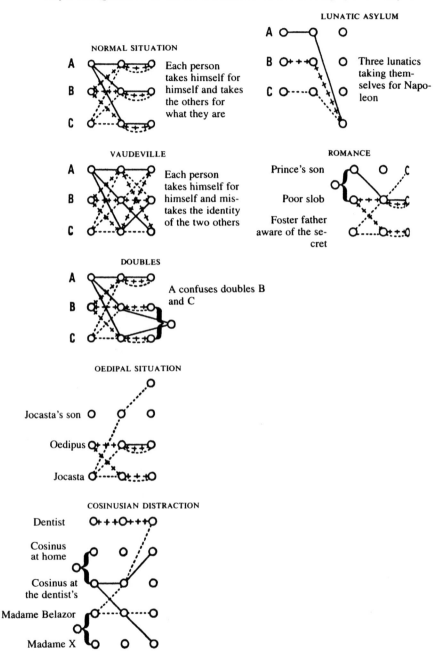

LUNATIC ASYLUM

Three lunatics taking themselves for Napoleon

NORMAL SITUATION

Each person takes himself for himself and takes the others for what they are

VAUDEVILLE

Each person takes himself for himself and mistakes the identity of the two others

ROMANCE

Prince's son

Poor slob

Foster father aware of the secret

DOUBLES

A confuses doubles B and C

OEDIPAL SITUATION

Jocasta's son

Oedipus

Jocasta

COSINUSIAN DISTRACTION

Dentist

Cosinus at home

Cosinus at the dentist's

Madame Belazor

Madame X

Figure 5

Tree representing the embedding of the parentheses in Raymond Roussel,
Nouvelles Impressions d'Afrique, *canto I (the encircled numbers*
represent the number of the verse wherein the parentheses are opened or
closed)

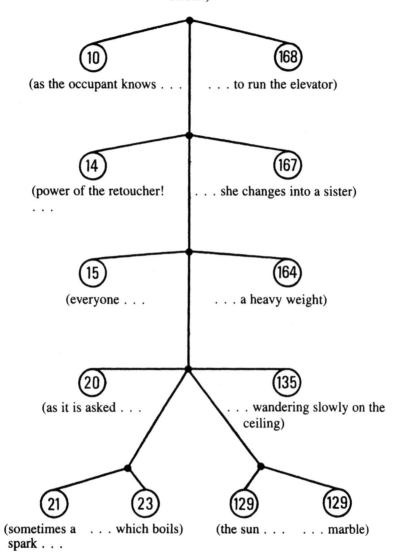

Figure 6

Representation by means of a bifurcating arborescence of the preceding system of parentheses

Figure 7

Representation by means of a bifurcating arborescence of another system of parentheses: [(   )] {[(   )]}

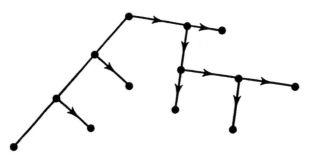

A Latin bi-square of order 10 is reproduced in figure 8; it is, moreover, an extremely rare specimen, and at the present time only two are known to exist. We thus proposed to write 10 stories (represented by the 10 lines of the table) wherein appear 10 characters (represented by the 10 columns of the table). Each character's attribute is determined by the letter of the corresponding square; his action is likewise determined by the number of the corresponding square.

Figure 8

*Specimen of the Latin bi-square of order 10; the letters represent a
characteristic attribute: A = violent lover, B = stupid as an ox,
C = rascal; etc. . . . . The numbers represent the dominant action of the
character: 0 = does nothing, 1 = steals and assassinates, 2 = behaves
in a strange and inexplicable way; etc. . . . .*

	Mr. Demaison	Paul	Mrs. Demaison	Count Bellerval	Archimedes	The goldfish	Destiny	Valerie	Don Diego	Mr. Member
Story number 1	A_0	G_7	F_8	E_9	J_1	I_1	H_5	B_3	C_4	D_6
2	H_6	B_1	A_7	G_8	F_9	J_2	I_4	C_3	D_5	E_0
3	I_5	H_0	C_2	B_7	A_8	G_9	J_3	D_4	E_6	F_1
4	J_4	I_6	H_1	D_3	C_7	B_8	A_9	E_5	F_0	G_2
5	B_9	J_5	I_0	H_2	E_4	D_7	C_8	F_6	G_1	A_3
6	D_8	C_9	J_6	I_1	H_3	F_5	E_7	G_0	A_2	B_4
7	F_7	E_8	D_9	J_0	I_2	H_4	G_6	A_1	B_3	C_5
8	C_1	D_2	E_3	F_4	G_5	A_6	B_0	H_7	I_8	J_9
9	E_2	F_3	G_4	A_5	B_6	C_0	D_1	I_9	J_7	H_8
10	G_3	A_4	B_5	C_6	D_0	E_1	F_2	J_8	H_9	I_7

These 10 stories contain thus all the possible combinations in the most
economical fashion possible. Moreover, they are the result of a century of
arduous mathematical research, for Euler conjectured that a Latin bi-
square of order 10 could not exist, and we had to wait until 1960 for Bose,
Parker, and Shrikhande to prove him wrong. . . .[7]

It is clear that the contribution of combinatorics to the domains of
words, rhymes, and metaphors is more complex than it seems, and that it
is far from the anagrams of the Rhétoriqueurs or the stammerings of the
Protean poets.

Harry Mathews

. . . .

Mathews's Algorithm

From the reader's point of view, the existence in literature of potentiality in its Oulipian sense has the charm of introducing duplicity into all written texts, whether Oulipian or not. It isn't merely a sonnet in Queneau's *100,000 Billion Poems* on which doubt is cast by the horde of alternatives waiting to take its place: the most practical work of prose, no matter how sturdy it may seem in its apparent uniqueness, will prove just as fragile as soon as one thinks of subjecting it to the procedures of S + 7 or Semo-Definitional Literature.[1] Beyond the words being read, others lie in wait to subvert and perhaps surpass them. Nothing any longer can be taken for granted; every word has become a banana peel. The fine surface unity that a piece of writing proposes is belied and beleaguered; behind it, in the realm of potentiality, a dialectic has emerged.

The algorithm here discussed is a new means of tracking down this otherness hidden in language (and, perhaps, in what language talks about). It is one more way of saying two things at once. It has its particular attractions. First of all, it's a simple mechanism into which complex materials can be introduced. If these materials require a certain amount of care in their presentation to form an algorithmic table, their potential duplicity is realized through means that are virtually automatic. The algorithm can make use of existing material as well as of material specially invented for it (a point that will be abundantly demonstrated later on). Its creative potentiality can manifest itself either in the actual construction of the table or in its subsequent solution. It can be used both to decompose (or analyze) texts or to compose (or invent) them. Last, the algorithm can be applied to every one of the rows of Queneau's Table, "semantic" as well as "syntactic." (And why stop there? The limitations adopted here— which run from letters to rudimentary semantic elements—define only a small part of what the algorithm can handle. It is capable of dealing with *fragments* of letters, either graphic or phonetic, as well as *their* component

126

parts, not to mention amoebas, molecules, and quarks. It can juggle not only episodes of fiction, as will be shown later, but entire books, indeed entire literatures and civilizations, planets, solar systems, galaxies—anything in fact that can be manipulated either in its material or its symbolic form. . . .)

So: how does it work?

Here is what you do.

I. Materials: Several—at Least Two—Sets of Heterogeneous Elements Are Required

Comment: The heterogeneity can sometimes be minimal, but it is nonetheless essential for the proper functioning of the algorithm. The less it is respected, the more likely the machine will simply reproduce replicas of the original sets. In theory, to avoid any chance of this happening, the rule is that in a table of n elements, $n^2 - (n-2)$ elements must be different. (Example: in a table of 4 sets of 4 elements, 14 of the 16 elements must differ.) In practice, however, it is often possible to lower this level of heterogeneity.

II. Arrangement

1. All sets must contain the same number of elements.
2. Each element in a set must have a function equivalent to or consistent with the corresponding elements of the other sets. (If, for instance, the elements are words, the equivalence will be one of grammatical function.) In other words, the elements of each set must be arranged in the same order. (Not $a_1b_1c_1d_1$ and $c_2a_2d_2b_2$ but $a_1b_1c_1d_1$ and $a_2b_2c_2d_2$.)
3. The sets are superimposed one above the other to form a table consisting of rows (the sets) and columns (the corresponding elements). Here is a table of 4 sets of 4 elements:

1	a_1	b_1	c_1	d_1
2	a_2	b_2	c_2	d_2
3	a_3	b_3	c_3	d_3
4	a_4	b_4	c_4	d_4

Comment: In all the examples, the number of elements in each set equals the number of sets. This is a convenience, not a requirement.

III. Operation

1. Shift each set $n-1$ places left. (In other words, shift the second set one place left, the third two places, etc.)

$$
\begin{array}{llll}
1 & a_1 & b_1 & c_1 & d_1 \\
2 & b_2 & c_2 & d_2 & a_2 \\
3 & c_3 & d_3 & a_3 & b_3 \\
4 & d_4 & a_4 & b_4 & c_4
\end{array}
$$

2. Read the columns downward starting with the initial elements (a) of the sets. Four new sets result:

$$
\begin{array}{llll}
a_1 & b_2 & c_3 & d_4 \\
a_4 & b_1 & c_2 & d_3 \\
a_3 & b_4 & c_1 & d_2 \\
a_2 & b_3 & c_4 & d_1
\end{array}
$$

3. Perform the same manipulation with a shift *right:*

$$
\begin{array}{llll}
1 & a_1 & b_1 & c_1 & d_1 \\
2 & d_2 & a_2 & b_2 & c_2 \\
3 & c_3 & d_3 & a_3 & b_3 \\
4 & b_4 & c_4 & d_4 & a_4
\end{array}
$$

4. Read the results upward, still beginning with the initial elements (a) of the original sets:

$$
\begin{array}{llll}
a_1 & b_4 & c_3 & d_2 \\
a_2 & b_1 & c_4 & d_3 \\
a_3 & b_2 & c_1 & d_4 \\
a_4 & b_3 & c_2 & d_1
\end{array}
$$

In this way, from n sets $2n$ sets can be obtained.

IV. Uses

The applications of the algorithm considered here are classified according to the *elements* forming the sets: a, b, c, etc. will be in turn letters, words, word groups, groups of word groups, and, finally, semantic elements. At every stage, two examples will be given, one involving existing material, the other new material.

1. Letters

(a) Using existing material: here, the words of all known languages, living or dead. From English:

```
T   I   N   E
S   A   L   E
M   A   L   E
V   I   N   E
```

After a shift left:

```
T   I   N   E
A   L   E   S
L   E   M   A
E   V   I   N
```
(tale, vile, mine, sane)

After a shift right:

```
T   I   N   E
E   S   A   L
L   E   M   A
I   N   E   V
```
(tile, sine, mane, vale)

(b) Using new material, i.e., words that do not yet exist, in known or imaginary languages.

This example is drawn from the dialect of a Montagnard tribe in Pan-Nam (cf. H. Mathews, *The Sinking of the Odradek Stadium*) that uses a vocabulary at once spontaneous and combinatorial:

```
B   A   G   O
K   E   D   U
F   E   S   I
L   O   M   I
```

After a shift left:

```
B   A   G   O
E   D   U   K
S   I   F   E
I   L   O   M
```
(besi, ladi, fogu, kemo)

After a shift right:

```
B   A   G   O
U   K   E   D
S   I   F   E
O   M   I   L
```
(bosu, kami, fegi, ledo)

2. Words

Here the rule of equivalence (II, 2) becomes obligatory. Sets of words[2] must be arranged in identical grammatical sequence.

(a) Using existing material: take the first lines of four well-known sonnets of Shakespeare:

> Shall I compare thee to a summer's day?
> Music to hear, why hear'st thou music sadly?
> That time of year thou may'st in me behold . . .
> Farewell! thou art too dear for my possessing . . .

Arrangement: Reduce each line to four main words (the remaining words will be considered as their auxiliaries):

I, compare, summer, day	(shall, thee, to a)
music, hear, thou, music	(why, sadly)
time, year, thou, behold	(that, of, in me)
farewell, thou, art(dear), possessing	(too, for my)

Align these four sets according to corresponding parts of speech:

I	summer	day	compare	(shall, thee, to a)
thou	music	music	hear	(why, sadly)
thou	time	year	behold	(that, of, in me)
thou	farewell	possessing	art (dear)	(too, for my)

Apply a shift left to this table. The results will read as:

I	music	year	art (dear)
thou	summer	music	behold
thou	farewell	day	hear
thou	time	possessing	compare

Reintroducing the auxiliaries, compose four new lines in blank verse (the openings of four undiscovered Shakespearean sonnets):

> The music of the years, too dear for me . . .
> The summer's music sadly thou beholdest . . .
> Today thou may'st in me hear the farewell . . .
> Possessing thee, why doth my Time compare . . .

Similarly, after a shift right:

> Shall I, sadly hearing the year's farewell . . .
> Possessing me, thou hast beheld my summer . . .
> Too dear a music for a day thou art . . .
> Music thou art of Time, that doth compare thee . . .

(b) Using new material: in the following example, where words are taken one by one, four propositions are arranged according to the rules of the algorithm:

Truth	left	him	cold.
Wealth	made	her	glad.
Work	turned	you	sour.
Love	kept	me	free.

After a shift left:

Truth	made	you	free.
Love	left	her	sour.
Work	kept	him	glad.
Wealth	turned	me	cold.

After a shift right:

Truth	kept	you	glad.
Wealth	left	me	sour.
Work	made	him	free.
Love	turned	her	cold.

Extending the notion of word to include auxiliaries (cf. IV, 2, a), we can move on to a more elaborate table:

Frustrated members	of the Cabinet	were found conspiring in	local massage parlors.
Drivers	from the Sanitation Department	will go on strike against	the new garbage helicopters.
Six terrorists	of the Keep Kids Kleen Klub	have planted bombs in	sexually integrated restrooms.
Female impersonators	not licensed by their union	are not allowed into	nursing schools.

After a shift left we read:

| Frustrated members | from the Sanitation Department | have planted bombs in | nursing schools. |
| Female impersonators | of the Cabinet | will go on strike against | sexually integrated restrooms. |

| Six terrorists | not licensed by their union | were found conspiring in | the new gar-bage helicop-ters. |
| Drivers | of the Keep Kids Kleen Klub | are not allowed into | local massage parlors. |

And after a shift to the right:

Frustrated members	not licensed by their union	have planted bombs in	the new gar-bage helicop-ters.
Drivers	of the Cabinet	are not allowed into	sexually inte-grated rest-rooms.
Six terrorists	from the Sani-tation Depart-ment	were found conspiring in	nursing schools.
Female imper-sonators	of the Keep Kids Kleen Klub	will go on strike against	local massage parlors.

3. Word groups (verses, sentences)

(a) Using existent material: returning to Shakespeare, take 14 of his best known sonnets, arrange the verses of each sonnet horizontally so as to form a set, and superimpose the sets. After a shift left, here is the first of the 14 possible readings (slightly edited as to punctuation):

> Shall I compare thee to a summer's day
> And dig deep trenches in thy beauty's field?
> Why lov'st thou that which thou receiv'st not gladly,
> Bare ruin'd choirs where late the sweet birds sang?
> Anon permit the basest clouds to ride
> And do what'er thou wilt, swift-footed Time:
> Nor Mars his sword, nor war's quick fire, shall burn
> Even such a beauty as you master now.
> Love's not Time's fool, though rosy lips and cheeks
> (When other petty griefs have done their spite,
> And heavily) from woe to woe tell oe'r
> That Time will come and take my love away;
> For thy sweet love remembered such wealth brings
> As any she belied beyond compare.

Comment: It is perhaps at this point that the analytic potential of the algorithm clearly manifests itself. This new poem throws light on the structure and movement of the Shakespearean sonnet.

(b) Using new material: the following example demonstrates a table made up of 3 sets of 3 sentences. Each sentence refers to an event concerning three different characters.

The conductor wanted his orchestra to produce an utterly muffled sound.	He declared, "If we keep everything low-key, perhaps we can work out a satisfactory arrangement."	He kept insisting: "Please don't strike the drums with anything harder than a sponge!"
The young Laotian chiropodist wandered around New York with his phrase book, which was a fraud—a collection of useless, ridiculous expressions.	He kept repeating his request without ever managing to get what he wanted: an adequate supply of absorbent cotton.	It wasn't until he flashed a fat bankroll that a compassionate saleswoman at last took care of him.
A crafty sheik came to town to buy a wife on favorable terms.	He tried Macy's, Bloomingdale's, and Korvette's without finding what he needed.	Since it was hard to take him seriously, everyone simply ignored his words.

After a shift left:

The conductor wanted his orchestra to produce an utterly muffled sound.	He kept repeating his request without ever managing to get what he wanted: an adequate supply of absorbent cotton.	Since it was hard to take him seriously, everyone simply ignored his words.
The young Laotian chiropodist wandered around New York with his phrase book, which was a fraud—a collection of useless, ridiculous expressions.	He tried Macy's, Bloomingdale's, and Korvette's without finding what he needed.	He kept insisting: "Please don't strike the drums with anything harder than a sponge!"

A crafty sheik came	He declared, "If we	It wasn't until he
to town to buy a	keep everything	flashed a fat bank-
wife on favorable	low-key, perhaps we	roll that a compas-
terms.	can work out a sat-	sionate saleswoman
	isfactory arrange-	at last took care of
	ment."	him.

4. Groups of word groups (stanzas, paragraphs, episodes, etc.)

(a) Using existing material: Shakespeare is here joined by George Herbert, Ben Jonson, and John Donne.

Take four sonnets that follow the Shakespearean model and divide them into their four main components: three quatrains and the concluding couplet. Using these components as elements, align those of each poem horizontally to form a set. Arrange the sets as a table.

Here, after a shift left, is the first of four possible readings:

> Farewell! thou art too dear for my possessing,
> And like enough thou know'st thy estimate:
> The charter of thy worth gives thee releasing,
> My bonds in thee are all determinate,
> While mortal love doth all the title gain!
> Which siding with invention, they together
> Bear all the sway, possessing heart and brain
> (Thy workmanship) and give thee share in neither.
> But now thy work is done, if they that view
> The several figures languish in suspense
> To judge which passion's false, and which is true,
> Between the doubtful sway of reason and sense;
> That thou remember them, some claim as debt;
> I think it mercy if thou wilt forget.

(b) Using new material: here a process of condensation can be profitably introduced. Rather than manipulate lengthy paragraphs, it seems more interesting to apply the algorithm directly to more substantial entities. The elements in the following examples are fictional episodes, summed up in one or two sentences.

1. (a) A and B are husband and wife. (b) A is summoned to the bedside of his ailing mother. (c) At this very moment B becomes involved with someone else. (d) On his return, A feels disgust for B, whom he decides to exclude from his life. (e) B has a nervous breakdown.

2. (a) A loves B. B does not love A. (b) When he inherits a fortune, A at first thinks of letting B benefit from it. (c) In the meantime, B, who has fallen on evil days, starts thinking of A as a possible savior. (d) If B now looks on A with fresh eyes, A, absorbed in his new life, is gradually forgetting about B altogether. (e) A and B never see each other again.

3. (a) A owes B a great deal of money. (b) Having decided he must earn financial independence, A settles in a developing country, where he succeeds in amassing a fortune. (c) B's mother gives B an unexpected sum of money. She also tells B of the goal A has set himself. (d) These new circumstances move B to suggest to A that he forget his former obligations. (e) A never forgives B for nullifying the solicitude of so many years.

4. (a) A knows young B well, but he does not know that he is B's father. B is also ignorant of the fact. (b) A accidentally learns that he is the father of a child whom he has never known. He drops everything to look for his offspring. (c) B's mother falls ill; B is notified. (d) B thus finds A at the ailing woman's bedside. B's unexpected appearance is the immediate cause of her death. (e) The relationship between A and B remains unchanged.

5. (a) A and B know each other. A decides to kill B in order to experience an Existential "random act." (b) A falls in love with an acquaintance of B. (c) Quite involuntarily, B becomes violently resentful of this person for taking A away. (d) Furious at B's outrageous behavior, A abandons his plan. But A's anger starts B wondering if he isn't considering murder. (e) B kills A.

After a shift right:

1. (a) A and B are husband and wife. (b) A falls in love with an acquaintance of B. (c) B's mother falls ill; B is notified. (d) These new circumstances move B to suggest to A that he forget his former obligations. (e) A and B never see each other again.

2. (a) A loves B. B does not love A. (b) A is summoned to the bedside of his ailing mother. (c) Quite involuntarily, B becomes furiously resentful of this person for taking A away. (d) B thus finds A at the ailing woman's bedside. B's unexpected appearance is the immediate cause of her death. (e) A never forgives B for nullifying the solicitude of so many years.

3. (a) A owes B a great deal of money. (b) When he inherits a fortune, A at first thinks of letting B benefit from it. (c) At this very

moment B becomes involved with someone else. (d) Furious at B's outrageous behavior, A abandons his plan. But A's anger starts B wondering if he isn't considering murder. (e) The relationship between A and B remains unchanged.

4. (a) A knows young B well, but he does not know that he is B's father. B is also ignorant of the fact. (b) Having decided he must earn financial independence, A settles in a developing country, where he succeeds in amassing a fortune. (c) In the meantime, B, who has fallen on evil days, starts thinking of A as a possible savior. (d) On his return, A feels disgust for B, whom he decides to exclude from his life. (e) B kills A.

5. (a) A and B know each other. A decides to kill B in order to experience an Existential "random act." (b) A accidentally learns that he is the father of a child whom he has never known. He drops everything to look for his offspring. (c) B's mother gives B an unexpected sum of money. She also tells B of the goal A has set himself. (d) If B now looks on A with fresh eyes, A, absorbed in his new life, is gradually forgetting about B altogether. (e) B has a nervous breakdown.

5. Semantic elements

The OuLiPo divides constrictive structures into *syntactic* and *semantic*. The former affect the material aspects of language (letters, words, syntax); the latter affect what language talks about (subject, content, meaning). Obviously, in the last example we have already moved from syntactic to semantic objects. Perhaps it will suffice to speed the algorithm on its course toward the absolute by ending this demonstration with one or two examples in which the semantic factor is even stronger.

(a) Using existing material: in this case, *Hamlet*. We can sum up our perception of the play according to the rules of the algorithm:

1. Having received instructions,	the son	hesitantly	chooses revenge.	Death is the condition of success.
2. Irrepressibly erotic,	the widowed mother	hastily	remarries.	This is a deceptive pleasure.
3. In the clutches of resentment,	the uncle	desperately	indulges a posthumous passion.	Can we possibly approve?

4. Royally willful,	the dead man	obsessively	tries to re-write history.	Someone has to pay.
5. A prey to this inces-tuous vio-lence,	Ophelia	faithfully	abandons her reason and her life.	A father's death is also involved.

After a shift to the right:

1. Having re-ceived in-structions,	Ophelia	obsessively	indulges a posthumous passion.	This is a de-ceptive plea-sure.
2. Irrepressibly erotic,	the son	faithfully	tries to re-write history.	Can we possi-bly approve?
3. In the clutches of resentment,	the widowed mother	hesitantly	abandons her reason and her life.	Someone has to pay.
4. Royally willful,	the uncle	hastily	chooses re-venge.	A father's death is also involved.
5. A prey to this inces-tuous vio-lence,	the dead man	desperately	remarries.	Death is the condition of success.

Here is another way of handling the same subject:

1. With the husband dead,	the mother	marries	the brother-in-law.
2. With the fa-ther dead,	the son	chooses	the mother.
3. With Ophe-lia dead,	reason	takes	a holiday.
4. With the brother dead,	the uncle	falls victim to	the son.

After a shift right:

1. With the husband dead,	the uncle	takes	the mother.
2. With the fa-ther dead,	the mother	falls victim to	a holiday.

| 3. With Ophe-
lia dead, | the son | marries | the son. |
| 4. With the
brother
dead, | reason | chooses | the brother-in-
law. |

Comment: It is probably unnecessary to point out that, here as else-where, the results yielded by existing works can be used in two ways: either as a means of commenting on those works or as materials for in-venting new ones.

(b) Using new material: for this last example, the elements are far more abstract (although the abstraction falls short of actual concept); they represent situations or events that writers have used since the beginning of literature. They have been arranged in patterns of minimal causality.

Given love,	consummation;	therefore resumption.
Given possession,	danger;	therefore flight.
Given victory,	war;	therefore reassess- ment.

After a shift left:

Given love,	danger	therefore reassess- ment.
Given victory,	consummation;	therefore flight.
Given possession,	war;	therefore resumption.

After a shift right:

Given love,	war;	therefore flight.
Given possession,	consummation;	therefore reassess- ment.
Given victory,	danger;	therefore resumption.

Comment: Perhaps more clearly than the preceding ones, this example shows how the inventiveness of the algorithm (indeed, of Oulipian tech-niques in general) can be realized in two ways—(1) in the setting up of the constrictive structure and (2) in its solution. In most of the earlier examples, the algorithm has produced its effect by requiring the creation of a table that "works" (cf. what is involved in writing a snowball). In the last example, on the other hand, one's ingenuity must be exerted to com-plete or justify the table (cf. what is involved in working out a procedure like "The Relation X takes Y for Z"). This last table is a table of *provo-cation*.

It must be realized that whatever its semantic level, the material of the algorithm must always be manipulated syntactically. (In the examples drawn from *Hamlet,* the elements are *handled* as words or phrases, no matter what their meaning is.) The algorithm can approach abstraction only through simple linguistic systems.

And also, perhaps, through its actual operation: it is here, at any rate, that the "meaning" of the algorithm is to be found. This meaning is nothing new as far as the activity of the OuLiPo is concerned. First of all, two other Oulipian structures can be classed as special cases of the algorithm (that is, with sets composed of two elements): the perverbial poem and the equivoque (or "Poem for Moebius Strip"). Furthermore, the algorithm fits in with the OuLiPo's general interest in combinatorial literature: the results the algorithm produces are, after all, only segments of the much vaster range of circular permutations that each of its tables implies. The algorithm would thus have as its remote ancestor the *Ars Magna* of Ramon Lull (which inspired Giordano Bruno's admiration), Leibnitz's *Dissertatio de Arte Combinatoria,* and Martin Gardner's genuine, albeit skeptical, interest. In Lull's work, circular permutations are given literal shape in figures consisting of concentric circles. These circles are divided into sections; by turning, each circle is made to form with its neighbors all the combinations possible between their respective sections. If most of Lull's figures contain only two circles, one of them—the *figura universalis*—has as many as fourteen.

Fourteen concentric circles: wouldn't Lull then become a forerunner of one of the most extraordinary works the OuLiPo has produced, the *100,000 Billion Poems* of Raymond Queneau? It is perfectly possible to inscribe Queneau's sonnets on the *figura universalis.* Each circle need simply be divided into ten sections. The outermost circle would contain the first verses of the poems, the circle next to it the second verses, and so on. The arrangement would provide as complete a means of reading the work as it finds in book form (and, probably, a more convenient one). The suggestion that this work of Queneau's be assigned to the Lullian combinatorial tradition is made not for the sake of claiming it as a "relative" of the algorithm but in order to set the latter in its proper place among Oulipian structures. By the way they basically function, these structures can be divided into two complementary categories. The first category is that of the proliferation of possibilities; the second is that of their reduction. In the first we find forms like Semo-Definitional Literature, the Lescurian word square, and attempts at "record setting" (Perec's lipogram and palindrome). In the second are to be found, for instance, S + 7, phonetic translation, and antonymic poetry. In regard to our present subject, where *100,000 Billion Poems* uses a combinatorial system to extract a maximum of results from a limited amount of material, the algorithm—while still exploiting the potentiality of circular permutations—seeks to subject them to the harsh selectivity of a reductive form. Its aim is not to liberate potentiality but to coerce it.

Paul Fournel

. . . .

Computer and Writer

The Centre Pompidou Experiment

When the literary project of the A.R.T.A. was launched, rapid efforts had to be made to establish a basis for a possible agreement between computer science and literary creation.[1] Christian Cavadia entrusted the whole of the project to Paul Braffort (logician, computer scientist, and writer), whose first goal was to educate the public and the writers themselves about this new undertaking.

Aided Reading

At first, work was brought to bear on preexisting literary material. There are, in fact, a few combinatory or algorithmic works that may be read far more easily with the help of a computer. Here, the machine performs a simple task of selecting and editing.

Combinatory Literature

The *Cent Mille Milliards de poèmes*[2] by Raymond Queneau furnishes material particularly favorable to this type of experiment. It consists of ten sonnets composed such that each verse of each of them may be combined with any of the other verses in the ten texts, which gives a total of 10^{14} sonnets. The printed collection is very prettily conceived, but the manipulation of the strips on which each verse is printed is sometimes tedious.

The computer, though, makes a selection in the corpus in function of the length of the "reader's" name and the time which he takes to type it into the terminal, then prints the sonnet, which bears the double signature of Queneau and his reader.[3]

The author himself may profit from this process: when the combinations

140

are this numerous, he may take soundings of his work. The computer in this case serves as an assistant in the definitive fine-tuning of the text.

Algorithmic Literature

Same application in the domain of algorithmic literature: Dominique Bourguet has programmed Raymond Queneau's "A Story as You Like It"[4] so as to facilitate its reading. In this brief text, the reader is repeatedly invited to choose what follows in the tale through a system of double questions. The elements of narration being very short, the game dominates the reading of the text itself. This is unfortunate, since all of these possible texts have real charm. The computer first of all "speaks" with the reader, proposing the different choices to him, then prints the chosen text "cleanly" and without the questions. The pleasure of play and the pleasure of reading are thus combined.

In the same spirit and according to the same principles, a medieval tale was programmed by Jean-Pierre Enard and Paul Fournel,[5] and the 720 fairy tales of a work group directed by J. P. Balpe will be programmed.

Aided Creation

After all of this, the relation work→computer→reader must be replaced by other sorts of relations in which the author plays a role (without necessarily stripping the reader of *his* role). Among the different projects submitted by authors to Paul Braffort, one may already find examples of very different types of relations.

Type 1: Author→Computer→Work

In this type, only creation is aided. The computer is an integral part of the drafting process and its work serves to elaborate the definitive text. Italo Calvino proposes lists of characters, constraints, and events to the machine, asking it to determine through progressive refinement who may indeed have done what. The author thus chooses to work on material that the machine allows him to dominate.[6]

Type 2: Author→Computer→Work→Computer→Reader

The computer intervenes on two levels this time. For one of the chapters in the *Princesse Hoppy*, Jacques Roubaud elaborates, with the help of a machine, a chapter which the reader must read with this same machine.[7]

He will be called upon to solve a series of enigmas, and the machine will furnish him with clues (inspired by the game of cork-penny) as to his groping progression in the text.

Type 3: Author→Computer→Reader→Computer→Work

With this third type we enter into the domain of projects that are more distant and more technically complex. In Marcel Bénabou's "artificial aphorisms," the author furnishes a stock of empty forms and a stock of words destined to fill them; the reader then comes along to formulate a request, and, following this request, the machine combines words and forms to produce aphorisms.[8]

The reader's participation is limited, but it nonetheless necessitates a few elementary flexions in the resultant text. In spite of everything, one may affirm that the author dominates his material in these aphorisms; this is not so in the case of the S.S.A.Y.L.I. (Short Story As You Like It) project.

The goal of this enterprise is to produce diversified short stories in very large quantities according to the precise and various wishes formulated by the reader (he may choose the length, the theme, the decor, the characters, and the style).

Beginning with a few homosyntactic short stories, Paul Braffort and Georges Kermidjian attempt to establish an extremely supple general ossature and a stock of "agms," minimal unities of action or description. Their exact description is in permanent evolution, but one may say, roughly, that they are the intermediary unities between the word and the sentence, which in theory ought to permit one to avoid both the pitfalls of grammar and the feeling of suffocation provoked by sentence types that recur incessantly (as in the work of Sheldon Kline). Each of these agms receives specific attributes which will come into play according to the reader's wishes.

The interest of this project is triple: first, it allows one to produce short stories, and this is nice when one likes producing short stories; second, it enables one to elaborate a particular grammar prudently, step by step; third, it allows one to constitute a stock of agms that may be used on other occasions. But it is a long-term project that is only beginning. It will take patience, work, and time (= money).[9]

Italo Calvino

. . . .

Prose and Anticombinatorics

The preceding examples concerned the use of the computer as an aid to literary creation in the following situations:

The structures chosen by the author are relatively few in number, but the possible realizations are combinatorily exponential.

Only the computer may realize a number (more or less large) of these potentialities.

On the contrary, the assistance of the computer takes on an *anticombinatory* character when, among a large number of possibilities, the computer selects those few realizations compatible with certain constraints.

Order in Crime

I have been working for some time on a short story (perhaps a novel?) which might begin thus:

The fire in the cursed house

In a few hours Skiller, the insurance agent, will come to ask for the computer's results, and I have still not introduced the information into the electronic circuits that will pulverize into innumerable impulses the secrets of the Widow Roessler and her shady *pension*. Where the house used to stand, one of those dunes in vacant lots between the shunting yards and the scrapyards that the periphery of our city leaves behind itself like so many little piles of trash forgotten by the broom, nothing now remains but scattered debris. It might have been a cute little villa beforehand, or just as well nothing other than a ghostly hovel: the reports of the insurance company do not say; now, it has burned from the cellar to the attic, and nothing was found on the charred cadavers of its four inhabitants that might enable one to reconstitute the antecedents of this solitary massacre.

A notebook tells more than these bodies, a notebook found in the ruins,

143

entirely burned except for the cover, which was protected by a sheet of plastic. On the front is written: *Accounts of horrible acts perpetrated in this house,* and on the back there is an index divided into twelve headings, in alphabetical order: To Bind and Gag, To Blackmail, To Drug, To Prostitute, To Push to Suicide, To Rape, To Seduce, To Slander, To Spy Upon, To Stab, To Strangle, To Threaten with a Revolver.

It is not known which of the inhabitants of the house wrote this sinister report, nor what was its intent: denunciation, confession, self-satisfaction, fascinated contemplation of evil? All that remains to us is this index, which gives the names neither of the people who were guilty nor those of the victims of the twelve actions—felonious or simply naughty—and it doesn't even give the order in which they were committed, which would help in reconstituting a story: the headings in alphabetical order refer to page numbers obscured by a black stroke. To complete the list, one would have to add still one more verb: To Set Ablaze, undoubtedly the final act of this dark affair—accomplished by whom? In order to hide or destroy what?

Even assuming that each of these twelve actions had been accomplished by only one person to the prejudice of only one person, reconstituting the events is a difficult task: if the characters in question are four in number, they may represent, taken two by two, twelve different relations for each of the twelve sorts of relations listed. The possible solutions, in consequence, are twelve to the twelfth power; that is, one must choose among solutions whose number is in the neighborhood of eight thousand eight hundred seventy-four billion two hundred ninety-six million six hundred sixty-two thousand two hundred fifty-six. It is not surprising that our overworked police preferred to shelve the dossier, their excellent reasoning being that however numerous were the crimes committed, the guilty died in any case with the victims.

Only the insurance company needs to know the truth, principally because of a fire insurance policy taken out by the owner of the house. The fact that the young Inigo died in the flames only renders the question that much thornier: his powerful family, who undoubtedly had disinherited and excluded this degenerate son, is notoriously disinclined to renounce anything to which it may have a claim. The worst conclusions (included or not in that abominable index) may be drawn about a young man who, hereditary member of the House of Lords, dragged an illustrious title over the park benches that serve a nomadic and contemplative youth as beds, and who washed his long hair in public fountains. The little house rented to the old landlady was the only heritage that remained to him, and he had been admitted into it as sublessee by his tenant, against a reduction of the already modest rent. If he, Inigo, had been both guilty incendiary and victim of a criminal plot carried out with the imprecision and insouciance that apparently characterized his behavior, proof of fraud would relieve the company from payment of damages.

But that was not the only policy that the company was called upon to honor after the catastrophe: the Widow Roessler herself each year renewed a life insurance policy whose beneficiary was her adopted daughter, a fashion model familiar to anyone who leafs through the magazines devoted to *haute couture.* Now Ogiva too is dead, burned along with the collection of wigs that transformed her glacially charming face—how else to define a beautiful and delicate young woman with a totally bald head?—into hundreds of different and delightfully asymmetric characters. But it so happened that Ogiva had a three-year-old child, entrusted to relatives in South Africa, who would soon claim the insurance money, unless it were proved that it was she who had killed (*To Stab? To Strangle?*) the Widow Roessler. And since Ogiva had even thought to insure her wig collection, the child's guardians may also claim this indemnization, except if she were responsible for its destruction.

Of the fourth person who died in the fire, the giant Uzbek wrestler Belindo Kid, it is known that he had found not only a diligent landlady in the Widow Roessler (he was the only paying tenant in the *pension*) but also an astute impresario. In the last few months, the old woman had in fact decided to finance the seasonal tour of the ex–middleweight champion, hedging her bets with an insurance policy against the risk of contract default through illness, incapacity, or accident. Now a consortium of promoters of wrestling matches is claiming the damages covered by the insurance; but if the old lady *pushed him to suicide,* perhaps through *slandering* him, *blackmailing* him, or *drugging* him (the giant was known in international wrestling circles for his impressionable character), the company could easily silence them.

My hero intends to *solve the enigma,* and from this point of view the story belongs thus to the *detective mystery* genre.

But the situation is also characterized by an eminently combinatory aspect, which may be schematized as follows:

4 characters: A, B, C, D.

12 transitive, nonreflexive actions (see list below).

All the possibilities are open: one of the 4 characters may (for example) rape the 3 others or be raped by the 3 others.

One then begins to eliminate the impossible sequences. In order to do this, the 12 actions are divided into 4 classes, to wit:

appropriation of will 	{ to incite
to blackmail
to drug

$$\text{appropriation of a secret} \begin{cases} \text{to spy upon} \\ \text{to brutally extort a confession from} \\ \text{to abuse the confidence of} \end{cases}$$

$$\text{sexual appropriation} \begin{cases} \text{to seduce} \\ \text{to buy sexual favors from} \\ \text{to rape} \end{cases}$$

$$\text{murder} \begin{cases} \text{to strangle} \\ \text{to stab in the back} \\ \text{to induce to commit suicide} \end{cases}$$

Objective Constraints

Compatibility between relations

For the actions of murder: If A strangles B, he no longer needs to stab him or to induce him to commit suicide.

It is also improbable that A and B kill each other.

One may then postulate that for the murderous actions the relation of two characters will be possible only once in each permutation, and it will not be reversible.

For sexual actions: If A succeeds in winning the sexual favors of B through seduction, he need not resort to money or to rape for the same object.

One may also exclude, or neglect, the reversibility of the sexual rapport (the same or another) between two characters.

One may then postulate that for the sexual acts, the relation of two characters will be possible only once in each permutation, and it will not be reversible.

For the appropriation of a secret: If A secures B's secret, this secret may be defined in another relation that follows in the sequence, between B and C, or C and B (or even C and D, or D and C), a sexual relation, or a relation of murder, or of the appropriation of will, or of the appropriation of another secret. After that, A no longer needs to obtain the same secret from B by another means (but he may obtain a different secret by a different means from B or from other characters). Reversibility of the acts of appropriation of a secret is possible, if there are on both sides two different secrets.

For the appropriation of will: If A imposes his will on B, this imposition may provoke a relation between A (or another) and B, or even between B and C (or A), a relation that may be sexual, murderous, the appropriation of a secret, the appropriation of another will. After that, A no longer needs to impose the same will on B by another means (but he may, etc.).

Reversibility is possible, obviously, between two different wills.

Order of sequences

In each permutation, after an action of murder has taken place, the victim may no longer commit or submit to any other action.

Consequently, it is impossible for the three acts of murder to occur in the beginning of a permutation, because no characters would then be left to accomplish the other actions. Even two murders in the beginning would render the development of the sequence impossible. One murder in the beginning dictates permutations of 11 actions for 3 characters.

The optimal case is that in which the three acts of murder occur at the end.

The sequences given by the computer must be able to reveal chains of events held together by possible logical links. We have seen that the acts of will and of secret can imply others. In each permutation will be found privileged circuits, to wit:

the appropriation of a secret ⎰ of a sexual appropriation / of a murder ⎱ — determines an appropriation of will that determines ⎰ a murder / a sexual appropriation ⎱

or:

the appropriation of a will — leads to ⎰ a murder / a sexual appropriation that determines, etc. / an appropriation of a secret ⎱

Each new relation in the chain excludes others.

Subjective Constraints

Incompatibility of each character with certain actions committed or submitted to. The 12 actions may also be divided according to a second sort of system, classifying them in *4 subjective categories*.

acts of physical strength	acts of persuasion	disloyal acts	acts that exploit another's weakness
to extort	to incite	to abuse the confidence	to buy good graces
to rape	to seduce	to stab in the back	to blackmail
to strangle	to induce to commit suicide	to spy upon	to drug

—Of A it is known that he is a man of enormous physical strength, but that he is also an almost inarticulate brute.

A cannot submit to acts of physical strength.

A cannot commit acts of persuasion.

—Of B it is known that she is a woman in complete control of herself, with a strong will; she is sexually frigid; she hates drugs and drug addicts; she is rich enough to be interested only in herself.

B cannot submit to acts of persuasion.

B is not interested in acts that exploit another's weakness (she is not interested in buying sexual favors, she does not touch drugs, she has no motive for blackmail).

—Of C it is known that he is a very innocent Boy Scout, that he has a great sense of honor; if he takes drugs, he vomits immediately; his innocence protects him from all blackmail.

C cannot submit to acts that exploit another's weakness.

C cannot commit disloyal acts.

—Of D it is known that she is a terribly mistrustful woman and physically very weak.

D cannot submit to disloyal acts.

D cannot commit acts of strength.

An ulterior complication could be introduced!!!!

Each character could *change* in the course of the story (after certain actions committed or submitted to): each might lose certain incompatibilities and acquire others!!!!!!!!

For the moment, we forgo the exploration of this domain.

Esthetic Constraints (or subjective on the part of the programmer)

The programmer likes order and symmetry. Faced with the huge number of possibilities and with the chaos of human passions and worries, he tends to favor those solutions that are the most harmonious and economical.

He proposes a model, such that:

—each action be perpetrated by one and only one character and have one and only one character as a victim;

—the 12 actions be equally distributed among the 4 characters; that is, each of them perpetrates 3 actions (one on each of the others) and is the victim of 3 actions (each perpetrated by one of the others);

—each of the 3 actions perpetrated by a character belongs to a different (objective) class of actions;

—the same as above for each of the three actions submitted to by any given character;

—between two characters there be no commutativity within the same class of actions (if A kills B, B cannot kill A; likewise, the three sexual relations will occur between differently assorted couples).

Is it possible at the same time to take account of the subjective constraints and of the so-called esthetic constraints?

This is where the computer comes in; this is where the notion of "computer-aided literature" is exemplified.

Let us consider, for instance, 4 characters whom we shall call:

ARNO
CLEM
DANI
BABY

A very simple program permits us to engender selections of 12 misdeeds. Each of these selections might be, in theory, the scenario our hero is trying to reconstitute.

Here are a few examples of such scenarios:

SELEC1

ARNO	BUYS	CLEM
CLEM	EXTORTS A CONFESSION FROM	ARNO
ARNO	CONSTRAINS	ARNO
ARNO	EXTORTS A CONFESSION FROM	BABY
CLEM	RAPES	DANI
ARNO	CUTS THE THROAT OF	DANI
DANI	CONSTRAINS	BABY
BABY	EXTORTS A CONFESSION FROM	ARNO
CLEM	POISONS	ARNO
DANI	EXTORTS A CONFESSION FROM	CLEM
ARNO	ABUSES	ARNO
CLEM	EXTORTS A CONFESSION FROM	CLEM

SELEC1

ARNO	POISONS	ARNO
DANI	SEDUCES	DANI
BABY	SPIES UPON	CLEM
BABY	RAPES	CLEM
BABY	EXTORTS A CONFESSION FROM	DANI
CLEM	SPIES UPON	ARNO
CLEM	THREATENS	CLEM
DANI	CONSTRAINS	BABY
DANI	EXTORTS A CONFESSION FROM	BABY
DANI	EXTORTS A CONFESSION FROM	ARNO
CLEM	ABUSES	BABY
BABY	BLACKMAILS	ARNO

SELEC1

DANI	SEDUCES	ARNO
BABY	CONSTRAINS	ARNO
ARNO	SPIES UPON	DANI
BABY	ABUSES	ARNO
CLEM	RAPES	CLEM
BABY	CUTS THE THROAT OF	DANI
ARNO	STRANGLES	ARNO
DANI	BUYS	ARNO
ARNO	ABUSES	ARNO
DANI	CUTS THE THROAT OF	CLEM
DANI	SEDUCES	CLEM
ARNO	CONSTRAINS	BABY

The absurdity of these scenarios is obvious. In fact, the program used is completely *stupid:* it permits a character to commit a misdeed against himself.

The program can be improved in imposing:

—that autocrimes be excluded;

—that each character figure only 3 times as criminal and 3 times as victim.

One then obtains scenarios like the following:

SELEC2

DANI	POISONS	ARNO
BABY	THREATENS	CLEM
BABY	SPIES UPON	ARNO
CLEM	BLACKMAILS	ARNO

CLEM	EXTORTS A CONFESSION FROM	BABY
DANI	SEDUCES	BABY
DANI	STRANGLES	CLEM
ARNO	RAPES	BABY
BABY	CUTS THE THROAT OF	DANI
ARNO	CONSTRAINS	CLEM
ARNO	ABUSES	DANI
CLEM	BUYS	DANI

SELEC2

ARNO	CONSTRAINS	CLEM
CLEM	BLACKMAILS	ARNO
DANI	BUYS	ARNO
ARNO	CUTS THE THROAT OF	BABY
ARNO	EXTORTS A CONFESSION FROM	DANI
BABY	RAPES	CLEM
CLEM	SEDUCES	BABY
DANI	THREATENS	CLEM
CLEM	ABUSES	DANI
BABY	STRANGLES	DANI
BABY	POISONS	ARNO
DANI	SPIES UPON	BABY

SELEC2

BABY	SPIES UPON	CLEM
ARNO	CUTS THE THROAT OF	DANI
DANI	STRANGLES	CLEM
DANI	THREATENS	ARNO
BABY	BLACKMAILS	ARNO
DANI	BUYS	BABY
CLEM	EXTORTS A CONFESSION FROM	BABY
BABY	RAPES	DANI
CLEM	CONSTRAINS	DANI
ARNO	ABUSES	BABY
ARNO	SEDUCES	CLEM
CLEM	POISONS	ARNO

This new program still comprises obvious insufficiencies.

Thus, in the first scenario it is not possible for Clem to blackmail Arno who has already been poisoned by Dani. In the second scenario, Baby cannot rape Clem, because Arno has already cut the latter's throat, etc.

Paul Braffort, who ensures the development in computer science necessary to the progress of our work, has also written a series of programs for selections that progressively account for the *constraints* our story must respect in order to remain "logically" and "psychologically" acceptable.

This clearly demonstrates, we believe, that the aid of a computer, far from *replacing* the creative act of the artist, permits the latter rather to liberate himself from the slavery of a combinatory search, allowing him also the best chance of concentrating on this "clinamen" which, alone, can make of the text a true work of art.

Raymond Queneau

· · · · · · · · · · · · · · · ·

The Relation X Takes Y for Z

I

As Paul Braffort remarked during the meeting of 14 January 1966, the ternary relation "X takes Y for Z" may be represented by a multiplication: XY = Z. The "graphs" of 26 December 1965 (see Claude Berge, "For a Potential Analysis of Combinatory Literature") will be replaced by multiplication tables (see II for the difficult cases).

Examples:

Normal Situation

	a	b	c
a	a	b	c
b	a	b	c
c	a	b	c

Vaudeville Situation

	a	b	c
a	a	c	b
b	c	b	a
c	b	a	c

Amphitryon

	J	M	Am	S	Al
Jupiter	J	M	Am	S	Al
Mercury	J	M	Am	S	Al
Amphitryon	J	M	Am	S	Al
Sosia	Am	S	Am	S	Al
Alcmene	Am	S	Am	S	Al

153

If every character takes himself for himself (that is, if $a^2 = a$, $b^2 = b$, etc.) and takes no other for himself (that is, if $ax \neq a$, $bx \neq b$, etc.), there will result only one possible situation for two characters, 12 for 3 characters, 108 for 4, and, more generally, $(n - 1)^{n-1}$, n for n characters $(n > 2)$.

Consider the following interesting theorem.

The multiplication table of a group (Abelian or not) corresponds to the following situation: nobody takes himself for what he is, nor takes the others for what they are, with the exception of the unity-element, which takes itself for what it is and takes the others for what they are.

In other words, the multiplication table of a group corresponds to a situation both vaudevillesque and mad, as seen by a lucid observer (the author for example).

Commutativity of the multiplication: The multiplication is commutative when $ab = ba = c$, that is, when Paul takes John for Peter and John also takes Paul for Peter (always in the case where nobody takes himself for somebody else).

Exercise: Find concrete examples of this situation in French or foreign literature, theater or novel.

Exercises: Find concrete situations corresponding to the following semi-groups proposed by R. Croisot in "Propriétés des complexes forts et symétriques de demi-groupes," *Bulletin de la Société Mathématique de France,* vol. 80 (1952), pp. 217–227.

	a	b	c	d			a	b	c	d
a	c	c	d	a		a	a	a	a	a
b	c	c	d	a		b	a	a	a	c
c	d	d	a	c		c	a	a	a	a
d	a	a	c	d		d	a	c	a	b

	a	b	c			a	b	c
a	a	b	c		a	a	c	c
b	b	c	c		b	c	b	c
c	c	c	c		c	c	c	c

II

We have assumed until now that the multiplication was defined globally, which is not always the case. When there are isolated points in the "graph," we may assume that the product is then 0.

Three madmen (a, b, c) take themselves for Napoleon (n) and each of them takes the two others for what they are:

	a	b	c	n
a	n	b	c	a
b	a	n	c	b
c	a	b	n	c
n	0	0	0	0

Another convention might be that n (fictive) would take a, b, c, for what they are and, on the other hand, that a, b, c would take n for what he was. One would then have:

	a	b	c	n
a	n	b	c	n
b	a	n	c	n
c	a	b	n	n
n	a	b	c	n

Oedipus

		a	b	c	d
son of Jocasta	= a	b	b	c	d
Oedipus	= b	0	b	c	d
stepfather	= c	b	a	c	d
Jocasta	= d	0	b	c	d

Exercise: Find a formulation of this situation without zero.

Raymond Queneau

. . . .

A Story as You Like It

This text, submitted at the 83rd meeting of the Ouvroir de Littérature Potentielle, was inspired by the presentation of the instructions given to computers, and by programmed teaching. It is a structure analogous to the "tree" literature proposed by François Le Lionnais at the 79th meeting.

1. Do you wish to hear the story of the three alert peas?
   if yes, go to 4
   if no, go to 2
2. Would you prefer the story of the three big skinny beanpoles?
   if yes, go to 16
   if no, go to 3
3. Would you prefer the story of the three middling mediocre bushes?
   if yes, go to 17
   if no, go to 21
4. Once upon a time there were three peas dressed in green who were fast asleep in their pod. Their round faces breathed through the holes in their nostrils, and one could hear their soft and harmonious snoring.
   if you prefer another description, go to 9
   if this description suits you, go to 5
5. They were not dreaming. In fact, these little creatures never dream.
   if you prefer that they dream, go to 6
   if not, go to 7
6. They were dreaming. In fact, these little creatures always dream and their nights secrete charming dreams.
   if you wish to know these dreams, go to 11
   if you don't care about it, go to 7
7. Their cute little feet were covered in warm stockings and in bed they wore black velvet gloves.

156

if you prefer gloves of another color, go to 8

if this color suits you, go to 10

8. In bed, they wore blue velvet gloves.

if you prefer gloves of another color, go to 7

if this color suits you, go to 10

9. Once upon a time there were three peas rolling along on the great highway. When evening came, they fell fast asleep, tired and worn.

if you wish to know the rest, go to 5

if not, go to 21

10. All three were dreaming the same dream; indeed, they loved each other tenderly and, like proud mirrors, always dreamed similarly.

if you wish to know their dream, go to 11

if not, go to 12

11. They dreamed that they were getting their soup at the soup kitchen, and that upon uncovering their bowl they discovered that it was ers soup. Horrified, they woke up.

if you wish to know why they woke up horrified, consult the word "ers" in Webster, and let us hear no more of it

if you judge it a waste of time to investigate this question further, go to 12

12. Opopoï! they cried when they opened their eyes. Opopoï! what a dream we dreamed! A bad omen, said the first. Yessir, said the second, that's a fact, and now I'm sad. Don't worry like that, said the third, who was the sharpest of the three. We must comprehend rather than despair; in short, I will analyze it for you.

if you wish to know the interpretation of this dream right away, go to 15

if you wish on the contrary to know the reactions of the other two, go to 13

13. You bore us to tears, said the first. Since when do you know how to analyze dreams? Yes, since when? added the second.

if you too wish to know since when, go to 14

if not, go to 14 anyway, because in any case you won't learn a thing

14. Since when? cried the third. How should I know? The fact is that I practice analysis. You'll see.

if you too wish to see, go to 15

if not, go to 15 also, for you will see nothing

15. Well then, let's see! cried his brothers. Your irony doesn't please me a bit, replied the other, and you'll not learn a thing. Moreover, during this rather sharp conversation, hasn't your sense of horror been blurred, or even erased? What use then to stir up the mire of your papilionaceous unconscious? Let's rather go wash ourselves in the fountain and greet this

gay morning in hygiene and saintly euphoria! No sooner said than done: they slip out of their pod, let themselves roll gently to the ground, and trot joyously to the theater of their ablutions.

if you wish to know what happens at the theater of their ablutions, go to 16

if you do not wish to know, go to 21

16. Three big beanpoles were watching them.

if the three big beanpoles displease you, go to 21

if they suit you, go to 18

17. Three middling mediocre bushes were watching them.

if the three middling mediocre bushes displease you, go to 21

if they suit you, go to 18

18. Seeing themselves voyeurized in this fashion, the three alert peas, who were very modest, fled.

if you wish to know what they did after that, go to 19

if you do not wish to know, go to 21

19. They ran very hard back to their pod and, closing the latter after them, went back to sleep.

if you wish to know the rest, go to 20

if you do not wish to know, go to 21

20. There is no rest and the story is finished.

21. In this case, the story is likewise finished.

Paul Fournel

in collaboration with Jean-Pierre Énard

. . . .

The Theater Tree:

A Combinatory Play

Principle: At the outset, the objective was to produce a play using the structure of the tree. The problems encountered in a project of this sort are numerous, and some of them appeared practically insoluble. A "tree" play would, more particularly, demand an almost superhuman effort of memory on the part of the actors.

We thus elaborated a new graph which gives the audience all the appearances of the tree, but avoids the disadvantages for the actors:

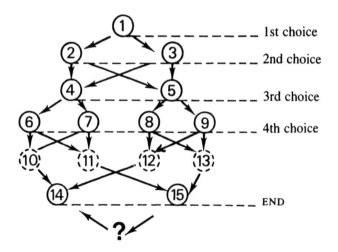

Directions for use: The actors play the first scene, then invite the audience to determine that which follows, in choosing between two possible scenes (II and III). The modalities of this choice should be determined in

159

function of the locality: the audience in a theater may, for example, vote by a show of hands; in the case of a radio play, by telephone, etc. The essential point is that the vote should not take too much time.

In the example which we have elaborated, the audience will be asked to choose four times, which means that there will be five scenes in the play. Given that our "tree" contains fifteen scenes (four of which do not lead to choices), sixteen different plays of five scenes each may be engendered. In order to produce these sixteen plays in traditional fashion, one would have to write eighty scenes (16 × 5). We have thus economized sixty-seven scenes.

The Theater Tree: In order that the structure be immediately recognized by the audience, we have tried to construct simple plots and intrigues, for which the choices offered to the audience are both real and functional.

Scene 1: The king is unhappy; misfortune reigns in the palace. The queen, returning from a journey, cannot comfort him. He is unhappy for one of the following reasons, between which the audience will choose:

—His daughter the princess has lost her smile. (see scene 2)
—The princess has been kidnapped. (see scene 3)

Scene 2: The princess appears upon the stage. She is unhappy. The king offers a reward to him who will make her smile again. The queen, step-mother of the princess, rejoices secretly. The candidates come and go with no success. The masked hero arrives; the princess smiles.

The king and the queen argue. The king learns that the queen has a lover, by whom she is pregnant, and the queen learns that the king has a lost son. Is the masked hero:

—The king's son? (see scene 5)
—The queen's lover? (see scene 4)

Scene 3: The queen wails hypocritically in the presence of the king. With the princess gone, the child whom the queen is carrying will reign.

In the forest, the enchained princess falls in love with her kidnapper, and asks him to take her back to the palace as proof of his love. At the palace, the king and queen argue. The queen has a lover, by whom she is pregnant, the king has a lost son. During this argument, the masked man and the princess arrive. Who is the masked man?

—Is he the king's son? (see scene 5)
—Is he the queen's lover? (see scene 4)

Scene 4: The masked man is the queen's lover. The princess faints. The king, beside himself with rage, commands that the instruments of torture be brought to him.

—Will he kill his wife? (see scene 6)
—Will he challenge the lover to a duel? (see scene 7)

Scene 5: The hero avers that he is the king's son. The princess faints. The queen demands proof and perfidiously asks that the young man be thrown into the noble-pit in order to determine if he is a blueblood.[1] The king fails to recognize the absurd character of the situation, and accepts. Only the princess can save the masked man:

—Will she awaken? (see scene 8)
—Will she remain unconscious? (see scene 9)

Scene 6: The king puts his wife in the torture machine. He will use this device to eliminate her.

—Would you like a happy ending? (see scenes 10 + 14)
—Would you like an unhappy ending? (see scenes 11 + 15)

Scene 7: The king challenges the lover to a duel. In the course of the fight, the queen is killed.

—Happy ending? (see scenes 10 + 14)
—Unhappy ending? (see scenes 11 + 15)

Scene 8: The princess awakens. She demonstrates the absurdity of the situation to her father. In a fit of rage, he forces his wife to test the device; she dies.

—Happy ending? (see scenes 12 + 14)
—Unhappy ending? (see scenes 13 + 15)

Scene 9: The princess does not awaken. The king, before throwing his son into the noble-pit, wishes to see if it is in working order, and throws his wife in. She dies.

—Happy ending? (see scenes 12 + 14)
—Unhappy ending? (see scenes 13 + 15)

Scene 10: The queen is dead. The king and the lover are relieved. In fact, the lover had seduced the queen in order to get into the palace. But he loves the princess. He is sad, however, to be her brother (recognition).

—Go to scene 14.

Scene 11: The lover, mad with rage, kills the king.

—Go to scene 15.

Scene 12: The king recognizes his son. The hero and the princess are unhappy, since, although they love each other, they cannot marry, being brother and sister.

—Go to scene 14.

Scene 13: The hero, mad with rage, kills the king (he loved the queen).

—Go to scene 15.

Scene 14: In fact, through a complicated play of marriages and adoptions, the hero and the princess are not brother and sister, and are thus free to marry.

Scene 15: The king is dead. The princess kills the hero and throws herself into the noble-pit (she is rejected, but if the spectator wishes to know why, he must come back to see the play again, because the reason for this rejection is explained in scene 14).

Examples of possible combinations: 1–2–4–6–10–14; 1–2–5–8–12–14; 1–3–5–9–13–15; etc.

N.B.: It is obvious that a résumé such as this cannot pretend to replace the rigorous coherence we have tried to maintain throughout the play.

Oulipians and Their Works

· ·

Much of the bibliographical material that follows appeared in *Atlas de littérature potentielle*. This section has been supplemented and updated with new material for this revised edition, but it does not pretend to exhaustivity: these are, then, selective bibliographies. No attempt has been made to distinguish between works directly influenced by the group and pre-Oulipian or non-Oulipian texts by members of the Oulipo. Texts published in the "Bibliothèque Oulipienne" are listed at the end of this section, under the rubric "Collective Works." The material used in the brief biographical sketches was in most cases supplied by the members themselves; additional material was kindly furnished by Noël Arnaud, Marcel Bénabou, Ross Chambers, Jacques Jouet, and Harry Mathews.

NOËL ARNAUD was born on 15 December 1919 in Paris. In the late 1930s he was a member of a neo-Dada group that published the review *Les Réverbères* and performed plays by authors such as Tristan Tzara, Guillaume Apollinaire, Georges Ribemont-Dessaignes, and Erik Satie. He also directed a jazz club. In 1940 he joined the Surrealist group *La Main à la Plume*, the only one of its kind operating in the occupied zone; between 1941 and 1944 it published forty-odd texts, including Paul Eluard's *Poésie et vérité*, which contains the famous poem "Liberté." During this period, Noël Arnaud was an active member of the armed resistance. In 1950 he joined the Collège de 'Pataphysique, where he serves as a Regent of General 'Pataphysics and the Clinic of Rhetoriconosis, and Major Conferant of the Order of the Grande Gidouille. In 1960 he became a founding member of the Oulipo. As a friend of Boris Vian, Arnaud oversaw the publication of most of Vian's works, and wrote his biography. He was a cofounder and then president of the Association des Amis d'Alfred Jarry and the Association des Amis de Valentin Brû. On 30 March 1984, after François Le Lionnais's death, Noël Arnaud was elected president of the Oulipo.

Semis sur le ciel. Paris: Editions des Réverbères, 1940.
L'illusion réelle ou Les apparences de la réalité. Paris: La Main à la Plume, 1942.
Aux absents qui n'ont pas toujours tort. Paris: La Main à la Plume, 1943.
Duke Ellington. Paris: Le Messager Boiteux de Paris, 1950.

163

L'état d'ébauche. Paris: Le Messager Boiteux de Paris, 1950.

"Avènement d'un Queneau glorieux." *Temps Mêlés* 5-6 (1953).

"Louis de Neufgermain, poète hétéroclite." *Bizarre* 4 (1956).

"Norge ou l'éloge de la langue vivante." *Critique* 107 (1956).

"Les métamorphoses historiques de Dada." *Critique* 134 (1958).

La religion et la morale de Francis Picabia. Verviers: Temps Mêlés, 1958.

"La vie nouvelle d'Alfred Jarry." *Critique* 151 (1959).

"Littérature combinatoire." *Critique* 171-72 (1961).

Encyclopédie des farces et attrapes et des mystifications. With François Caradec. Paris: Pauvert, 1964.

"Vers une littérature illettrée." *Bizarre* 32-33 (1964).

Les vies parallèles de Boris Vian. Paris: Pauvert, 1966.

La langue verte et la cuite. With Asger Jorn. Paris: Pauvert, 1968.

Poèmes algol. Foreword by François Le Lionnais. Illustrations by Jacques Carelman. Verviers: Temps Mêlés, 1968.

"Les champs d'épandage de la littérature." In *Entretiens sur la littérature*. Paris: Plon, 1970.

Alfred Jarry d'Ubu au Docteur Faustroll. Paris: La Table Ronde, 1974.

Le dossier de l'affaire "J'irai cracher sur vos tombes." Paris: Bourgois, 1974.

"Queneau, l'humour et la 'pataphysique." *Magazine Littéraire* 94 (1974).

"Et naquit l'Ouvroir de Littérature Potentielle." Foreword in Jacques Bens, *Oulipo 1960-1963*. Paris: Bourgois, 1980.

"Mais où est donc passé *Chêne et chien?*" In *Actes du premier colloque international Raymond Queneau*. Verviers: Temps Mêlés, 1983.

"Un Queneau honteux?" *Europe* 650-51 (1983).

"Gérard Genette et l'Oulipo." *Sureau* 1 (1984).

"Pierre MacOrlan à travers la 'pataphysique." *Cahiers du C.E.R.C.L.E.F* (1984).

L'agence Quenaud: La vie de Jean Queval par un témoin. Bassac: Plein Chant, 1987.

L'œcuménisme de Raymond Queneau. Limoges: Centre International de Documentation, de Recherche et d'Edition Raymond Queneau, 1995.

Vers une sexualisation de l'alphabet. Paris: Limon, 1996.

MARCEL BENABOU was born in Meknès, Morocco in 1939. He studied at the Ecole Normale Supérieure and earned his doctorate at the Sorbonne. He is a professor of Roman history at the Université de Paris VII. Bénabou joined the Oulipo in 1969, and he serves as the group's Definitively Provisional Secretary.

"Le P.A.L.F." With Georges Perec. *Change* 14 (1973).

"Suétone, les Césars et l'histoire." In *Suétone*. Paris: Gallimard, 1975.

La résistance africaine à la romanisation. Paris: Maspero, 1976.

"La vie de Tacfarinas." *Les Africains* 9 (1978).

"La vie de Juba II." *Les Africains* 11 (1979).

"L'apprentis." *Littératures* 7 (1983).

"La règle et la contrainte." *Pratiques* 39 (1983).

Pourquoi je n'ai écrit aucun de mes livres. Paris: Hachette, 1986.

Jette ce livre avant qu'il soit trop tard. Paris: Seghers, 1992.

Jacob, Ménahem et Mimoun: Une épopée familiale. Paris: Seuil, 1995.

Vie des douze Césars. Paris: Gallimard, 1996.

In English:

Why I Have Not Written Any of My Books. Trans. David Kornacker.
Preface Warren F. Motte, Jr. Lincoln and London: University of Nebraska Press, 1997.

Jacob, Ménahem, and Mimoun: A Family Epic. Trans. Steven Rendall.
Preface Warren F. Motte, Jr. Lincoln and London: University of Nebraska Press, 1998.

JACQUES BENS studied natural sciences at the university before becoming a
writer. He is a founding member of the Oulipo and served from 1960 to
1963 as its first Provisionally Definitive Secretary.

Chanson vécue. Paris: Gallimard, 1958.

Valentin. Paris: Gallimard, 1958.

La plume et l'ange. Paris: Gallimard, 1959.

Sept jours de liberté. Paris: Gallimard, 1961.

Queneau. Paris: Gallimard, 1962.

41 sonnets irrationnels. Paris: Gallimard, 1965.

La trinité. Paris: Gallimard, 1965.

Guide des jeux d'esprit. Paris: Albin Michel, 1967.

Le retour au pays. Paris: Gallimard, 1968.

Adieu Sidonie. Paris: Gallimard, 1969.

Boris Vian. Paris: Bordas, 1976.

Rouge grenade. Paris: Grasset, 1976.

La semence d'Horus: Contes de l'Egypte des pharaons. Paris: Garnier,
1979.

Oulipo 1960-1963. Foreword by Noël Arnaud. Paris: Bourgois, 1980.

"Oulipien à 97%." *Magazine Littéraire* 193 (1983).

Gaspard de Besse. Paris: Ramsay, 1986.

Nouvelles des enchanteurs. Paris: Ramsay, 1988.

La cinquantaine à Saint-Quentin: Confession enrichie d'un "Eloge des

dames et des motocyclettes." Paris: Seghers, 1989.
Nouvelles désenchantées. Paris: Seghers, 1989.
Les dames d'onze heures. Paris: Julliard, 1994.
Pagnol. Paris: Seuil, 1994.
Le pain perdu. Paris: Julliard, 1995.

CLAUDE BERGE studied literature and mathematics at the Université de Paris. He is currently a professor of mathematics at the Université de Paris VI and Director of Research at the Centre National de la Recherche Scientifique. Berge was a founding member of the Oulipo; within the group, he is principally responsible for combinatory structures.

Sur une théorie ensemble des jeux alternatifs. Paris: Gauthier-Villars, 1953.
Séminaire sur les méthodes algébriques de la cybernétique. Paris: Institut de Statistique de l'Université de Paris, 1956.
Théorie générale des jeux à n personnes. Paris: Gauthier-Villars, 1957.
Théorie des graphes et ses applications. Paris: Dunod, 1958.
Espaces topologiques, fonctions multivoques. Paris: Dunod, 1959.
"Problèmes plaisants et délectables." Column in *Le Journal de l'A.F.I.R.O.,* 1960-64.
Programmes, jeux, réseaux de transport. With A. Ghouila-Houri. Paris: Dunod, 1962.
Sculptures multipètres. Paris: Minotaure, 1965.
Principes de combinatoire. Paris: Dunod, 1968.
Graphes et hypergraphes. Paris: Dunod-Bordas, 1969.
Introduction à la théorie des hypergraphes. Montreal: Les Presses de l'Université de Montréal, 1973.
Hypergraphes: Combinatoire des ensembles. Paris: Gauthier-Villars, 1987.

In English:
Theory of Graphs and its Applications. London: Methuen, 1958.
The Theory of Graphs. New York: Methuen and Wiley, 1961.
Topological Spaces. London: Oliver and Boyd, 1963.
Programming, Games, Transportation Networks. With A. Ghouila-Houri. London: Methuen and Wiley, 1965.
Lectures on Graph Theory. Bombay: Tata Institute, 1967.
Principles of Combinatorics. New York: Academic Press, 1971.
Graphs and Hypergraphs. Amsterdam: North Holland, 1973.
Hypergraph Seminar. With D. K. Ray-Chaudhuri. Berlin: Springer Verlag, 1974.
Fractional Graph Theory. Delhi: McMillan Company of India, 1978.

Hypergraphs: Combinatorics of Finite Sets. Amsterdam: North Holland, 1989.

Graph Theory and Combinatorics. Amsterdam: North Holland, 1993.

ANDRE BLAVIER is a librarian, bibliographer, editor, and publisher. His journal, *Les Temps Mêlés,* was the first to devote a special issue to the work of Raymond Queneau (nos. 5-6, 1953), and his publishing house, Temps Mêlés, has brought forth many works by members of the Oulipo. He was elected to the Oulipo on 13 February 1961. He published a special issue of *Les Temps Mêlés* on the group in 1964. Blavier established the Centre de Documentation Raymond Queneau in Verviers, Belgium, and has sponsored three international colloquia on Queneau's work.

"Tics et mystiques du verbe." *Cahiers du Collège de 'Pataphysique* 8-9 (1952).
"Raymond Queneau." *Temps Mêlés* 5-6 (1953).
Sept graphismes colorés. Illustrations by Joseph Peukenne. Verviers: Temps Mêlés, 1954.
La roupie de cent sonnets. Illustrations by René Lambert. Verviers: Temps Mêlés, 1955.
"Cinq siècles de pensée nationale." *Bizarre* 4 (1956).
De quelques inventions belges utiles et "tolérables." Verviers: Temps Mêlés, 1960.
Les lettres belges sous la chape de laine. Verviers: Temps Mêlés, 1960.
"De l'humour (?) à la sagesse." *Temps Mêlés* 50-52 (1961).
"L'harmonimètre." *Bizarre* 32-33 (1964).
"Solvique et Phonique." *Bizarre* 32-33 (1964).
"A Khan Abdul Hamid." *Les Soirées d'Anvers* 12 (1965).
"S + 7 en wallon." *Les Soirées d'Anvers* 12 (1965).
L'Ubu rwé. Liège: AA Editions, 1970.
Ceci n'est pas une pipe. Verviers: Temps Mêlés and Fondation René Magritte, 1973.
"A propos d'un errata." *L'Herne* 29 (1975).
Occupe-toi d'homélies. Paris: Cheval d'Attaque, 1976.
Ecrits complets de René Magritte. Ed. André Blavier. Paris: Flammarion, 1979.
Les fous littéraires. Paris: Veyrier, 1982.
Le mal du pays ou les travaux forc[en]és. Illustrations by Lionel Vinche. Brussels: A La Pierre d'Alun, 1983.
Cinémas de quartier, suivi de La cantilène de la mal-baisée avec les remembrances du vieux barde idiot, et Une conclusion provisoire. Bassac: Plein Chant, 1985.

Raymond Queneau. Bruxelles: Editions Labor, 1988.

PAUL BRAFFORT, having studied mathematics and philosophy, is a computer scientist by trade, but is also a musician and a composer. He joined the Oulipo in 1961, and has been instrumental in the group's efforts to interface computer technology and literature.

L'intelligence artificielle. Paris: Presses Universitaires de France, 1968.
In English:
Computer Programming and Formal Systems. Ed. Paul Braffort and D. Hirschberg. Amsterdam: North Holland, 1963.
Automation in Language Translation and Theorem Proving: Some Applications of Mathematical Logic. Ed. Paul Braffort and F. van Scheepen. Brussels: Commission of Eurorean Communities, 1968.

ITALO CALVINO was born in Cuba of Italian parents; he spent his youth in San Remo. He fought in the Italian resistance during the Second World War, an experience reflected in his first novel, *Il sentiero dei nidi di ragno.* He lived in France and Italy, and served as an editor for the Einaudi publishing firm. He joined the Oulipo in 1973. Italo Calvino died on 19 September 1985.

Il sentiero dei nidi di ragno. Turin: Einaudi, 1947.
"La formica argentina." *Botteghe Oscure* 10 (1952).
Il visconti dimezzato. Turin: Einaudi, 1952.
Fiabe italiane. Turin: Einaudi, 1956.
Il barone rampante. Turin: Einaudi, 1957.
Il cavaliere inesistente. Turin: Einaudi, 1958.
I racconti. Turin: Einaudi, 1958.
Ultima viene il corvo. Turin: Einaudi, 1958.
La giornata d'uno scrutatore. Turin: Einaudi, 1963.
Marcovaldo, ovvero: Le stagioni in città. Turin: Einaudi, 1963.
Le cosmicomiche. Turin: Einaudi, 1965.
Ti con zero. Turin: Einaudi, 1967.
Le città invisibili. Turin: Einaudi, 1972.
Il castello dei destini incrociati. Turin: Einaudi, 1973.
Se una notte d'inverno un viaggiatore. Turin: Einaudi, 1979.
Palomar. Turin: Einaudi, 1983.
La strada di San Giovanni. Milan: Mondadori, 1990.
In English:
Adam, One Afternoon, and Other Stories. Trans. Archibald Colquhoun and Peggy Wright. London: Collins, 1957.

Cosmicomics. Trans. William Weaver. New York: Harcourt Brace Jovanovich, 1968.

t zero. Trans. William Weaver. New York: Harcourt Brace Jovanovich, 1969.

The Watcher and Other Stories. Trans. Archibald Colquhoun and William Weaver. New York: Harcourt Brace Jovanovich, 1971.

Invisible Cities. Trans. William Weaver. New York: Harcourt Brace Jovanovich, 1974.

The Path to the Nest of Spiders. Trans. Archibald Colquhoun. New York: Ecco, 1976.

The Baron in the Trees. Trans. Archibald Colquhoun. New York: Harcourt Brace Jovanovich, 1977.

The Castle of Crossed Destinies. Trans. William Weaver. New York: Harcourt Brace Jovanovich, 1977.

The Nonexistent Knight and The Cloven Viscount. Trans. Archibald Colquhoun. New York: Harcourt Brace Jovanovich, 1977.

Italian Folktales. Trans. George Martin. New York: Harcourt Brace Jovanovich, 1980.

If on a winter's night a traveler. Trans. William Weaver. New York: Harcourt Brace Jovanovich, 1981.

Marcovaldo, or The seasons in the city. Trans. William Weaver. New York: Harcourt Brace Jovanovich, 1983.

Difficult Loves. Trans. Archibald Colquhoun, William Weaver, and Peggy Wright. New York: Harcourt Brace Jovanovich, 1984.

Mr. Palomar. Trans. William Weaver. New York: Harcourt Brace Jovanovich, 1985.

The Uses of Literature. Trans. Patrick Creagh. New York: Harcourt Brace Jovanovich, 1986.

Six Memos for the Next Millennium. Trans. Patrick Creagh. Cambridge: Harvard University Press, 1988.

Under the Jaguar Sun. Trans. William Weaver. New York: Harcourt Brace Jovanovich, 1988.

The Road to San Giovanni. Trans. Tim Parks. New York: Pantheon, 1993.

FRANCOIS CARADEC is a man of letters. He joined the Oulipo in 1983.

Christophe Colomb. Paris: Grasset, 1956.

L'affaire de la Gazette de Lausanne. Paris: Collège de 'Pataphysique, 1958.

Monsieur Tristecon, chef d'entreprise. Verviers: Temps Mêlés, 1960.

Le parfait secrétaire, ou, L'alphabet par les méthodes actives. Paris:

Collège de 'Pataphysique, 1961.

Encyclopédie des farces et attrapes et des mystifications. With Noël Arnaud. Paris: Pauvert, 1964

Guide de Paris mystérieux. Ed. François Caradec and Jean-Robert Masson. Paris: Tchou, 1966.

Le Pétomane, 1857-1945: Sa vie, son oeuvre. Paris: Pauvert, 1967.

Fregoli, 1867-1936: Sa vie et ses secrets. With Jean Nohain. Paris: La Jeune Parque, 1968.

La vie exemplaire de la femme à barbe: Clementine Delait, 1865-1939. Paris: La Jeune Parque, 1969.

Alphonse Allais en verve. Ed. François Caradec. Paris: Horay, 1970.

Isidore Ducasse, comte de Lautéamont. With Albano Rodriguez. Paris: La Table Ronde, 1970.

Trésors du rire. Ed. François Caradec. Paris: Horay, 1970.

Trésors du pastiche. Ed. François Caradec and Noël Arnaud. Paris: Horay, 1971.

Vie de Raymond Roussel. Paris: Pauvert, 1972.

Les Goncourt en verve. Ed. François Caradec. Paris: Horay, 1973.

Mon oeil! With Christiane Sabatier. Paris: Denoël, 1973.

A la recherche d'Alfred Jarry. Paris: Seghers, 1974.

La logique mène à tout / Alphonse Allais. Ed. François Caradec. Paris: Horay, 1976.

Dictionnaire du français argotique et populaire. Paris: Larousse, 1977.

La farce et le sacré: Fêtes et farceurs, mythes et mystificateurs. Paris: Casterman, 1977.

Histoire de la littérature enfantine en France. Paris: Albin Michel, 1977.

Le café-concert. With Alain Weill. Paris: Hachette-Massin, 1980.

Christophe. Foreword by Raymond Queneau. Paris: Horay, 1981.

Nous deux mon chien: Portrait d'artiste. Paris: Horay, 1983.

Feu Willy. Paris: Pauvert, 1984.

La compagnie des zincs. Paris: Ramsay, 1986.

N'ayons pas peur des mots: Dictionnaire du français argotique et populaire. Paris: Larousse, 1988.

Alphonse Allais. Paris: Belfond, 1994.

Craquements (doux). Paris: Editions Plurielle, 1997.

Raymond Roussel. Paris: Fayard, 1997.

In English:

Le Pétomane. London: Souvenir, 1967.

BERNARD CERQUIGLINI is a linguist, philologist, and medievalist who teaches at the Université de Paris VII. He has studied the history of French orthographical conventions, and has been closely involved with the movement to reform French orthography. He joined the Oulipo in 1995.

Grammaires du texte médiéval. Paris: Larousse, 1978.
La représentation du discours dans les textes narratifs du Moyen Age français. Doctoral dissertation, Université de Provence, 1979.
La parole médiévale: discours, syntaxe, texte. Paris: Minuit, 1981.
Le roman du Graal: Manuscrit de Modène. Ed. Bernard Cerquiglini. Paris: UGE, 1981.
Histoire de la littérature française. Paris: Nathan, 1984.
Eloge de la variante: Histoire critique de la philologie. Paris: Seuil, 1989.
La naissance du français. Paris: Presses Universitaires de France, 1991.
L'accent du souvenir. Paris: Minuit, 1995.
Le roman de l'orthographe: Au paradis des mots, avant la faute 1150-1694. Paris: Hatier, 1996.
Le Jabberwocky de Lewis Carroll: Onze mots-valise dans huit traductions. Bordeaux: Le Castor Astral, 1997.

ROSS CHAMBERS was born on 19 November 1932 in Australia. After earning three degrees at the University of Sydney, he completed a doctorate in French literature at the Université de Grenoble; his thesis there won the Prix des Amis de l'Université de Grenoble. He has taught in France, Australia, and the United States, and is currently the Marvin Felheim Distinguished Professor of French and Comparative Literature at the University of Michigan. Elected to the Oulipo in 1961, Ross Chambers insists on the appellation "pseudo-Oulipian," since he is no longer an active member of the group.

Gérard de Nerval et la poétique du voyage. Paris: Corti, 1969.
L'ange et l'automate: Variations sur le mythe de l'actrice, de Nerval à Proust. Paris: Minard, 1971.
La comédie au château: Contribution à la poétique du théâtre. Paris: Corti, 1971.
"Spirite" de Théophile Gautier: Une Lecture. Paris: Minard, 1974.
In English:
Meaning and Meaningfulness: Studies in the Analysis and Interpretation of Texts. Lexington, KY: French Forum, 1979.
Story and Situation: Narrative Seduction and the Power of Fiction. Minneapolis: University of Minnesota Press, 1984.
Loiterature. Lincoln and London: University of Nebraska Press, 1988.
Room for Maneuver: Reading (the) Oppositional (in) Narrative. Chi-

cago: University of Chicago Press, 1991.

STANLEY CHAPMAN is an architect living in London. He is a Regent of the Collège de 'Pataphysique, for which he directs the Rogation London-in-Middlesex. Chapman was a friend of Boris Vian, with whom he coauthored several songs. He was elected to the Oulipo on 13 February 1961. Although he is no longer active in the group—and indeed has never attended an Oulipian luncheon—in the early years he corresponded regularly, submitting things as diverse as Shakespearean sonnets written backwards and a photoengraving of His Magnificence, the head of the Collège de 'Pataphysique, Baron Jean Mollet.

Onze mille verbes, cent virgules. Verviers: Temps Mêlés, 1969.
In English:
Heartsnatcher. London: Rapp and Whiting, 1968. [Translation of Boris Vian's *L'arrache-coeur.*]
Froth on the Daydream. Harmondsworth: Penguin, 1970. [Translation of Boris Vian's *L'écume des jours.*]

MARCEL DUCHAMP was born on 28 July 1887. He studied painting at the Académie Julian in Paris from 1904 to 1905, and first exhibited his work in 1909 at the Salon des Indépendants. In 1911 he began work on *Nude Descending a Staircase.* Duchamp helped to arrange the first New York Independents exhibition in 1917, and assisted with *The Blind Man* and *Rongwrong,* New York Dada magazines. With Man Ray, he edited and published *New York Dada.* His first one-man show was at the Arts Club of Chicago in 1937; this was followed by exhibitions at the Sidney Janis Gallery in New York (1959), the Pasadena Art Museum (1963), and the Tate Gallery in London (1966). He joined the Oulipo in 1962. Marcel Duchamp died in Paris on 1 October 1968.

"Calembours." *Littérature* 5 (1922).
Obligations pour la roulette de Monte-Carlo. Paris: 1924.
Disques. With inscribed puns, for the film *Anemic Cinema.* Paris: 1925-26.
L'opposition et les cases conjuguguées sont réconciliées. With V. Halberstadt. Paris: L'Echiquier, 1932.
Rotorelief. Paris: 1935.
La mariée mise à nu par ses célébataires, même. Paris: Rrose Sélavy, 1939.
Rrose Sélavy. Paris: G. L. M., 1939.
Boîte-en-valise. New York: Art of this Century Gallery, 1941.

Comment il faut commencer une partie d'échecs. Paris: Marcel Ledun, 1954. [French version of the book by E. Znosko-Borovsky.]
In English:
The Large Glass and Related Works, with Nine Original Etchings by Marcel Duchamp. Milan: Galleria Schwarz, 1967.

JACQUES DUCHATEAU, after having studied philosophy, became a writer and a journalist. He has worked in radio and in film criticism. According to Jacques Bens, Duchateau was by far the most taciturn member of the Oulipo in the early days. A founding member of the group, and consistently present at its subsequent meetings, Duchateau spoke for the first time during the meeting of 17 August 1961.

Zinga huit. Paris: Gallimard, 1967.
Boris Vian. Paris: La Table Ronde, 1969.
Boris Vian ou les facéties du destin. Paris: La Table Ronde, 1982.
La colonne d'air. Paris: Ramsay, 1987.

LUC ETIENNE (a pseudonym for Luc Etienne Périn) was a professor of mathematics in Reims, a Regent of the Collège de 'Pataphysique, and, under the name of "The Countess," a contributor to the satirical weekly *Le Canard Enchaîné.* He joined the Oulipo in 1970. In addition to his literary activity, he composed music and invented several instruments: an electronic orchestra conductor, an altocello, and an assisted bass flute. Luc Etienne died on 27 November 1984.

Triptykhon. Paris: Collège de 'Pataphysique, 1953.
"Adam et Eve en palindromes." *Bizarre* 8 (1957).
L'art du contrepet. Paris: Pauvert, 1957.
"Peut-on apprivoiser le palindrome?" *Bizarre* 8 (1957).
Polka des gidouilles: Branle ombilical pour cornet à pistons. Paris: Collège de 'Pataphysique, 1957.
"Le gidouillographe de Boris Vian." *Dossiers du Collège de 'Pataphysique* 12 (1960).
L'art de la charade à tiroirs. Paris: Pauvert, 1965.
La méthode à Mimile. With Alphonse Boudard. Paris: La Jeune Parque, 1970.
"Les jeux de langage chez Lewis Carroll." *L'Herne* 17 (1971).
"Poèmes à métamorphoses pour rubans de Moebius." *Subsidia 'Pataphysica* 15 (1973).
"Le sonnet à triple sens d'Adoré Floupette." *Cymbalum 'Pataphysicum* 11 (1979).

"Le trio 'des paradoxes.'" *Petit Archimède* (1979).

Palindromes bilingues. Paris: Editions du Fourneau, 1984.

Textes à expurger: Comment écrire des textes moralement irreprochables *pour l'enseignement de la lecture aux enfants.* Paris: Collège de 'Pataphysique, 1984.

PAUL FOURNEL was born on 20 May 1947 in Saint-Etienne. He studied literature at the Ecole Normale Supérieure de Saint Cloud, and earned his doctorate at the Université de Paris. He taught for a year at Princeton and during a summer session at the University of Colorado. For several years, he was an editor at the Ramsay and Seghers publishing houses in Paris. He is currently the Executive Director of the Alliance Française in San Francisco. Fournel joined the Oulipo in 1971 or 1972, and serves as the group's Provisionally Definitive Secretary.

Clefs pour la littérature potentielle. Paris: Denoël, 1972.

L'équilatère. Paris: Gallimard, 1972.

L'histoire véritable de Guignol. Lyon: Fédérop, 1975.

"Queneau et la lipo." *L'Herne* 29 (1975).

Les petites filles respirent le même air que nous. Paris: Gallimard, 1978.

Les aventures très douces de Timothée le rêveur. Paris: Hachette, 1979.

La reine de la cour. Paris: Gallimard, 1979.

Les grosses rêveuses. Paris: Seuil, 1982.

Les marionnettes. Paris: Bordas, 1982.

"Georges Perec mode d'emploi." *Magazine Littéraire* 193 (1983).

Un rocker de trop. Paris: Balland, 1983.

Les athlètes dans leur tête. Paris: Ramsay, 1988.

Un homme regarde une femme. Paris: Seuil, 1994.

Guignol: Les Mourguet. Paris: Seuil, 1995.

Le jour que je suis grand. Paris: Gallimard, 1995.

Norbert amoureux. Paris: Editions Plurielle, 1997.

In English:

Little Girls Breathe the Same Air As We Do. Trans. Lee Sahnestock. New York: Braziller, 1979.

MICHELLE GRANGAUD is a poet specializing in anagrammatic verse, and a novelist. She joined the Oulipo in 1995.

Memento-fragments. Paris: POL, 1987.

Stations. Paris: POL, 1990.

Geste. Paris: POL, 1991.

Renaîtres. Paris: Ecbolade, 1991.

Jours le jour. Paris: POL, 1994.
On verra bien. Paris: Editions Plurielle, 1996.
Poèmes fondus: Traductions de français en français. Paris: POL, 1997.
Etat civil. Paris: POL, 1998.

JACQUES JOUET was born in 1947. He is a literary experimentalist in the no-
blest sense of that term. His published works are richly various in form:
he has experimented in poetry, prose narrative (both the novel and the
short story), theater, and the essay. He is a director of writers workshops
and a published lexicographer. Jouet is deeply concerned with literary
form, with economy of expression and, broadly speaking, with the ways
in which literature can be made to accommodate ordinary experience. He
joined the Oulipo in 1983.

Guerre froide, mère froide. Villelongue d'Aude: Atelier du Gué, 1978.
14 réguliers comprenant leur désir. Paris: Saint-Germain-des-Près,
    1978.
Le bestiaire inconstant. Paris: Ramsay, 1983.
Romillats. Paris: Ramsay, 1986.
L'anse. Paris: Editions du Limon, 1988.
Des ans et des ânes. Paris: Ramsay, 1988.
Qui s'endort. Remoulins-sur-Gardon: Editions Jacques Brémond, 1988.
Raymond Queneau. Lyon: La Manufacture, 1988.
Les mots du corps dans les expressions de la langue française. Paris:
    Larousse, 1990.
107 âmes. Paris: Ramsay, 1991.
Le chantier. Paris: Editions du Limon, 1993.
Actes de la machine ronde. Paris: Julliard, 1994.
Le Directeur du Musée des Cadeaux des Chefs d'Etat de l'Etranger.
    Paris: Seuil, 1994.
Le point de vue de l'escargot. Strasbourg: L'Alsace and Le Verger, 1994.
La scène est sur la scène. Paris: Editions du Limon, 1994.
Histoire de Paul Gauguin et de son divan. Paris: Editions Plurielle, 1996.
La montagne R. Paris: Seuil, 1996.
Les annexes de l'oeil. Antibes: Editions Anna Tanaquilli, 1997.
L'évasion de Rochefort. Saint-Quentin: Festival de la Nouvelle, 1997.
Kayserberg. With Claudine Capdeville, Pierre Laurent, and Georges
    Kolebka. Paris: Editions Plurielle, 1997.
La scène usurpée. Monaco: Editions du Rocher, 1997.

LATIS (a pseudonym for Emmanuel Peillet) was a professor of philosophy
and Private General Secretary to the Baron Vice-Curator of the Collège

de 'Pataphysique. A founding member of the Oulipo, Latis proposed that the original abbreviation of "Ouvroir de Littérature Potentielle," "Olipo," be changed to "Oulipo," and he designed the group's symbol. Latis died in 1973.

L'organiste athée. Paris: Collège de 'Pataphysique, 1964.
Lettre au T S. Queneau G.C.O.G.G. Paris: Collège de 'Pataphysique, 1969.

FRANCOIS LE LIONNAIS, a chemical engineer and mathematician, was born in Paris on 3 October 1901. In the early 1920s, Le Lionnais wrote poetry, frequenting Dada groups with Max Jacob, Jean Dubuffet, and others. At the age of twenty-six, he was named director of a large industrial concern, the Forges d'Aquigny. In 1939 he began to prepare *Les grands courants de la pensée mathématique.* An active member of the armed resistance during World War II, Le Lionnais was arrested and deported to the Dora concentration camp. After the war, he served as a professor at the Ecole de Guerre, head of the Division of Teaching and Diffusion of Sciences at UNESCO, scientific advisor to the National Museums, and Regent of the Collège de 'Pataphysique. He was also an international authority on chess; it was through that game that he met Raymond Roussel and Marcel Duchamp. In 1960 he cofounded the Oulipo with Raymond Queneau. In later years, he cofounded the Oulipopo (detective fiction), the Oumupo (music), the Oupeinipo (painting), the Oucinépo (film), and the Oucuipo (cooking). François Le Lionnais died on 13 March 1984.

L'ouverture française: e4-e6. Paris: Cahiers de l'Echiquier Français, 1932.
Le jardin des échecs: Tournoi de Moscou, 1935. Paris: Cahiers de l'Echiquier Français, 1936.
Les prix de beauté aux échecs. Paris: Payot, 1939.
"La peinture à Dora." *Confluences* 10 (1946).
Les grands courants de la pensée mathématique. Ed. François Le Lionnais. Paris: Cahiers du Sud, 1948.
La mesure du temps. Paris: Dupont, 1948.
"Eloge du faux." In *Le faux dans l'art et dans l'histoire.* Paris: Catalogue of the Exhibition at the Grand Palais des Champs-Elysées, 17 June -16 July 1955.
La méthode dans les sciences modernes. Ed. François Le Lionnais. Paris: Science et Industrie, 1958.
Le temps. Paris: Encyclopédie Essentielle, 1959.
Magnelli. Paris: Galerie de France, 1960.

"A propos de la littérature expérimentale." Afterword in Raymond Queneau, *Cent mille milliards de poèmes*. Paris: Gallimard, 1961.

La prévision du temps. Paris: Les Yeux Ouverts, 1962.

Dictionnaire des échecs. Paris: Presses Universitaires de France, 1967.

"Ivresse algolique." Foreword in Noël Arnaud, *Poèmes algol*. Verviers: Temps Mêlés, 1968.

"Les mathématiques modernes sont-elles un jeu?" *Science Progrès Découverte* 3427 (1970).

"Alice joue aux échecs." *L'Herne* 17 (1971).

"Art et ordinateur." In *Traité d'informatique*. Paris: Techniques de l'Ingénieur, 1972.

"La querelle des maths modernes a 1000 *ans.*" *Sciences et Avenir* 310 (1972).

"Le troisième secteur." *Les Lettres Nouvelles*, September-October 1972.

"Changement de titre." In *La critique générative*. Paris: Seghers-Laffont, 1973.

"Un nouveau joueur d'échecs: L'ordinateur." *IBM-Informatique* 10 (1973).

Le jeu d'échecs. Paris: Presses Universitaires de France, 1974.

"Qu'est-ce que l'Oulipo." Interview with François Le Lionnais and Raymond Queneau. *L'Education* 209 (1974).

"Queneau à/et l'Oulipo." *L'Herne* 29 (1975).

"Queneau et les mathématiques." *L'Herne* 29 (1975).

"L'antéantépénultième." In Oulipo, *A Raymond Queneau*. Paris: Bibliothèque Oulipienne 4, 1977.

"Echecs et maths." In *Abécédaire: L'oeuvre de Marcel Duchamp*. Paris: Catalogue of the Marcel Duchamp Exhibition at the Centre Georges Pompidou, February 1977.

"Raymond Queneau et l'amalgame des mathématiques et de la littérature." *Nouvelle Revue Française* 290 (1977). [Reprinted in Oulipo, *Atlas de littérature potentielle*.]

"Lewis Carroll, précurseur de l'Oulipo." In Lewis Carroll, *Le magazine du presbytère*. Paris: Veyrier, 1978.

Dictionnaire des mathématiques. With Alain Bouvier and Michel George. Paris: Presses Universitaires de France, 1979.

Tempêtes sur l'échiquier. Paris: Pour La Science, 1981.

Les nombres remarquables. Paris: Hermann, 1983.

In English:

Time. London: Prentice-Hall International, 1963.

Great Currents of Mathematical Thought. Trans. Howard Bergmann, R. A. Hall, Helen Kline, and Charles Pinter. New York: Dover, 1971.

JEAN LESCURE was born on 14 September 1912 in the suburbs of Paris. He studied philosophy and literature at the Sorbonne and joined the Comité de Vigilance des Intellectuels Antifascistes in 1934. From 1934 to 1936 he was Jean Giono's secretary. Beginning in 1938, he edited the review *Messages*. The latter was forced to go underground during the Occupation; *Messages* 3 was published in Brussels (1942) and *Messages* 4 in Geneva (1943). Lescure was also involved with other organs of the clandestine press, notably the Editions de Minuit and Les Lettres Françaises. During this period, he was a member of an armed resistance unit operating in the western suburbs of Paris. After the Liberation, he became the literary director of French National Radio. Lescure was elected president of the Association Française des Cinémas d'Art et Essai in 1966, and of the Confédération Internationale des Cinémas d'Art et Essai in 1979. In addition to the works listed below, he produced translations, and essays on a score of painters. Jean Lescure is a founding member of the Oulipo and Regent of Anabathmology of the Collège de 'Pataphysique.

Le voyage immobile. Paris: Flory, 1938.
Exercice de la pureté. Paris: Messages, 1942.
Une anatomie du secret. Neuchâtel: Ides et Calendes, 1946.
1848, poème dramatique en trois journées. Geneva: Trois Collines, 1948.
La plaie ne se ferme pas. Paris: Charlot, 1949.
Les falaises de Taormina. Limoges: Rougerie, 1950.
Une rose de Vérone. Paris: 1953 .
Lapicque. Paris: Flammarion, 1956.
Treize poèmes. Paris: Gallimard, 1960.
Noires campagnes de mes murs. Avignon: Mouret, 1961.
La Saint-Jean d'été. Paris: Galanis, 1963.
Un herbier des dames. Paris: Bucher, 1964.
Images d'images. Paris: Galanis, 1965.
D'une obscure clarté. Paris: Villand et Galanis, 1966.
Drailles. Paris: Gallimard, 1968.
Non dicible cible. Paris: Lorenzelli, 1969.
L'étang. Paris: Galanis, 1972.
Treize proverbes smyrniotes. Izmir: Dayez, 1973.
Blason du corps blessé. Rouen: Société Normande des Amis du Livre, 1974.
Jardins déserts peut-être. Braunschweig: Schmücking, 1976.
Procession des monts. Paris: Benichou, 1976.
De l'arbre au masque. Paris: Benichou, 1977.
Malignes salignes. Paris: Orycte, 1977.
Quatre portes sur le jour quatre portes sur la mort. Paris: Orycte, 1978.

Le traité des couleurs. Paris: Orycte, 1980.
Ultra crepidam ou mort à l'élément terre. Paris: Orycte, 1981.
Itinéraires de la nuit. Paris: Clancier-Guénaud, 1982.
Un été avec Bachelard. Paris: Luneau Ascot, 1983.
La belle jardinière. Paris: Clancier-Guénaud, 1988.
Dayez. Paris: J. P. Joubert, 1991.
In English:
Creative Art and Cinematographic Production vis-à-vis the State in Europe. Strasbourg: Council of Europe, 1982.

HERVE LE TELLIER was born in 1957. He studied science and journalism at the university. A creative writer, a journalist, and a teacher, Le Tellier also participated in the *"Des Papous dans la tête"* series, directed by Bertrand Jérôme and Françoise Treussard on France Culture Radio. He joined the Oulipo in December 1992, and serves as the group's Treasurer.

Sonates de bar. Paris: Seghers, 1991.
Le voleur de nostalgie. Paris: Seghers, 1992.
L'athlète dans les étoiles. Paris: La Grande Halle-La Villette: Sport WND, 1993.
La France, l'industrie, la crise: Chroniques d'un déclin inévitable. Bordeaux: Le Castor Astral, 1993.
De sincerita with las mujeres. Paris: Editions Plurielle, 1996.
Les amnésiques n'ont rien vécu d'inoubliable, ou, Mille réponses à la question "A quoi tu penses?" Bordeaux: Le Castor Astral, 1997.

HARRY MATHEWS was born in New York in 1930. He studied music and musicology at Harvard, and later at the Ecole Normale de Musique in Paris. After 1953 he worked as a writer, living principally in France. Along with John Ashberry, Kenneth Koch, and James Schuyler, he edited and published the review *Locus Solus* (1960-62). He has translated works by Marie Chaix, Jeanne Cordelier, Georges Bataille, and Georges Perec. He became a member of the Oulipo in 1973. Since 1978, Mathews has taught courses in fiction and creative writing at various colleges and universities in France and the United States. He was awarded a National Endowment for the Arts grant in fiction writing in 1981.

"Le Catalogue d'une vie." *Magazine Littéraire* 193 (1983).
"Still Life." *Littératures* 7 (1983).
Le verger. Paris: POL, 1986.
Cuisine de pays. Châteauneuf-sur-Charente: Plein Chant, 1990.
In English:

The Conversions. New York: Random House, 1962; Normal, IL: Dalkey Archive Press, 1997.

Tlooth. New York: Doubleday, 1966; Normal, IL: Dalkey Archive Press, 1998.

The Ring: Poems, 1956-1969. Leeds: Julliard, 1970.

'*The Planisphere.* Providence, RI: Burning Deck, 1974.

The Sinking of the Odradek Stadium and Other Novels. New York: Harper and Row, 1975 [Includes *The Conversions* and *Tlooth.*]; *The Sinking of the Odradek Stadium,* Normal, IL: Dalkey Archive Press, 1999.

"Oulipo." *Word Ways: The Journal of Recreational Linguistics* 9.2 (1976).

Selected Declarations of Dependence. Calais, VT: Z Press, 1977.

Trial Impressions. Providence, RI: Burning Deck, 1977.

Country Cooking and Other Stories. Providence, RI: Burning Deck, 1980.

"G. Perec and the Oulipo." In *The Avant-Garde Tradition in Literature.* Ed. Richard Kostelanetz. Buffalo: Prometheus, 1982.

"Georges Perec." *Grand Street* 3.1 (1983).

Armenian Papers: Poems, 1954-1984. Princeton: Princeton University Press, 1987.

Cigarettes. New York: Weidenfeld & Nicholson, 1987; Normal, IL: Dalkey Archive Press, 1998.

20 Lines a Day. Normal, IL: Dalkey Archive Press, 1988.

The Orchard: A Remembrance of Georges Perec. Flint, MI: Bamberger Books, 1988.

Singular Pleasures. New York: Grenfell Press, 1988; Normal, IL: Dalkey Archive Press, 1993.

The Way Home. New York: Grenfell Press, 1988.

Out of Bounds. Providence, RI: Burning Deck, 1989.

The American Experience. London: Atlas, 1991.

Immeasurable Distances: The Collected Essays. Venice, CA: Lapis Press, 1991.

A Mid-Season Sky: Poems 1954-1991. Manchester: Carcanet, 1992.

The Journalist. Boston: Godine, 1994; Normal, IL: Dalkey Archive Press, 1997.

MICHELE METAIL studied music and languages. She is a poet, and has directed poetry workshops. Métail joined the Oulipo in 1974.

Première décennie: Compléments de noms 1973-1983. Issy-les-Moulineaux, 1983.

OSKAR PASTIOR is a poet who lives in Berlin. He has worked on the anagram, the palindrome, and the sestina forms. He joined the Oulipo in 1995.

Offne Worte. Bucharest: Literatur, 1964.
Vom Sichersten ins Tausendste. Frankfurt: Suhrkamp, 1969.
Höricht: Sechzig Ubertragungen aus einem Frequenzbereich. Spenge: Ramm, 1975.
An die neue Aubergine, Zeichen und Plunder. Berlin: Rainer, 1976.
Fleischeslust. Lichtenberg: Ramm, 1976.
Gedichtgedichte. Munich: Heyne, 1976.
Höricht; Gedichtgedichte. Düsseldorf: S Press Tapes, 1977. [Sound recording.]
Summatorium. Düsseldorf: S Press Tapes, 1977. [Sound recording.]
Der krimgotische Fächer. Munich: Renner, 1978.
Ein Tangopoem und andere Texte. Berlin: Literarisches Colloquium, 1978.
Der krimgotische Fächer. Düsseldorf: S Press Tapes, 1979. [Sound recording.]
Tango. Düsseldorf: S Press Tapes, 1979. [Sound recording.]
Wechselbalg: Gedichte, 1977-1980. Spenge: Ramm, 1980.
Gedichtgedichte; Höricht, Fleischeslust. Munich: Heyne, 1982.
33 Gedichte. Munich: Hanser, 1983.
Sonetburger. Berlin: Rainer, 1983.
Anagrammgedichte. Munich: Renner, 1985.
Ingwer und Jedoch: Texte aus diversem Anlass. Göttingen: Herodot, 1985.
Lesungen mit Tinnitus: Gedichte 1980-1985. Munich: Hanser, 1986.
Jalousien aufgemacht: Ein Lesebuch. Munich: Hanser, 1987.
Eine Scheibe Dingsbums: Gedichte. Ravensburg: Maier, 1990.
Kopfnuss Januskopf: Gedichte in Palindromen. Munich: Hanser, 1990.
Poèmepoèmes. Brussels: TXT, 1990.
Feiggehege: Listen, Schnüre, Häufungen. Berlin: Literarisches Colloquium, 1991.
Urologe kuesst Nabelstrang: Verstreute Anagramme 1979-1989. Augsburg: Maro Verlag, 1991.
Der Fakir als Anfänger: Gedichte undAnsichten. Munich: Hanser, 1992.
Vokalisen & Gimpelstifte. Munich: Hanser, 1992.
Das Unding an sich. Frankfurt: Suhrkamp, 1994.
Eine kleine Kunstmaschine: 34 Sestinen. Munich: Hanser, 1994.
In English:

Poempoems. London: Atlas Press, 1990.

GEORGES PEREC was born on 7 March 1936 into a family of Polish Jews who had emigrated to France in the 1920s. His father died at the front in 1940 on the day of the armistice; his mother and other members of his family were murdered in the Nazi camps. Perec studied sociology at the Sorbonne and later worked as a research librarian in neurophysiology at the Centre National de la Recherche Scientifique, where he remained until 1979. His first published novel, *Les choses,* won the Prix Renaudot and was translated into sixteen languages. He joined the Oulipo in 1967, and was awarded the Prix Médicis in 1978 for *La vie mode d'emploi.* Apart from the works listed below, Perec was active in film, musical theater, translation, and radio plays; he contributed the weekly crossword puzzle to *Le Point* from 1976 until his death on 3 March 1982.

Les choses: Une histoire des années soixante. Paris: Julliard, 1965.
Quel petit vélo à guidon chromé au fond de la cour? Paris: Denoël, 1966.
Un homme qui dort. Paris: Denoël, 1967.
La disparition. Paris: Denoël, 1969.
Petit traité invitant à la découverte de l'art subtil du go. With Pierre
  Lusson and Jacques Roubaud. Paris: Bourgois, 1969.
Die Maschine. Trans. Eugen Helmlé. Stuttgart: Reclam, 1972.
Les revenentes. Paris: Julliard, 1972.
La boutique obscure: 124 rêves. Paris: Denoël, 1973.
Espèces d'espaces: Journal d'un usager de l'espace. Paris: Galilée,
  1974.
Alphabets. Paris: Galilée, 1975.
W ou le souvenir d'enfance. Paris: Denoël, 1975.
Je me souviens. Paris: Hachette, 1978.
La vie mode d'emploi. Paris: Hachette, 1978.
Un cabinet d'amateur: Histoire d'un tableau. Paris: Balland, 1979.
Les mots croisés. Paris: Mazarine, 1979.
La clôture et autres poèmes. Paris: Hachette, 1980.
Récits d'Ellis Island: Histoires d'errance et d'espoir. With Robert
  Bober. Paris: Sorbier, 1980
Théâtre I. Paris: Hachette, 1981.
Tentative d'épuisement d'un lieu parisien. Paris: Bourgois, 1982.
Penser/Classer: Textes du XXᵉ siècle. Paris: Hachette, 1985.
Les mots croisés II. Paris: POL and Mazarine, 1986.
"53 jours." Paris: POL, 1989.
L'infra-ordinaire. Paris: Seuil, 1989.
Voeux. Paris: Seuil, 1989.

Je suis né. Paris: Seuil, 1990.

Cantatrix Sopranica L. et autres écrits scientifiques. Paris: Seuil, 1991.

L. G.: Une aventure des années soixante. Paris: Seuil, 1992.

Cahier des charges de La vie mode d'emploi. Ed. Hans Hartje, Bernard Magné, and Jacques Neefs. Paris and Cadeilhan: CNRS and Zulma, 1993.

Le voyage d'hiver. Paris: Seuil, 1993.

Beaux présents, belles absentes. Paris: Seuil, 1994.

"Cher, très cher, admirable et charmant ami..." With Jacques Lederer. Paris: Flammarion, 1997.

Perec/rinations. Cadeilhan: Zulma, 1997.

In English:

Les Choses: A Story of the Sixties. Trans. Helen Lane. New York: Grove, 1967.

Life A User's Manual. Trans. David Bellos. Boston: Godine, 1987.

W, or The Memory of Childhood. Trans. David Bellos. Boston: Godine, 1988.

Things: A Story of the Sixties and A Man Asleep. Trans. David Bellos. Boston: Godine, 1990.

"53 Days." Trans. David Bellos. London: Harvill, 1992.

A Void. Trans. Gilbert Adair. London: Harvill, 1994.

RAYMOND QUENEAU was born on 21 February 1903 in Le Havre. He studied literature, philosophy, psychology, and sociology at the Sorbonne and frequented the Surrealist group in the mid-1920s (he broke with the Surrealists in 1930). In 1941, Queneau became General Secretary of the Gallimard publishing house. The same year, Picasso's *Le désir attrapé par la queue* was performed at Michel Leiris's home; Queneau played The Onion. His friendship with Noël Arnaud and François Le Lionnais dates from the following year. He joined the Collège de 'Pataphysique in 1950, where he was to become a Transcendent Satrap. In 1956, Gallimard proposed the Encyclopédie de la Pléiade, for which Queneau was to be principally responsible. He cofounded the Oulipo with François Le Lionnais in 1960. Raymond Queneau died on 25 October 1976.

Un cadavre. With Jacques Baron, Georges Bataille, J. A. Boiffard, Robert Desnos, Michel Leiris, Georges Limbour, Max Morise, Jacques Prévert, Georges Ribemont-Dessaignes, and Roger Vitrac. Paris: 1930.

Le chiendent. Paris: Gallimard, 1933.

Gueule de Pierre. Paris: Gallimard, 1934.

Les derniers jours. Paris: Gallimard, 1936.

Chêne et chien. Paris: Denoël, 1937.

Odile. Paris: Gallimard, 1937.

Les enfants du limon. Paris: Gallimard, 1938.

Un rude hiver. Paris: Gallimard, 1939.

Les temps mêlés. Paris: Gallimard, 1941.

Pierrot mon ami. Paris: Gallimard, 1942.

Les ziaux. Paris: Gallimard, 1943.

En passant. Lyon: Barbezat, 1944.

Foutaises. Lyon: Barbezat, 1944.

Loin de Rueil. Paris: Gallimard, 1944.

A la limite de la forêt. Paris: Fontaine, 1947.

Bucoliques. Paris: Gallimard, 1947.

Exercices de style. Paris: Gallimard, 1947.

On est toujours trop bon avec les femmes. Paris: Scorpion, 1947.

Une trouille verte. Paris: Minuit, 1947.

Le cheval troyen. Paris: Visat, 1948.

L'instant fatal. Paris: Gallimard, 1948.

Monuments. Paris: Moustié, 1948.

Petite suite. Paris: Gallimard, 1948.

"La place des mathématiques dans la classification des sciences." In *Les grands courants de la pensée mathgmatique*. Ed. François Le Lionnais. Paris: Cahiers du Sud, 1948.

Saint Glinglin. Paris: Gallimard, 1948.

Rendez-vous de juillet. With Jean Queval. Paris: Chavane, 1949.

Texticules. Paris: Galerie Louise Leiris, 1949.

Bâtons, chiffres et lettres. Paris Gallimard, 1950. Rev. ed., Paris: Gallimard, 1965.

Le journal intime de Sally Mara. Paris: Scorpion, 1950.

Petite cosmogonie portative. Paris: Gallimard, 1950.

Le dimanche de la vie. Paris: Gallimard, 1952.

Si tu t'imagines. Paris: Gallimard, 1952.

Histoire des littératures. Ed. Raymond Queneau. Paris: Gallimard, 1956.

Lorsque l'esprit. Paris: Collège de 'Pataphysique, 1956.

Pour une bibliothèque idéale. Paris: Gallimard, 1956.

Le chien à la mandoline. Verviers: Temps Mêlés, 1958.

Sonnets. Paris: Hautefeuille, 1958.

Zazie dans le métro. Paris: Gallimard, 1959.

Cent mille milliards de poèmes. Afterword by François Le Lionnais. Paris: Gallimard, 1961.

Entretiens avec Georges Charbonnier. Paris: Gallimard, 1962.

Les oeuvres complètes de Sally Mara. Paris: Gallimard, 1962. [Includes *On est toujours trop bon avec les femmes, Le Journal intime de Sally Mara,* and *Foutaises.*]

Bords. Paris: Hermann, 1963.

"Sur la multiplication croisée de spécimens. . ." *Temps Mêlés* 66-67 (1964).

Les fleurs bleues. Paris: Gallimard, 1965.

"Note complémentaire sur la sextine." *Subsidia 'Pataphysica* 1 (1965).

"Boule de neige." *Subsidia 'Pataphysica* 2 (1966).

Une histoire modèle. Paris: Gallimard, 1966.

Meccano ou l'analyse matricielle du langage. Illustrations by Enrico Baj. Milan: Sergio Tosi and Paolo Bellasich, 1966.

"Notre ami." *Réforme,* February 1966. [On Albert-Marie Schmidt.]

"Un conte à votre façon." *Les Lettres Nouvelles,* July-September 1967. [Reprinted in Oulipo, *La littérature potentielle.*]

Courir les rues. Paris: Gallimard, 1967.

"Poésie et mathématiques." *Le Monde,* 18 May 1967.

Battre la campagne. Paris: Gallimard, 1968.

Le vol d'Icare. Paris: Gallimard, 1968.

Fendre les flots. Paris: Gallimard, 1969.

"David Hilbert." In *Enzyklopädie die Grossen der Weltgeschichte.* Zurich: Kindler Verlag, 1971.

"De quelques langages animaux et notamment du langage chien dans *Sylvie et Bruno.*" *L'Herne* 17 (1971).

"La relation x prend y pour z." *Subsidia 'Pataphysica* 5 (1972). [Reprinted in part and modified in Oulipo, *La Littérature potentielle.*]

Le voyage en Grèce. Paris: Gallimard, 1973.

Classification des travaux de l'Oulipo. Poster distributed at Europalia 75. London Imprimerie, 1974. [Reprinted in Oulipo, *Atlas de littérature potentielle.*]

"Qu'est-ce que l'Oulipo?" Interview with François Le Lionnais and Raymond Queneau. *L'Education* 209 (1974).

Morale élémentaire. Paris: Gallimard, 1975.

Contes et propos. Paris: Gallimard, 1981.

Journal 1939-1940. Paris: Gallimard, 1986.

Oeuvres complètes. Vol. 1. Paris: Gallimard, 1989.

Gustave le Bon. Limoges: Sixtus, 1990.

Dormi pleure. Bordeaux: Le Castor Astral, 1996.

Journaux 1914-1965. Paris: Gallimard, 1996.

In English:

A Hard Winter. Trans. Betty Askwith. London: Lehmann, 1948.

The Skin of Dreams. Trans. H. J. Kaplan. New York: New Directions, 1948.

Pierrot. Trans. J. Maclaren-Ross. London: Lehmann, 1950.

The Trojan Horse and At the Edge of the Forest. Trans. Barbara Wright.

London: Gaberbocchus, 1954.
Exercises in Style. Trans. Barbara Wright. New York: New Directions, 1958.
Zazie. Trans. Barbara Wright. New York: Harper, 1960.
The Blue Flowers. Trans. Barbara Wright. New York: Atheneum, 1967.
The Bark Tree. Trans. Barbara Wright. New York: New Directions, 1971.
The Flight of Icarus. Trans. Barbara Wright. New York: New Directions, 1973.
The Sunday of Life. Trans. Barbara Wright. New York: New Directions, 1977.
We Always Treat Women Too Well. Trans. Barbara Wright. New York: New Directions, 1981.
One Hundred Million Million Poems. Trans. John Crombie. Paris: Kickshaws, 1983.
Pounding the Pavements, Beating the Bushes, and other 'Pataphysical Poems. Trans. Teo Savory. Greensboro, North Carolina: Unicorn Press, 1985.
Odile. Trans. Carol Sanders. Normal, IL: Dalkey Archive Press, 1988.
Pierrot Mon Ami. Trans. Barbara Wright. Normal, IL: Dalkey Archive Press, 1989.
The Last Days. Trans. Barbara Wright. London: Atlas, 1990; Normal, IL: Dalkey Archive Press, 1990.
Saint Glinglin. Trans. James Sallis. Normal, IL: Dalkey Archive Press, 1993.
Raymond Queneau's Chêne et chien: *A Translation with Commentary.* Trans. Madeleine Velguth. New York: Land, 1995.
Children of Clay. Trans. Madeleine Velguth. Los Angeles, CA: Sun & Moon Press, 1998.

JEAN QUEVAL was born in Paris in 1913. He wrote poems, novels, plays, and critical essays. Queval was also very active in translating things as diverse as *Beowulf,* Iris Murdoch, and texts from Swedish. He won the Hans Christian Andersen Translation Prize and the Prix MacOrlan. A founding member of the Oulipo, Jean Queval died in December 1990.

Communauté d'entreprise. Paris: Fayard, 1943.
Première page, cinquième colonne. Paris: Fayard, 1945.
L'air de Londres. Paris: Julliard, 1947.
Rendez-vous de juillet. With Raymond Queneau. Paris: Chavane, 1949.
Jacques Prévert. Paris: Mercure de France, 1950.
Marcel Carne. Paris: Editions du Cerf, 1952.
De l'Angleterre. Paris: Gallimard, 1956.

TV. Paris: Gallimard, 1957.

Tout le monde descend. Paris: Mercure de France, 1959.

Essai sur Raymond Queneau. Paris: Seghers, 1960.

Jacques Becker. Paris: Seghers, 1962.

Etc. Paris: Gallimard, 1963.

Lieux-dits. Paris: Mercure de France, 1963.

Le point. Verviers: Temps Mêlés, 1967.

Lexique des dieux. Paris: Delpire, 1968.

Max-Pol Fouchet. Paris: Seghers, 1969.

En somme. Paris: Gallimard, 1970.

Raymond Queneau. Paris: Seghers, 1971.

Henri Storck, ou, La traversée du cinéma. Brussels: Festival National du Film Belge, 1976.

"Queneau, discours et rêve." *Nouvelle Revue Française* 290 (1977).

Raymond Queneau, portrait d'un poète. Paris: Veyrier, 1984.

Tout est bien qui finit mieux. Paris: Bordas, 1984.

Nestor et Agamemnon. Paris: Messidor, 1986.

In English:

Marcel Carne. London: British Film Institute, 1950.

PIERRE ROSENSTIEHL is a mathematician who specializes in the theory of labyrinths and graphs. He is a Directeur d'Etudes in mathematics at the Ecole des Hautes Etudes en Sciences Sociales. He joined the Oulipo in 1986.

Les choix économiques: Décisions séquentielles et simulation. With Alain Ghouila-Houri, and the collaboration of D. A. Emery et al. Paris: Dunod, 1960.

Mathématiques de l'action, langage des ensembles des statistiques et des aléas. Paris: Dunod, 1965.

Paris-Pékin par le Transsibérien. Paris: Gallimard, 1980.

L'à-peu-près: Aspects anciens et modernes de l'approximation. Paris: Ecole des Hautes Etudes en Sciences Sociales, 1988.

In English:

Mathematics in Management: The Language of Sets, Statistics and Variables. Amsterdam: North Holland, 1969.

Recilinear Planar Layouts of Planar Graphs and Bipolar Orientations. Princeton: Princeton University Department of Computer Science, 1985.

JACQUES ROUBAUD is a poet, novelist, critic, and a professor of mathematics at the Université de Paris. He joined the Oulipo in 1966. He currently teaches poetics at Ecole des Hautes Etudes en Sciences Sociales.

E Paris: Gallimard, 1967.

"Morphismes rationnels et algébriques dans les types d'A-algèbres discrets à une dimension." *Publications de l'Institut de Statistique de l'Université de Paris* 17.4 (1968).

Petit traité invitant à la découverte de l'art subtil du go. With Pierre Lusson and Georges Perec. Paris: Bourgois, 1969.

Mono no aware: Le sentiment des choses. Paris: Gallimard, 1970.

Trente et un au cube. Paris: Gallimard, 1973.

"Un problème combinatoire posé par la poésie lyrique des troubadours." *Mathématiques et Sciences Humaines* 27 (n. d.).

"Quelques méthodes anciennes et nouvelles de traduction à partir du français." *Change* 19 (1974).

Etoffe. Geneva: G. K. Editions, 1975.

Mezura. Paris: Atelier, 1975.

Tombeau de Pétrarque. Paris: Solaire, 1975.

Autobiographie, chapitre dix. Paris: Gallimard, 1977.

"La mathématique dans la méthode de Raymond Queneau." *Critique* 359 (1977). [Reprinted in Oulipo, *Atlas de littérature potentielle.*]

Graal fiction. Paris: Gallimard, 1978.

La vieillesse d'Alexandre: Essai sur quelques états récents du vers français. Paris: Maspero, 1978.

"Préparation d'un portrait formel de Georges Perec." *L'Arc* 76 (1979).

"L'aventure de l'astronome" and "Poutsas du soir." [Chapters 3 and 4 of *La princesse Hoppy ou Le conte du Labrador.*] *Change* 38 (1980).

Vingt poètes américains. Ed. Michel Deguy and Jacques Roubaud. Paris: Gallimard, 1980.

Dors, précédé de Dire la poésie. Paris: Gallimard, 1981.

Les troubadours. Paris: Seghers, 1981.

Les animaux de tout le monde. Paris: Ramsay, 1983.

La belle Hortense. Paris: Ramsay, 1985.

La fleur inverse: Essai sur l'art formel des troubadours. Paris: Ramsay, 1986.

Quelque chose noir. Paris: Gallimard, 1986.

L'enlèvement d'Hortense. Paris: Ramsay, 1987.

Le grand incendie de Londres. Paris: Seuil, 1989.

La princesse Hoppy ou Le conte du Labrador. Paris: Hatier, 1990.

L'exil d'Hortense. Paris: Seghers, 1990.

Les animaux de personne. Paris: Seghers, 1991.

La pluralité des mondes de Lewis. Paris: Gallimard, 1991.

La boucle. Paris: Seuil, 1993.

Monsieur Goodman rêve de chats. Paris: Gallimard, 1994.

Poésie, etcetera, ménage. Paris: Stock, 1995.

L'abominable tisonnier de John McTaggart Ellis McTaggart. Paris: Seuil, 1997.

Mathématique:. Paris: Seuil, 1997.

(...(((Titre provisoire(titre provisoire))(titre provisoire))...)(titre provisoire). Paris: Editions Plurielle, 1997.

In English:

Our Beautiful Heroine. Trans. David Kornacker. Woodstock, New York: Overlook Press, 1987.

Hortense Is Abducted. Trans. Dominic Di Bernardi. Elmwood Park, IL: Dalkey Archive Press, 1989.

Some Thing Black. Trans. Rosmarie Waldrop. Elmwood Park, IL: Dalkey Archive Press, 1990.

The Great Fire of London. Trans. Dominic Di Bernardi. Normal, IL: Dalkey Archive Press, 1991.

Hortense in Exile. Trans. Dominic Di Bernardi. Normal, IL: Dalkey Archive Press, 1992.

The Princess Hoppy or, The Tale of Labrador. Trans. Bernard Hœpffner. Normal, IL: Dalkey Archive Press, 1993.

The Plurality of Worlds of Lewis. Trans. Rosmarie Waldrop. Normal, IL: Dalkey Archive Press, 1995.

ALBERT-MARIE SCHMIDT was born in Paris on 16 October 1901. In 1922, he earned a Diplôme d'Etudes Supérieures, with a thesis on French translations of Plato between 1536 and 1550. From 1922 on, he participated in the famous Pontigny (later to become Cerisy) Colloquia, where he met André Gide, Roger Martin du Gard, and others. He taught at the Ecole Alsacienne and defended his doctoral thesis, *La poésie scientifique en France au XVIᵉ siècle* in 1939. He taught at the Université de Caen and, from 1945 until his death, was a professor of literature at the Université de Lille. Schmidt was a founding member of the Oulipo; moreover, it was he who proposed that the name "Ouvroir de Littérature Potentielle" replace "Séminaire de Littérature Expérimentale." Schmidt placed his enormous literary erudition at the disposal of the group. He was a specialist in all forms of literature under constraint, in particular the work of the Grands Rhétoriqueurs and the Baroque poets. He and Noël Arnaud were principally responsible for the History of Experimental Literature project; at his death, the project was temporarily abandoned (it will be pursued by Noël Arnaud and Jacques Roubaud). Albert-Marie Schmidt died on 8 February 1966.

Saint-Evremond ou l'humaniste impur. Paris: Cavalier, 1932.

Jean Calvin: Trois traités. Ed. Albert-Marie Schmidt. Paris: Je Sers, 1935.

Pierre de Ronsard: Hymne des Daimons. Ed. Albert-Marie Schmidt. Paris: Albin Michel, 1938.

La poésie scientifique en France au XVIᵉ siècle. Paris: Albin Michel, 1938.

La jeune poésie et ses harmoniques. Ed. Albert-Marie Schmidt. Paris: Albin Michel, 1942.

La littérature symboliste. Paris: Presses Universitaires de France, 1942.

"Haute science et poésie française au seizième siècle." *Les Cahiers d'Hermès* 1 (1947).

"Théologie et préciosité dans les sonnets de Laurent Drelincourt." *Les Cahiers d'Hermès* 2 (1947).

Poètes et romanciers du moyen âge. With Albert Pauphilet and Régine Pernoud. Paris: Gallimard, 1952.

Poètes du XVIᵉ siècle. Paris: Gallimard, 1953.

Jean Calvin et la tradition calvinienne. Paris: Seuil, 1957.

"La littérature humaniste à l'époque de la Renaissance." In Raymond Queneau, ed., *Histoire des littératures.* Vol. 3. 165-254. Paris: Gallimard, 1958.

La mandragore. Paris: Flammarion, 1958.

L'amour noir. Ed. Albert-Marie Schmidt. Monaco: Rocher, 1959.

Maupassant: Romans. Ed. Albert-Marie Schmidt. Paris: Albin Michel, 1959.

Maupassant par lui-même. Paris: Seuil, 1962.

Francesco Colonna: Le songe de Poliphile. Ed. Albert-Marie Schmidt. Paris: Club des Libraires de France, 1963.

Le roman de Renart. Ed. Albert-Marie Schmidt. Paris: Albin Michel, 1963.

Pierre de Ronsard: Les amours. Ed. Albert-Marie Schmidt. Paris: Gallimard, 1964.

XIVᵉ et XVᵉ siècles français: Les sources de l'humanisme. Paris: Seghers, 1964.

Crébillon: Le Sopha. Ed. Albert-Marie Schmidt. Paris: U.G. E., 1966.

Etudes sur le XVIᵉ siècle. Ed. Albert-Marie Schmidt. Paris: Albin Michel,1967.

Paracelse ou la force qui va. Paris: Plon, 1967.

Chronique de la Réforme. Lausanne: Rencontre, 1970.

In English:

John Calvin and the Calvinistic Tradition. Trans. Ronald Wallace. New York: Harper, 1960.

COLLECTIVE WORKS

"Exercices de littérature potentielle." In *Dossiers du Collège de 'Pataphysique* 17 (1961).

"Oulipo." *Temps Mêlés* 66-67 (1964).

La littérature potentielle: Créations, recréations, récréations. Paris: Gallimard, 1973.

Atlas de littérature potentielle. Paris: Gallimard, 1981.

The "Bibliothèque Oulipienne" (1974 to the present; each volume is printed in a limited edition of 150 copies):

1 Georges Perec, *Ulcérations.*
2 Jacques Roubaud, *La princesse Hoppy ou Le conte du Labrador.*
3 Raymond Queneau, *Les fondements de la littérature d'après David Hilbert.*
4 Oulipo, *A Raymond Queneau.*
5 Harry Mathews, *Le savoir des rois.*
6 Italo Calvino, *Piccolo Sillabario Illustrato.*
7 Jacques Roubaud, *La princesse Hoppy ou Le conte du Labrador. Chapitre 2: Myrtilles et Béryl.*
8 Paul Fournel, *Elémentaire moral.*
9 Paul Braffort, *Mes hypertropes.*
10 Paul Fournel and Jacques Roubaud, *L'Hôtel de Sens.*
11 Jacques Bens, *Rendez-vous chez François.*
12 Noël Arnaud, *Souvenirs d'un vieil Oulipien.*
13 Marcel Bénabou, *Un aphorisme peut en cacher un autre.*
14 Jacques Duchateau, *Les sept coups du tireur à la ligne en apocalypse lent, occupé à lire "Monnaie de singe" de William Faulkner.*
15 Jacques Roubaud, *Io et le loup.*
16 Oulipo, *La cantatrice sauve.*
17 Jacques Duchateau, *Sanctuaire à tiroirs.*
18 Paul Braffort, *Le désir (les désirs) dans l'ordre des amours.*
19 Georges Perec, *Epithalames.*
20 Italo Calvino, *Comment j'ai écrit un de mes livres.*
21 Michèle Métail, *Portraits-robots.*
22 Claude Berge, *La princesse aztèque.*
23 Oulipo, *A Georges Perec.*
24 Jean Queval, *,;:!?!?!()[ ].*
25 Marcel Bénabou, *Locutions introuvables.*
26 Jacques Roubaud, *Le train traverse la nuit.*
27 Luc Etienne, *L'art du palindrome phonétique.*
28 Jacques Jouet, *L'éclipse.*

29 Marcel Bénabou, *Alexandre au greffoir.*

30 [There is no volume 30.]

31 Jean Queval, *Insecte contemplant la préhistoire.*

32 Jean Queval, *Ecrits sur mesure.*

33 Michèle Métail, *Cinquante poèmes corpusculaires.*

34 Michèle Métail, *Filigranes.*

35 Michèle Métail, *Cinquante poèmes oscillatoires.*

36 Jean Lescure, *Ultra crepidam.*

37 François Caradec, *Fromage ou dessert?*

38 Jacques Jouet, *L'oulipien démasqué.*

39 Michèle Métail, *Petit atlas géo-homophonique des départements de la France métropolitaine et d'outre-mer.*

40 Marcel Bénabou, *Bris de mots.*

41 Jacques Roubaud, *Vers une oulipisation conséquente de la littérature.*

42 Noël Arnaud, *Le dernier compte rendu.*

43 Jacques Roubaud, *Secondes litanies de la Vierge.*

44 Jacques Jouet, *Espions.*

45 François Caradec, *La voie du troisième secteur.*

46 Paul Fournel, *Banlieue.*

47 Jacques Roubaud, *La disposition numérologique du* rerum vulgarium fragmenta, *précédé d'une vie brève de François Pétrarque.*

48 Paul Braffort, *Les bibliothèques invisibles.*

49 François Caradec, *Veuillez trouver ci-inclus.*

50 Michèle Métail, *Cinquante poèmes oligogrammes.*

51 Harry Mathews, *Ecrits français.*

52 Jacques Jouet, *Les sept règles de Perec.*

53 Jacques Roubaud, *Le voyage d'hier.*

54 Oulipo, *S + 7, le retour.*

55 Oulipo, *Autres morales élémentaires.*

56 Jacques Jouet, *Glose de la Comtesse de Die et de Didon.*

57 Harry Mathews, *Une soirée oulipienne.*

58 Paul Braffort, *Trente-quatre brazzles.*

59 Marcel Bénabou, *Rendre à Cézanne.*

60 François Caradec, *105 proverbes liftés, suivis de quelques proverbes soldés.*

61 Jacques Roubaud, *Crise de théâtre.*

62 Jacques Jouet, *Le chant d'amour grand-singe, recueilli, traduit et commenté par Jacques Jouet.*

63 Noël Arnaud, *Gérard Genette et l'Oulipo.*

64 Jacques Jouet and Jacques Roubaud, *[ə].*

65 Oulipo, *N-ines, autrement dit quenines.*

66 Jacques Roubaud, *N-ine, autrement dit quenine (encore).*

67 Claude Berge, *Qui a tué le duc de Densmore?*

68 Oulipo, *Troll de tram (le tramway de Strasbourg).*

69 Jacques Duchateau, *Le cordon de saint François.*

70 Harry Mathews, *A l'oeil.*

71 Oulipo, *Bibliothèques invisibles, toujours.*

72 Jacques Jouet, *Monostication de La Fontaine.*

73 Oskar Pastior, *Spielregel, Wildwuchs, Translation (Règle du jeu, Ulcérations, Translations).*

74 Hervé Le Tellier, *Mille pensées (premiers cents).*

75 Michelle Grangaud, *Formes de l'anagramme.*

76 Michelle Grangaud, *D'une petite haie, si possible belle, aux Regrets.*

77 Hervé Le Tellier, *A bas Carmen!*

78 Jacques Jouet, *Une chambre close.*

79 Oulipo, *La guirlande de Paul.*

80 Jacques Bens, *L'art de la fuite.*

81 Jacques Roubaud, *Trois ruminations.*

82 Jacques Jouet, *Exercices de la mémoire.*

83 Jacques Roubaud, *La terre est plate, 99 dialogues dramatiques, mais brefs, précédé de Petite rumination du 150.*

84 Hervé Le Tellier, *Un sourire indéfinissable, Mona Lisa, dite La Joconde, sous 53 jours différents.*

85 François Le Lionnais, *Un certain disparate (fragments), suivi d'un témoignage de Jacques Roubaud.*

86 Walter Henry [Paul Braffort], *Chu dans la mer sale ou la rumination polymorphe.*

87 Marcel Bénabou, *L'Hannibal perdu.*

88 Jacques Bens, *J'ai oublié.*

89 Claude Berge, *Raymond Queneau et la combinatoire.*

90 Oulipo, *Sexe: ce xé.*

91 Georges Perec, Harry Mathews, and Oskar Pastior, *Variations, variations, variationen.*

La Bibliothèque Oulipienne. Collects and reprints volumes 1-16. Geneva: Slatkine, 1981.

La Bibliothèque Oulipienne. Vol. 1. Collects and reprints volumes 1-18. Paris: Ramsay, 1987.

La Bibliothèque Oulipienne. Vol. 2. Collects and reprints volumes 19-37. Paris: Ramsay, 1987.

La Bibliothèque Oulipienne. Vol. 3. Collects and reprints volumes 38-52. Paris: Seghers, 1990.

La Bibliothèque Oulipienne. Vol. 4. Collects and reprints volumes 53-62. Bordeaux: Le Castor Astral, 1997.

In English:

Oulipo Laboratory: Texts from the Bibliothèque Oulipienne. Trans. Harry Mathews, Warren F. Motte, Jr., and Iain White. Intro. Alastair Brotchie. London: Atlas, 1995. [Includes translations of François Le Lionnais's "Two Manifestos" and volumes 3, 20, 46, 62, 67, and 70 of the Bibliothèque Oulipienne.]

Notes

. . . .

INTRODUCTION

1. In alphabetical order: Noël Arnaud, Jacques Bens, Claude Berge, Jacques Duchateau, Latis, François Le Lionnais, Jean Lescure, Raymond Queneau, Jean Queval, Albert-Marie Schmidt.

2. The new members: Marcel Bénabou, André Blavier, Paul Braffort, Italo Calvino, François Caradec, Ross Chambers, Stanley Chapman, Marcel Duchamp, Luc Etienne, Paul Fournel, Jacques Jouet, Harry Mathews, Michèle Métail, Georges Perec, Jacques Roubaud. It must be noted that the Oulipo draws no distinction between living and dead members; Italo Calvino, Marcel Duchamp, Luc Etienne, Latis, François Le Lionnais, Georges Perec, Raymond Queneau, and Albert-Marie Schmidt are now deceased.

3. See "Entretien: Perec / Jean-Marie Le Sidaner," *L'Arc* 76 (1979): 7. (All translations are mine unless otherwise specified.)

4. According to some, the first utterance on earth, addressed by Adam to Eve, was a palindrome: "Madam, I'm Adam." Although this theory may seem rather esoteric to non-Anglophones, it rejoins a broader tradition of myth which postulates the formal purity and rigor of original language. See Claude-Gilbert Dubois, *Mythe et langage au seizième siècle* (Bordeaux: Ducros, 1970).

5. See "Deux Principes parfois respectés par les travaux oulipiens," *Atlas de littérature potentielle*, 90. (For full references to Oulipian works, see the bibliographies in the foregoing section, "Oulipians and Their Works.")

6. "Entretien: Perec / Jean-Marie Le Sidaner," 8. In fact, only one of Perec's poems, entitled simply "Un Poème," seems to have been written freely. See his *La Clôture et autres poèmes*, 85.

7. See Paul Braffort, "Un Système formel pour l'algorithmique littéraire," *Atlas de littérature potentielle*, 110.

8. See Harold Bloom, *The Anxiety of Influence* (New York: Oxford University Press, 1973), 14–16, 19–45; *Kabbalah and Criticism* (New York: Seabury, 1975), 25–27, 36–37, 54–55, 62–67, 78–79, 86–89, 122–23; *A Map of Misreading* (New York: Oxford University Press, 1975), 70–75, 84, 95–99, 106–09, 126, 149, 179, 195, 200; *Poetry and Repression* (New Haven: Yale University Press, 1976), 1, 16–21, 47, 66, 99–100, 124–26, 164, 183, 223, 248–49; *Agon: Toward a Theory of Revisionism* (New York: Oxford University Press, 1982), 200–223; *The Breaking of the Vessels* (Chicago: University of Chicago Press, 1982), 23–31. See also Michel Serres, *La Naissance de la physique dans le texte de Lucrèce: Fleuves et turbulences* (Paris: Minuit, 1977), and "Lucretius: Science and Religion," in *Hermes: Literature, Science, Philosophy,* ed. Josué V. Harari and David Bell (Baltimore, Md.: Johns Hopkins University Press, 1982), 98–124; Jeffrey Mehlman, *Cataract: A Study in Diderot* (Middletown, Conn.: Wes-

leyan University Press, 1979), esp. 1–32. Essays from the Thom polemic are offered in *Sub-Stance* 40 (1983).

9. "Entretien: Perec / Ewa Pawlikowska," *Littératures* 7 (1983): 70–71.

LIPO: FIRST MANIFESTO

1. How can sap rise in a debate? We shall leave this question aside, since it arises not from poetry but from vegetal physiology.

2. The Lettrists, as the name suggests, focused their aesthetics on the alphabetical letter. See Isidore Isou, *Le Lettrisme et l'hypergraphie dans la peinture et la sculpture contemporaines* (Paris: Grassin, 1961), *Les Champs de force de la peinture lettriste: Nouvelles Précisions sur la mécanique, le* [sic] *matière, le rythme et l'anecdote de l'hypergraphie* (Paris: R. Altmann, I. Isou, 1964), and *Ballets ciselants polythanasiques, hypergraphiques et infinitésimaux* (Paris: R. Altmann, I. Isou, 1965). See also Maurice Lemaître, *Le Lettrisme devant Dada et les nécrophages de Dada!* (Paris: Centre de Créativité, 1967) and *Le Lettrisme dans le roman et les arts plastiques, devant le "pop-art" et la bande dessinée* (Paris: Centre de Créativité, 1970). The latter constitutes the first number of the review *Lettrisme*, published by the Centre de Créativité. For a history of the movement, see Jean-Paul Curtay's excellent *La Poésie lettriste* (Paris: Seghers, 1974), esp. 68–98. (WM)

3. The Russian mathematician A. A. Markov (1856–1922), principally known for his work in theory of probability. (WM)

4. Raymond Queneau's *Cent Mille Milliards de poèmes,* discussed in the Introduction to the present volume. Boolian haikus: a literary application of the work of the British mathematician George Boole (1815–64). See François Le Lionnais, "Poèmes booléens" and "Théâtre booléen," *La Littérature potentielle,* 262–66 and 267–68. (WM)

5. "Crows, foxes" may be an allusion to La Fontaine's fable, "The Crow and the Fox." Nonetheless, François Le Lionnais was genuinely interested in animal language, and proposed to the Oulipo on 1 July 1963 that the group undertake to write poems using only those human vocables understood by certain animals: poems for dogs, for crows, for foxes, and so forth. This provoked the following exchange:

> Jean Lescure: "One of my clients, who trains racehorses, told me one day that he often reads Baudelaire to his horses, and they seem to adore it. . . ."
> Raymond Queneau: "That's what's called doping. It's because of Baudelaire that Off-Track Betting is going to Hell in a basket."

See Jacques Bens, *Oulipo 1960–1963,* 230–31. As to Algol, both Le Lionnais and Noël Arnaud experimented in the 1960s with Algol poems. See Le Lionnais, "Ivresse algolique," *La Littérature potentielle,* 217–22; Arnaud, "Poèmes algol," *La Littérature potentielle,* 223–27; and Bens, *Oulipo 1960–1963,* 54–55. (WM)

6. A fine autoreferential example of Villon's acrostics is furnished by the *envoi* of the "Ballade des contre-vérités":

Voulez vous que verté vous die?
Il n'est jouer qu'en maladie,
Lettre vraie que tragédie,
Lâche homme que chevalereux,
Orrible son que mélodie,
Ne bien conseillé qu'amoureux.

(Shall I tell you the truth?
There is no joy except in sickness,
No truth except in tragedy,
No coward like a brave man,
No sound more horrible than melody,
No wisdom except that of lovers.)

On the use of acrostics in Psalms and Lamentations, see Ralph Marcus, "Alphabetic Acrostics in the Hellenistic and Roman Periods," *Journal of Near Eastern Studies* 6 (1947): 109–15. Auguste Herbin (1882–1960) was a French painter. The B.A.C.H. acrostic was used by Bach in the theme of the last fugue of his *Art of the Fugue;* it was later adopted in works by Liszt, Schumann, Reger, and Barblan. See Albert Schweitzer, *J. S. Bach* (New York: Macmillan, 1935), I, 425. (WM)

SECOND MANIFESTO

1. A systematic exploration of the detective novel has already been undertaken in this perspective. [See François Le Lionnais, "Les Structures du roman policier: Qui est le coupable?" and Jacques Duchateau, "Lecture marginale de Peter Cheyney," *La Littérature potentielle,* 66–69 and 70–74, respectively. (WM)]

2. This is a bilingual homophonic translation of the first line of Keats's *Endymion:* "A thing of beauty is a joy for ever." Le Lionnais's ejaculation can be literally (if nonhomophonically) translated as: "A beautiful monkey is a toy for winter." (WM)

BRIEF HISTORY OF THE OULIPO

1. The Collège de Pataphysique takes its name from "pataphysics," the discipline proposed by Alfred Jarry, which he defined in his *Gestes et opinions du Docteur Faustroll* (II, viii) as "the science of imaginary solutions." Jarry himself spelled the word with an initial apostrophe, perhaps to suggest *épataphysique,* or "shocking physics." The Collège itself was founded on 11 May 1948, the fiftieth anniversary of *Faustroll;* its principal (if by no means exclusive) function is to promote work on Jarry. Publications of the group include the *Cahiers du Collège de Pataphysique* and the *Dossiers du Collège de Pataphysique.* See Linda Klieger Stillman, *Alfred Jarry* (Boston: Twayne, 1983), 41–42. Several of the founding members of the Oulipo held titles within the Collège de Pataphysique: Queneau, for example, was a Transcendent Satrap; Latis was the Private General Secretary to the Baron Vice-Curator; Noël Arnaud is the Regent of General Pataphysics and

the Clinic of Rhetoriconosis, as well as Major Conferant of the Order of the Grande Gidouille. (WM)

2. See Noël Arnaud, "Et naquit l'Ouvroir de Littérature Potentielle," in Jacques Bens, *Oulipo 1960–1963*, 8. (WM)

3. Raymond Queneau's first novel, published by Gallimard in 1933. (WM)

4. In the penultimate quatrain of his "Booz endormi," Victor Hugo rhymes *Jérimadeth* with *se demandait*. As the former place name figures in no known atlas, it has been conjectured that *Jérimadeth* may be read as *je rime à dait*, or "I rhyme with *dait*." (WM)

5. According to Bens's minutes, this meeting took place not on April 5 but on April 17. See *Oulipo 1960–1963*, 42–43. (WM)

6. Again, according to Bens, the date of the meeting was not April 20 but April 28. See *Oulipo 1960–1963*, 45–52. (WM)

7. Lady Godiva was a female tortoise who lived in François Le Lionnais's garden. See *Oulipo 1960–1963*, 71. (WM)

8. Baudelaire, of course.

9. Years become centuries in Oulipospeak. (WM)

10. Let us recall the names of the old ones: Noël Arnaud, Jacques Bens, Claude Berge, Paul Braffort, Jacques Duchateau, François Le Lionnais, Jean Lescure, Raymond Queneau, Jean Queval. Foreign correspondents: André Blavier, Ross Chambers, Stanley Chapman.

RULE AND CONSTRAINT

1. Queneau's attack was directed against André Breton and orthodox surrealism; see also "Raymond Queneau and the Amalgam of Mathematics and Literature" and "Mathematics in the Method of Raymond Queneau." Queneau, distressed by Breton's autocratic rule, left the surrealist group. Along with Jacques Baron, Georges Bataille, J.-A. Boiffard, Robert Desnos, Michel Leiris, Georges Limbour, Max Morise, Jacques Prévert, Georges Ribemont-Dessaignes, and Roger Vitrac, Queneau signed *Un Cadavre*, the 1930 pamphlet condemning Breton. Its language is very vituperative (if perhaps not quite as harsh as certain passages of Breton's *Second Manifesto*); the most commonly occurring epithets are *flic* (cop) and *curé* (priest). See Maurice Nadeau, *Histoire du surréalisme* (Paris: Seuil, 1964), 131–37. (WM)

2. Bénabou is of course alluding to *La Disparition*. (WM)

3. This diagram, previously unpublished, was furnished by Marcel Bénabou as a complement to "Rule and Constraint." The three circles should be imagined as rotating freely; thus, in elaborating a given structure, any combination of linguistic object, semantic object, and operation is possible. (WM)

THE COLLÈGE DE PATAPHYSIQUE AND THE OULIPO

1. See "Brief History of the Oulipo," n. 1. The text here translated served as the introduction to a body of work submitted by the Oulipo to the Collège de Pataphysique. (WM)

2. "Art is long! And life so short," *Faust*, I, 558–59. (WM)
3. See "Brief History of the Oulipo," n. 1. (WM)

POTENTIAL LITERATURE

1. A group of French mathematicians who worked and published collectively under the pseudonym of Nicolas Bourbaki. Principally dealing with set theory, Bourbaki's work was highly influential for the amateur and professional mathematicians in the Oulipo. (WM)
2. See Georges Perec's "History of the Lipogram" for discussions of these figures and their lipogrammatic works. (WM)
3. The philosopher H. M. Sheffer, who taught at Harvard, published a paper in 1913 in which he reduced all the symbols of sentential logic (e.g., "and," "or," "not," "if/then,") to a single stroke. Queneau evokes the Sheffer Stroke as a model of methodological elegance. (WM)
4. The German mathematician George Cantor (1845–1918), known for his work on the theory of numbers. (WM)
5. Literally, "leaves," "sun," "fickle," "banks," "vermilion," "sleep." (WM)
6. The catalogue of the Bibliothèque Nationale informed me that in 1867 he had published *L'Arithmétique de Mademoiselle Lili*.
7. Keith Bosley, in *Mallarmé: The Poems* (Harmondsworth: Penguin, 1977), 167–69, translates the sonnet as follows:

> Will lovely, lively, virginal today
> Shatter for us with a wing's drunken bow
> This hard, forgotten lake haunted in snow
> By the sheer ice of flocks not flown away!
>
> A swan that was remembers it is he
> Hopelessly yielding for all his fine show
> Because he did not sing which way to go
> When barren winter beamed its apathy.
>
> His neck will shake off that white agony
> Space deals out to the bird that will deny,
> But not earth's horror where the plumes are clamped.
>
> A ghost whom to this place his lights assign,
> He stiffens in the cold dream of contempt
> Donned amid useless exile by the Swan. (WM)

8. Here, I again rely on Keith Bosley (169–71):

> While high her sheer nails offer up their pink
> Agate this midnight, lanternary Anguish
> Upholds a crowd of evening dreams now sunk
> In phoenix fires: no urn gathers their ash

On sideboards in the empty room, no conch,
No cancelled trinket resonantly foolish
(The Master took it to the Styx to drink
Tears for the Void regards all else as trash).

But near the blank north casement a gold gash
Gasps where perhaps painted unicorns lash
Fire cornering a nymph, dead, naked, lank

In the mirror, while still in the frame's ambush
Obliviously embraced, the septet wink
And forthwith in their distant fastness flash. (WM)

9. The entire text of Athalie's dream (from Racine's *Athalie*, II, v) is as follows:

C'était pendant l'horreur d'une profonde nuit.
Ma mère Jézabel devant moi s'est montrée,
Comme au jour de sa mort pompeusement parée.
Ses malheurs n'avaient point abattu sa fierté;
Même elle avait encor cet éclat emprunté
Dont elle eut soin de peindre et d'orner son visage,
Pour réparer des ans l'irréparable outrage.
Tremble, m'a-t-elle dit, *fille digne de moi.*
Le cruel Dieu des Juifs l'emporte aussi sur toi.
Je te plains de tomber dans ses mains redoutables,
Ma fille. En achevant ces mots épouvantables,
Son ombre vers mon lit a paru se baisser;
Et moi, je lui tendais les mains pour l'embrasser.
Mais je n'ai plus trouvé qu'un horrible mélange
D'os et de chair meurtris, et traînés dans la fange,
Des lambeaux pleins de sang, et des membres affreux. . . .

Samuel Solomon's translation of this passage, from *Jean Racine: Complete Plays*
(New York: Random House, 1967), II, 400, is as follows:

It was a brooding, horror-breathing night.
My mother Jezebel appeared before me,
Arrayed in pomp, as on the day she died.
Her pride was quite untamed by her misfortunes;
Immaculate as ever were the unguents
With which she never failed to deck her face
To hide the hideous ravages of time.
"Tremble," she said to me, "my worthy daughter.
You, too, the cruel Jewish God must slaughter.
I pity you, when in His fearful hands
You fall, my child." With these words, big with dread,
Her spirit seemed to lean towards my bed;
And I, I stretched my hands out to embrace her.
Yet all I found was but a horrid mush

Of bones and mangled flesh, dragged in the slush,
Of bloody strips, and limbs all shameless scarred. . . .(WM)

10. The efficacy of transformations of this sort depends largely on the shock they produce as they run into the original: that is, the reader must ideally "hear" the original and the transformation simultaneously, and the latter must jar the former (this is also true of the S + 7 Method). To produce this effect, the *untransformed* part of the new text (in Queneau's example, the vocalic structure) must follow the original faithfully. Granted this, literal translation of the passage would not be effective. (WM)

11. Named after Leonardo of Pisa, also known as Fibonacci, a thirteenth-century Italian mathematician, author of *Liber Abaci*. In a Fibonacci series, the first two terms are chosen arbitrarily (although by convention they are generally either 0 and 1 or 1 and 1); each term thereafter is the sum of the two preceding terms, for example, 1, 1, 2, 3, 5, 8, 13, 21, 34, 55, etc. Perhaps Fibonacci's greatest achievement was his popularization in the Western world of the Hindu-Arabic numerals. (WM)

12. According to François Le Lionnais, Estoup was a stenography teacher in the early part of this century who, while doing research for a treatise on the frequency of words, discovered a law. Raymond Queneau formulated the latter as follows: "The place of a word in the list ordered according to frequencies is constant when multiplied by its own frequency." Queneau's evocation and attempted explanation of this law at an early meeting of the Oulipo was met, according to Jacques Bens, by glassy-eyed incomprehension. See *Oulipo 1960–1963*, 42, 88, 90–91. (WM)

13. Text of a lecture delivered in M. J. Favard's Quantitative Linguistics Seminar on 29 January 1964. The activity of the Ouvroir de Littérature Potentielle having grown considerably since then, this report of its work is already dated.

On the Oulipo, see F. Le Lionnais, preface to *Cent Mille Milliards de poèmes;* R. Queneau, *Entretiens avec Georges Charbonnier;* dossier 17 of the *Cahiers du Collège de Pataphysique:* numbers 66–67 of *Temps Mêlés*.

I recall the names of the members of the Oulipo: Noël Arnaud, Jacques Bens, Claude Berge, Jacques Duchateau, Latis, François Le Lionnais, Jean Lescure, Jean Queval, A.-M. Schmidt, and foreign residents: André Blavier, Paul Braffort, Stanley Chapman, Ross Chambers, and Marcel Duchamp.

The reader will find a more developed account of the matrical analysis of language in an article (to appear) in *Etudes de linguistique quantitative*, no. 3, published by the Faculté de Lettres et des Sciences humaines of the University of Besançon.

QUENEAU OULIPIAN

1. Claude Simonnet, *Queneau déchiffré* (Paris: Julliard, 1962), 13–14.
2. Claude Simonnet, ibid.

3. Paul Gayot, "Madagascar et Valentin Brû," *Dossiers du Collège de Pataphysique* 20.

4. Paul Gayot, "A travers le Paris de Zazie et de Valentin Brû," ibid.

5. This article originally appeared in *L'Arc* 28 [1966] under the title "Littérature Potentielle."

RAYMOND QUENEAU AND THE AMALGAM
OF MATHEMATICS AND LITERATURE

1. Christian Goldbach was a Russian mathematician who conjectured in a letter to Leonhard Euler in 1742 that every even integer greater than four could be expressed as the sum of two odd prime numbers. His conjecture is an example of "incomplete induction" since, although it has never been proved false, it cannot be verified for *every* even integer greater than four. The Prussian mathematician F. Klein (1849–1925) proposed the "Erlanger Program" in 1872. It drastically modified the existing classification of geometry and remained the authoritative model for nearly fifty years. It was finally rendered obsolete by the new geometries that followed the general theory of relativity (1916). (WM)

2. The "Disparate Luncheons" (for instance, several years ago, the one with Pierre Auger, François Jacob, André Lichnerowicz, Stanislas Ulam), the "Mathematical Luncheons" (for instance, in the spring of 1976, with Henri Cartan, Nicolaas Kuiper, Casimir Kuratowski, Christine Phili), and other agapes.

3. He was an honorable member of the "Confrérie des Dégustateurs de Nombres," which I founded some years ago (but which has never met).

4. S, because s is the first letter of "sum."

5. E. Waring (1734–98), an English mathematician specializing in number theory, conjectured in 1770 that every integer $n > 0$ is the sum of a fixed least number $g(s)$ of the sth power of integers $\geqq 0$. (WM)

6. Mathematicians who are richly informed about and passionately interested in art and poetry are far more numerous.

7. October third being both Janine's birthday and my own, we used to celebrate it by dining together with, at the most, our spouses; presents of ties and delicacies, and quatrains ("October" rhyming with "sober").

8. See François Le Lionnais, "Poèmes booléens," *La Littérature potentielle*, 262–66. (WM)

9. The allusion is to André Breton and the surrealist group; see "Rule and Constraint," n. 1. (WM)

10. It is not a question of *cadavres exquis*. Queneau's patent guarantees, in addition to the conservation of the rhyme (which is not at all extraordinary), the conservation of syntactic coherence (that is Oulipian) and aspires to the conservation of a semantic atmosphere (which is Quenellian).

11. It has already fostered works in France by Monique Bringer, Georges Guilbaud, and Jacques Roubaud, as well as works by American mathematicians.

12. This article was originally published in *Nouvelle Revue Française* 290 [1977].

MATHEMATICS IN THE METHOD OF RAYMOND QUENEAU

1. François Le Lionnais, "Raymond Queneau et l'amalgame des mathématiques et de la littérature," *Nouvelle Revue Française* 290 (1977): 76. ["Raymond Queneau and the Amalgam of Mathematics and Literature" appeared in the *Nouvelle Revue Française* prior to its publication in *Atlas de littérature potentielle*. (WM)]

2. See "Conjectures fausses en théorie des nombres," *Bords*, Hermann, 1963, 31–36.

3. *Bords*, 34.

4. *Bords*, 82.

5. *Critique*, 176 (1962). Reprinted in *Bords*. [By "right here," Roubaud means the journal *Critique*, where "Mathematics in the Method of Raymond Queneau" was published prior to its publication in *Atlas de littérature potentielle*. (WM)]

6. *Bords*, 12.

7. *Bords*, 29.

8. In the *Proceedings of the Académie des Sciences*.

9. Vol. 12, no. 1, January 1972.

10. See the first sixteen terms of the series 1.1.1.2. in the article cited above, 39.

11. This is a conscious choice: see, for example, in the article on the s-additive series, the remark on page 64: "For $s^1 = 1$, we discover with pleasure Fibonacci's numbers." These numbers, long linked to esthetic speculations, figure, for example, in the great medieval Georgian courtly work, *The Knight in the Tiger Skin*.

12. Reprinted in the "Queneau" issue of *L'Herne*.

13. *Bâtons, chiffres et lettres*, 340. [See Queneau's "Potential Literature." (WM)]

14. Or previously, perhaps, to the idea of matrical analysis, I do not know.

15. Reprinted in *Cahiers de l'Herne*.

16. "The black sun of melancholy" is an allusion to Gérard de Nerval's sonnet "El Desdichado," line 4, which is itself an allusion to Albrecht Dürer's *Melancholia*. (WM)

17. Notably, in the work of P. Braffort and J. Bens.

18. The issue of 29 *sable* 93, 79.

19. The quotation is from Pound's *Spirit of Romance*, ch. 2. (WM)

20. These are not the only "mutations" in the poem.

21. In J. Roubaud, *Etoffe* (Zurich: G. K. Editions, 1974).

22. G. Perec, *Ulcérations*, Bibliothèque Oulipienne 1.

23. See Claude Berge's article, "Pour une analyse potentielle de la littérature combinatoire," in Oulipo, *La Littérature potentielle*, "Idées," Gallimard, and, in the same volume, Queneau's article, "La Relation X prend Y pour Z." [Both articles appear in the present collection. (WM)]

24. Article cited, 63.

25. Bibliothèque Oulipienne 2.

26. See the book cited, note 23, principally Jean Lescure's historical article and

François Le Lionnais's two "manifestoes." [All three pieces appear in the present collection. (WM)]

27. "Littérature potentielle," in *Bâtons, chiffres et lettres*, 317.

28. Article cited, n. 27, 322.

29. Article cited, 323.

30. F. Le Lionnais, "Premier manifeste," in *La Littérature potentielle*, 20.

31. See n. 27. [See also Georges Perec's "History of the Lipogram." (WM)]

32. G. Perec, "Histoire du lipogramme."

33. *Lettres Nouvelles*, 1969.

34. *La Disparition*, 1.

35. See the texts cited in nn. 27 and 32.

36. *La Disparition*, 296. The disappearance of the *e* elicits an effervescence of punctuation. [Queneau's text also appears in *La Littérature potentielle*, 98. (WM)]

37. Queneau's table was published in *Atlas de littérature potentielle*, 74–77. (WM)

38. It is impossible for me to offer any more details, since these belong to the Oulipo.

39. Article cited, 322.

40. *Le Voyage en Grèce*, 94.

41. See section 4.

42. See also the testimony of F. Le Lionnais in the *Nouvelle Revue Française:* "A fan of whole numbers cannot help but yearn to confront the horrors and delights of those rebel angels, the prime numbers."

43. This position remains of current interest, if one may judge from certain recent oafish statements about the "Fascism" of language.

44. Gallimard.

45. J. Roubaud, *Mezura*, Editions de l'Atelier, 1976.

46. Introduction to the *Poésie des ensembles*.

47. Editions Caractères, 1958.

48. Editions Gallimard, 1961.

49. See *La Littérature potentielle* or *Bâtons, chiffres et lettres*.

50. See P. Lusson's work in the Cercle Polivanov on these questions.

51. The *other* basic example is of course Raymond Roussel's *Comment j'ai écrit certains de mes livres*.

52. See "La Littérature sémo-définitionnelle," in *La Littérature potentielle*, 123.

53. Bourbaki, introduction to *Topologie générale*.

54. *Topologie générale*, ch. 1, 186.

55. F. Le Lionnais is the representative, and almost the only one, of this tendency.

56. Bibliothèque Oulipienne 3.

57. Queneau, *Les Fondements de la littérature d'après David Hilbert*, 3.

58. Id., ibid., 4.

59. Id., 13.

60. Id., 12.

61. In the article "Technique du roman," *Bâtons, chiffres et lettres*, 33.

62. In the broad sense, the term "text" seems to be the term that most closely corresponds to "set," in its very great poverty.

63. See "Pour une analyse potentielle de la littérature combinatoire," *La Littérature potentielle*, 58. [Perec's work resulted in *La Vie mode d'emploi*. See also Perec, "Quatre figures pour *La Vie mode d'emploi*," *L'Arc* 76 (1979), 50–53. (WM)]

64. See Harry Mathews's experiments with Shakespeare's sonnets in "Mathews's Algorithm." (WM)

65. Not counting the places that advertise it.

66. *Bâtons, chiffres et lettres*, 29. The novels in question are *Le Chiendent, Gueule de Pierre*, and *Les Derniers Jours*.

67. *Odile*, 33.

68. We are not attacking the indivisibility of the man and the work.

69. See n. 11.

70. Still in "Technique du roman," in *Bâtons, chiffres et lettres*, 33.

71. This article was originally published in *Critique* 359 [1977].

HISTORY OF THE LIPOGRAM

1. Perec is alluding to Queneau's *Cent Mille Milliards de poèmes*. (WM)

2. Racine's *Phèdre*, line 1,112: "Le jour n'est pas plus pur que le fond de mon coeur" (The day is no more pure than my own heart). That this was the line Perec had in mind was confirmed by a personal letter from him to the editor in February 1982. (WM)

3. "It is shameful to have difficult trifles / And it is the foolish toil of buffoons." Martial, *Epigrams* II, 86, 9–10. (WM)

4. "I sing of Demeter and Kore, the bride of Klymenos." (WM)

5. Rittler speaks of twins, the Spanish also tell a story of brothers (*Los dos hermanos* . . .), and *La Disparition* tells the story of a large family: would the theme of brothers be somehow inherent to the lipogram?

6. Two translations are possible: "The enchantment struck down Apollo's son" and "I free Apollo's son from enchantment." (WM)

7. "And yet the R is a letter of the alphabet, a letter which recurs quite often, notwithstanding the paucity of our discourse. A letter which, although you might ignore all the others, cannot escape you. Now, of course, one can repeat that old and famous aphorism, NATURE IS CONQUERED BY ART." (WM)

8. "Various consequences of love, in five exemplary tales, and new devices for writing in prose and verse without one of the vowels." (WM)

9. "The vowel *e* is found in the majority of the most frequently used words in the language, such as . . . father, mother, benevolence . . . levity . . . jejune, pleasant, excellent . . . nevertheless . . . woe . . . zest!" (WM)

10. Literally (if not lipogrammatically) translated: "We camp in Malakoff, or rather, since Malakoff has entirely disappeared, neither seen nor heard, we camp where it used to rise up, so insulting (Vanity of vanities, all is vanity!)." (WM)

11. See Queneau's *L'Instant fatal*. (WM)

12. "The ancient power of language surges forth in the Lord's Prayer." (WM)

13. Efforts to locate the Conrad text and to identify the English female novelist have thus far failed to bear fruit. Marcel Bénabou suggested that Perec meant D. H. Lawrence rather than Conrad, but this cannot be confirmed. On the other hand, I am indebted to Bruce Kochis for an example of liponymy from Vladimir Mayakovsky: in his "About This," a poem of 1,500 lines about love, Mayakovsky never uses that word. The first part ends with a rhyme that seems to call for the word "love," whose absence is thus rendered conspicuous. See *Mayakovsky*, trans. and ed. Herbert Marshall (New York: Hill and Wang, 1965), 161–215. (WM)

RECURRENT LITERATURE

1. The authors wish to thank Bernard Jaulin and Pierre Rosenstiehl for their judicious advice.

2. The authors are referring to Jean Lescure's S + 7 method. See *La Littérature potentielle*, 143–54, and *Atlas de littérature potentielle*, 166–70. (WM)

3. Among the eleven texts offered in "Exercices d'homosyntaxisme" (*La Littérature potentielle*, 176–80), none is attributed to Latis. (WM)

FOR A POTENTIAL ANALYSIS OF
COMBINATORY LITERATURE

1. *Dissertatio de Arte Combinatoria*, J.-E. Erdmann (1666). It is surprising to note that this very rare work, written in Latin, has never to our knowledge been translated. We owe certain of the references we used in the inventory of combinatory literature to Y. Belaval. Let us also cite another famous mathematician, Leonhard Euler, who suggested principles for a Combinatory Art in his *Lettres à une princesse d'Allemagne sur divers sujets de physique et de philosophie*, Steidel (1770–74), 27.

2. One could mathematize the concept of configuration in defining it as an *application of a set of objects within an abstract finite set provided with a known structure;* for example, a permutation of n objects is a "bijective application of the set of objects within the set ordered 1, 2, . . . , n." Nevertheless, we are interested only in those applications that satisfy certain constraints, and the nature of these constraints is too varied to allow us to use this definition as the basis for a general theory.

3. "Honor, Art, Money, Property, Praise, Woman, and Child / One has, seeks, misses, hopes for, and disappears." G. P. Harsdörffer (1607–58), a founder of the "Pegnitz Shepherds," a Nuremberg society, wrote a *Poetischer Trichter* (*Poetic Funnel*) (1647–53) with which one could "pour" the art of poetry into anybody in six hours. See J. G. Robertson, *Outlines of the History of German Literature* (Edinburgh: Blackwood, 1950), 83. (WM)

4. Marc Saporta's *Composition No. 1* (Paris: Seuil, 1962) was published in 1962, not 1965. (WM)

5. The poem Berge has transformed is Ronsard's "Quand vous serez bien vieille":

> Quand vous serez bien vieille, au soir, à la chandelle,
> Assise auprès du feu, devidant et filant,
> Direz, chantant mes vers, en vous esmerveillant:
> Ronsard me celebroit du temps que j'estois belle.
>
> Lors vous n'aurez servante oyant telle nouvelle,
> Desja sous le labeur à demy sommeillant,
> Qui, au bruit de Ronsard, ne s'aille réveillant,
> Benissant vostre nom de louange immortelle.
>
> Je seray sous la terre, et, fantosme sans os,
> Par les ombres myrteux je prendray mon repos;
> Vous serez au fouyer une vieille accroupie,
>
> Regrettant mon amour et vostre fier desdain.
> Vivez, si m'en croyez, n'attendez à demain;
> Cueillez dés aujourd'hui les roses de la vie.

Humbert Wolfe, in Pierre de Ronsard, *Sonnets for Helen* (London: George Allen and Unwin, 1934), translates the poem as follows:

> When you are old, at evening candle-lit
> beside the fire bending to your wool,
> read out my verse and murmur, "Ronsard writ
> this praise for me when I was beautiful."
>
> And not a maid but, at the sound of it,
> though nodding at the stitch on broidered stool,
> will start awake, and bless love's benefit
> whose long fidelities bring Time to school.
>
> I shall be thin and ghost beneath the earth
> by myrtle shade in quiet after pain,
> but you, a crone, will crouch beside the hearth
>
> Mourning my love and all your proud disdain.
> And since what comes tomorrow who can say?
> Live, pluck the roses of the world to-day. (WM)

6. See the study Jean Ferry devoted to him in the journal *Bizarre* 34–35 (1964).

7. Work on the literary applications of the Latin bi-square was pursued by Georges Perec; in 1978 it resulted in his *La Vie mode d'emploi*. (WM)

MATHEWS'S ALGORITHM

1. S + 7: see *La Littérature potentielle*, 143–54 and *Atlas de littérature potentielle*, 166–70. Semo-Definitional Literature: "Littérature Sémo-Définitionnelle"

or "L.S.D.," a process elaborated by Marcel Bénabou and Georges Perec; see *La Littérature potentielle*, 123–40. (WM)

2. It is entirely possible to apply the algorithm to syllables. If we omit this example, it is only because its demonstration is somewhat fastidious.

COMPUTER AND WRITER:
THE CENTRE POMPIDOU EXPERIMENT

1. A.R.T.A.: "Atelier de Recherches et Techniques Avancées," or "Workshop of Advanced Studies and Techniques," a group working at the Centre Pompidou. For a time, the Oulipo used A.R.T.A. equipment in their work on computer-aided literature. Personal letter from Paul Fournel to the editor, 5 December 1983. (WM)

2. Gallimard.

3. In the same spirit and using a very similar technique, Michel Bottin programmed the 10^{67} poems contained in the XLIst kiss of love of Quirinus Kuhlman.

4. This story is published in Oulipo, *La Littérature potentielle*, Gallimard's "Idées" collection, 277. [It also appears in the present volume (WM).]

5. A prototype of this text may be found in Oulipo, *La Littérature potentielle*, Gallimard's "Idées" collection, 281. [Appearing here as "The Theater Tree: A Combinatory Play." (WM)]

6. See Calvino's "Prose and Anticombinatorics." (WM)

7. See Roubaud's *La Princesse Hoppy ou le conte du Labrador:* Bibliothèque Oulipienne 2 (ch. 1); Bibliothèque Oulipienne 7 (ch. 2); *Change* 38 (1980), 11–29 (chs. 3, 4). (WM)

8. See Bénabou, *Un Aphorisme peut en cacher un autre.* (WM)

9. This paper was presented at the "Writer-Computer" meetings of June 1977.

THE THEATER TREE: A COMBINATORY PLAY

1. The "noble-pit" (*trappe à nobles*) is an allusion to Alfred Jarry's *Ubu roi*, III, ii. (WM)

Glossary

· ·

Included here are names of Oulipian and pre-Oulipian poetic structures, as well as figures of classical rhetoric (many of the latter occur in Marcel Bénabou's "Table of Elementary Linguistic and Literary Operations"). In the few cases in which Oulipian use of a term differs from general usage, this has been noted. The reader may find examples of many of the structures in *La Littérature potentielle* and *Atlas de littérature potentielle,* referred to below as I and II, respectively.

ALPHABETICAL DRAMA
A short theatrical form in which the lines spoken by the actors homophonically mimic the sound of a person reciting the alphabet. See I, 111–14.

ANAGLYPHIC TEXT
A three-dimensional verbal text. See I, 289.

ANAPHORA
Repetition of a word at the beginning of successive utterances: e.g., "I came, I saw, I conquered."

ANASTROPHE
Unusual inversion of words or syntagms within an utterance: e.g., "Came the dawn."

ANTIRHYME
If one accepts the supposition that one may, for any given phoneme, postulate an "antiphoneme"—that is, a phoneme having opposite, complementary, or symmetrical characteristics—it would be possible to create antirhymes, or couplets ending in phonemes and their antiphonemes. Antirhyme is a special case of antonymic translation. See I, 291.

ANTONYMIC TRANSLATION
A process of textual production that involves the transformation of an utterance into its contrary, along a given axis of symmetry. The latter may be situated at any level: that of the individual word, of grammatical characteristics, or of the general signification of an utterance. See I, 204–05; II, 165.

APHAERESIS
The omitting of a syllable or a letter at the beginning of a word: e.g., "bo" for "hobo."

BEAU PRESENT
A form of acrostic encoding in which the letters of a given name appear, in order, in the text. According to the most doctrinaire, the letters of that name, once used, may not be used again in the text. Georges Perec practiced a special form

209

of the *beau présent,* using *only* the letters of a given name to construct the text. See II, 264, 291–92.

BELLE ABSENTE
A form of acrostic encoding in which the letters of a given name are the only letters not used in the text. In verse forms, one letter may be excluded in each verse: the name is thus progressively spelled out *in absentia.* See II, 213, 290–91, and Georges Perec, *La Clôture et autres poèmes,* 73–76.

BOOLIAN POEMS
A process of textual production devised by François Le Lionnais, a literary application of the work of the British mathematician George Boole (1815–64). See I, 262–68.

BRACHYLOGIA
An abridged expression: e.g., "And he to England shall along with you" (*Hamlet,* III, iii).

CENTO
A text composed of passages from other texts. See I, 172–75, 209–14.

CHRONOGRAM
A text in which certain letters, when placed together, form a date in Roman numerals. See II, 268–70.

COUPEUR A LA LIGNE
[Cutter on the line.] A variation of the TIREUR A LA LIGNE consisting of the progressive suppression of alternate sentences in a text. See II, 285.

CRASIS
Contraction of two letters or syllables into one.

DEPORTMANTEAU WORD
The division of a portmanteau word into its original constitutive elements.

DIAERESIS
In the Oulipian lexicon, the division of one syllable into two.

EDGES OF POEM
A process of textual production that uses the first and last verses, plus the first and last words of the intervening verses of a given poem. See I, 292–93.

EPANALEPSIS
Repetition at the end of an utterance of the word with which it began: e.g., "I would like that, would I."

EPENTHESIS
Insertion of a letter, phoneme, or syllable into the middle of a word: e.g., "visitating" for "visiting."

EURYPHALLIC VERSE
See SNOWBALL.

GEMINATION
In the Oulipian lexicon, the doubling of the initial syllable of an utterance.

HAIKUIZATION
A process that retains the rhyming parts of a poem to form a new poem. See Queneau's "Potential Literature," and I, 185–203.

HAPLOGRAPHY
An error through which a copyist deletes a segment of a text, due to the identity of the initial and final elements of the segment.

HENDIADYS
A figure of speech using two nouns and the conjunction "and," rather than a noun and an adjective, to express a given idea.

HETEROGRAM
A text in which no letter is repeated. A "perfect" heterogram is also a "perfect" pangram: a text of 26 letters using all the letters of the alphabet. Georges Perec practiced a form called "heterogrammatic poetry" in which each verse of a given text is an anagram of every other verse within that text. See II, 231–36, 337, and Perec, *Alphabets, Ulcérations,* and *La Clôture et autres poèmes.*

HOLOPOEMS
Following the principles of holography, holopoems are represented as images in space. As the reader moves under (or over, or around) them, new words or verses become apparent. See I, 290.

HOLORHYME
A form of homophonic verse. See I, 237–38. See also HOMOMORPHISM.

HOMOEUTELEUTON
The repetition of a phoneme at the end of successive utterances: e.g., rhymed verses.

HOMOMORPHISM
A process by which new texts are generated, which imitate the structure of a master text. The different types of homomorphisms are defined by the structure imitated: homosyntaxism, homovocalism, homophony, etc. See I, 115, 176–80; II, 159–164.

JAVANESE STUTTERING
A form of stuttering wherein syllables, rather than phonemes, are repeated. See Jean Lescure's "Poème pour bègue," I, 116.

LARDING
A form of TIREUR A LA LIGNE elaborated by Paul Fournel. In his example, a Queneau text is successively "larded" with 3, 1, 4, and 1 new sentences (this series, of course, corresponds to the first four figures of the number π). See II, 283.

LA RIEN QUE LA TOUTE LA
[The nothing but everything the.] A text without nouns, verbs, or adjectives, a structure proposed by François Le Lionnais. See I, 228–29.

LIPOGRAM
A text in which a given letter (or letters) of the alphabet does not appear. See Georges Perec, "History of the Lipogram," *La Disparition,* and *Les Revenentes.* See also I, 77–100; II, 211–17. Liponyms, lipophonemes, and liposyllables are texts in which (respectively) a given word, phoneme, or syllable does not appear.

L.S.D.
"Littérature Sémo-Définitionnelle": Semo-Definitional Literature, a procedure elaborated by Marcel Bénabou and Georges Perec. Various effects are obtained through the substitution of the definitions of given words within a text for the words themselves. See I, 123–40.

METATHESIS
The transposition of letters or phonemes in a word: e.g., "modren" for "modern."

PALINDROME
A written locution that reads the same backward or forward. Palindromes may be "positive" or "negative": that is, composed, respectively, of an even or odd number of integers. See I, 101–06; II, 218–26. Phonetic palindromes, syllabic palindromes, and word palindromes are texts in which the reflected integers are, respectively, phonemes, syllables, and words, rather than letters. See II, 220–21.

PANGRAM
A text containing all the letters of the alphabet. Obviously, the "value" of a pangram increases in inverse proportion to its length. A "perfect" pangram is a text of 26 letters including all the letters of the alphabet. See II, 231–32.

PARAGOGE
The addition of a letter or a syllable to the end of a word. This addition may be either functional (e.g., "drowned") or unnecessary (e.g., "drownded").

PARAGRAM
A printer's error consisting of the substitution of one letter for another. As Marcel Bénabou uses the word in his "Table of Elementary Linguistic and Literary Operations," it bears only a very distant relation to the Saussurian notion of "paragram."

PERVERB
A perverb juxtaposes the first part of one proverb to the second part of another. See II, 293–94, 344–45.

POEMS FOR MOEBIUS STRIP
A process elaborated by Luc Etienne, involving the disposition of a text on a Moebius strip. See I, 269–75.

PORTMANTEAU WORD
A word that formally and semantically conflates two other words: e.g., "smog," from "smoke" and "fog."

PROSTHESIS
The addition of a letter or a syllable to the beginning of a word: e.g., "irregard-less" for "regardless."

RHOPALIC VERSE
See SNOWBALL.

S + 7
A method of textual transformation elaborated by Jean Lescure in which each substantive in a given text is replaced by the seventh substantive following it in the dictionary. See I, 143–54; II, 166–70.

SNOWBALL
A form in which each segment of a text is one letter longer than the segment preceding it. Also called euryphallic verse and rhopalic verse. A number of variations are conceivable, such as the "melting snowball" (see Harry Mathews's "Liminal Poem"), in which, after its expansion, the poem contracts. See I, 107–10; II, 194–210.

SPOONERISM
A generally unintentional transposition of sounds in two or more words: e.g., "tee many martoonis." Named after the Reverend W. A. Spooner (1844–1930) of New College, Oxford, renowned for this sort of verbal lapsus. In French literature, the conscious use of spoonerisms, or *contrepèterie,* is thought to have originated with Rabelais. Luc Etienne's *L'Art du contrepet* serves as a spoonerism primer.

SQUARE POEM
A form proposed by Jean Lescure that exploits all possible permutations of a given set of four words. See his *Drailles,* 277–84, and I, 155–65.

SYNCOPE
The dropping of letters or syllables in the middle of a word or expression: e.g., "Halloween" for "all hallow even."

TAUTOGRAM
A text whose words all begin with the same letter. See I, 117.

TIREUR A LA LIGNE
[Puller on the line.] A form elaborated by Jacques Duchateau. Consists of taking two sentences in a given text and interpolating a new sentence, then two new sentences in the interstices thus created, and so forth. See Duchateau, *Les Sept Coups du tireur à la ligne en apocalypse lent, occupé à lire "Monnaie de singe" de William Faulkner,* and II, 271–85. See also COUPEUR A LA LIGNE and LARDING.

TMESIS

Insertion of one or more words between the parts of a compound word: e.g.,
"what person soever" for "whatsoever person."

UNTRACEABLE LOCUTIONS

A form elaborated by Marcel Bénabou. See his *Locutions introuvables*. See also
PERVERB.

ZEUGMA

A figure in which a single modifier applies in different ways to two or more
words: e.g., "The room was not light, but his fingers were."

INDEX

· ·

SELECTED DALKEY ARCHIVE PAPERBACKS

PETROS ABATZOGLOU, *What Does Mrs. Freeman Want?*
PIERRE ALBERT-BIROT, *Grabinoulor.*
YUZ ALESHKOVSKY, *Kangaroo.*
FELIPE ALFAU, *Chromos.*
   Locos.
IVAN ÂNGELO, *The Celebration.*
   The Tower of Glass.
DAVID ANTIN, *Talking.*
ALAIN ARIAS-MISSON, *Theatre of Incest.*
DJUNA BARNES, *Ladies Almanack.*
   Ryder.
JOHN BARTH, *LETTERS.*
   Sabbatical.
DONALD BARTHELME, *The King.*
   Paradise.
SVETISLAV BASARA, *Chinese Letter.*
MARK BINELLI, *Sacco and Vanzetti Must Die!*
ANDREI BITOV, *Pushkin House.*
LOUIS PAUL BOON, *Chapel Road.*
   Summer in Termuren.
ROGER BOYLAN, *Killoyle.*
IGNÁCIO DE LOYOLA BRANDÃO, *Teeth under the Sun.*
   Zero.
BONNIE BREMSER, *Troia: Mexican Memoirs.*
CHRISTINE BROOKE-ROSE, *Amalgamemnon.*
BRIGID BROPHY, *In Transit.*
MEREDITH BROSNAN, *Mr. Dynamite.*
GERALD L. BRUNS,
   Modern Poetry and the Idea of Language.
EVGENY BUNIMOVICH AND J. KATES, EDS.,
   Contemporary Russian Poetry: An Anthology.
GABRIELLE BURTON, *Heartbreak Hotel.*
MICHEL BUTOR, *Degrees.*
   Mobile.
   Portrait of the Artist as a Young Ape.
G. CABRERA INFANTE, *Infante's Inferno.*
   Three Trapped Tigers.
JULIETA CAMPOS, *The Fear of Losing Eurydice.*
ANNE CARSON, *Eros the Bittersweet.*
CAMILO JOSÉ CELA, *Christ versus Arizona.*
   The Family of Pascual Duarte.
   The Hive.
LOUIS-FERDINAND CÉLINE, *Castle to Castle.*
   Conversations with Professor Y.
   London Bridge.
   North.
   Rigadoon.
HUGO CHARTERIS, *The Tide Is Right.*
JEROME CHARYN, *The Tar Baby.*
MARC CHOLODENKO, *Mordechai Schamz.*
EMILY HOLMES COLEMAN, *The Shutter of Snow.*
ROBERT COOVER, *A Night at the Movies.*
STANLEY CRAWFORD, *Some Instructions to My Wife.*
ROBERT CREELEY, *Collected Prose.*
RENÉ CREVEL, *Putting My Foot in It.*
RALPH CUSACK, *Cadenza.*
SUSAN DAITCH, *L.C.*
   Storytown.
NIGEL DENNIS, *Cards of Identity.*
PETER DIMOCK,
   A Short Rhetoric for Leaving the Family.
ARIEL DORFMAN, *Konfidenz.*
COLEMAN DOWELL, *The Houses of Children.*
   Island People.
   Too Much Flesh and Jabez.
RIKKI DUCORNET, *The Complete Butcher's Tales.*
   The Fountains of Neptune.
   The Jade Cabinet.
   Phosphor in Dreamland.
   The Stain.
   The Word "Desire."
WILLIAM EASTLAKE, *The Bamboo Bed.*
   Castle Keep.
   Lyric of the Circle Heart.
JEAN ECHENOZ, *Chopin's Move.*
STANLEY ELKIN, *A Bad Man.*
   Boswell: A Modern Comedy.
   Criers and Kibitzers, Kibitzers and Criers.
   The Dick Gibson Show.
   The Franchiser.
   George Mills.
   The Living End.
   The MacGuffin.
   The Magic Kingdom.
   Mrs. Ted Bliss.
   The Rabbi of Lud.
   Van Gogh's Room at Arles.
ANNIE ERNAUX, *Cleaned Out.*

LAUREN FAIRBANKS, *Muzzle Thyself.*
   Sister Carrie.
LESLIE A. FIEDLER,
   Love and Death in the American Novel.
GUSTAVE FLAUBERT, *Bouvard and Pécuchet.*
FORD MADOX FORD, *The March of Literature.*
JON FOSSE, *Melancholy.*
MAX FRISCH, *I'm Not Stiller.*
   Man in the Holocene.
CARLOS FUENTES, *Christopher Unborn.*
   Distant Relations.
   Terra Nostra.
   Where the Air Is Clear.
JANICE GALLOWAY, *Foreign Parts.*
   The Trick Is to Keep Breathing.
WILLIAM H. GASS, *A Temple of Texts.*
   The Tunnel.
   Willie Masters' Lonesome Wife.
ETIENNE GILSON, *The Arts of the Beautiful.*
   Forms and Substances in the Arts.
C. S. GISCOMBE, *Giscome Road.*
   Here.
DOUGLAS GLOVER, *Bad News of the Heart.*
   The Enamoured Knight.
WITOLD GOMBROWICZ, *A Kind of Testament.*
KAREN ELIZABETH GORDON, *The Red Shoes.*
GEORGI GOSPODINOV, *Natural Novel.*
JUAN GOYTISOLO, *Count Julian.*
   Marks of Identity.
PATRICK GRAINVILLE, *The Cave of Heaven.*
HENRY GREEN, *Blindness.*
   Concluding.
   Doting.
   Nothing.
JIŘÍ GRUŠA, *The Questionnaire.*
GABRIEL GUDDING, *Rhode Island Notebook.*
JOHN HAWKES, *Whistlejacket.*
AIDAN HIGGINS, *A Bestiary.*
   Bornholm Night-Ferry.
   Flotsam and Jetsam.
   Langrishe, Go Down.
   Scenes from a Receding Past.
   Windy Arbours.
ALDOUS HUXLEY, *Antic Hay.*
   Crome Yellow.
   Point Counter Point.
   Those Barren Leaves.
   Time Must Have a Stop.
MIKHAIL IOSSEL AND JEFF PARKER, EDS., *Amerika:*
   Contemporary Russians View
   the United States.
GERT JONKE, *Geometric Regional Novel.*
JACQUES JOUET, *Mountain R.*
HUGH KENNER, *The Counterfeiters.*
   Flaubert, Joyce and Beckett:
   The Stoic Comedians.
   Joyce's Voices.
DANILO KIŠ, *Garden, Ashes.*
   A Tomb for Boris Davidovich.
AIKO KITAHARA,
   The Budding Tree: Six Stories of Love in Edo.
ANITA KONKKA, *A Fool's Paradise.*
GEORGE KONRÁD, *The City Builder.*
TADEUSZ KONWICKI, *A Minor Apocalypse.*
   The Polish Complex.
MENIS KOUMANDAREAS, *Koula.*
ELAINE KRAF, *The Princess of 72nd Street.*
JIM KRUSOE, *Iceland.*
EWA KURYLUK, *Century 21.*
VIOLETTE LEDUC, *La Bâtarde.*
DEBORAH LEVY, *Billy and Girl.*
   Pillow Talk in Europe and Other Places.
JOSÉ LEZAMA LIMA, *Paradiso.*
ROSA LIKSOM, *Dark Paradise.*
OSMAN LINS, *Avalovara.*
   The Queen of the Prisons of Greece.
ALF MAC LOCHLAINN, *The Corpus in the Library.*
   Out of Focus.
RON LOEWINSOHN, *Magnetic Field(s).*
D. KEITH MANO, *Take Five.*
BEN MARCUS, *The Age of Wire and String.*
WALLACE MARKFIELD, *Teitlebaum's Window.*
   To an Early Grave.
DAVID MARKSON, *Reader's Block.*
   Springer's Progress.
   Wittgenstein's Mistress.
CAROLE MASO, *AVA.*

FOR A FULL LIST OF PUBLICATIONS, VISIT:
www.dalkeyarchive.com

SELECTED DALKEY ARCHIVE PAPERBACKS

FOR A FULL LIST OF PUBLICATIONS, VISIT:
www.dalkeyarchive.com